*The Sceptic's Guide*

*to*

# READING THE BIBLE

# The Sceptic's Guide

## to

# READING THE BIBLE

# HILARY BRAND

*A 'no-strings' exploration for those*
*who have given up or never really tried*

Text copyright © Hilary Brand 2000
The author asserts the moral right
to be identified as the author of this work

**Published by**
**The Bible Reading Fellowship**
Peter's Way, Sandy Lane West
Oxford OX4 6HG
ISBN 1 84101 084 7

First published 2000
10 9 8 7 6 5 4 3 2 1 0

**Acknowledgments**
Unless otherwise stated, scripture quotations are taken from
The New Revised Standard Version of the Bible, Anglicized Edition,
copyright © 1989, 1995 by the Division of Christian Education of
the National Council of the Churches of Christ in the USA, and are
used by permission. All rights reserved.

Scripture quotations taken from the *Holy Bible, New International*
*Version*, copyright © 1973, 1978, 1984 by International Bible
Society, are used by permission of Hodder & Stoughton Limited.
All rights reserved. 'NIV' is a registered trademark of International
Bible Society. UK trademark number 1448790.

Extracts from the Authorized Version of the Bible (The King James
Bible), the rights in which are vested in the Crown, are reproduced
by permission of the Crown's patentee, Cambridge University Press.

A catalogue record for this book is available from the British Library

Printed and bound in Great Britain by
Omnia Books Limited, Glasgow

# Contents

# Part One
# INTRODUCTION

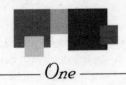

# One

# This book: what it's all about

## Why write it?

It's a question I've asked myself many times in the last few months!

It all began with the Thursday Group.

Where church is concerned, I've probably always been one of the awkward squad. I can't escape the need for a spiritual side to my existence and I'm irretrievably drawn to the character of Jesus Christ. But I have a love/hate relationship with organized religion. It was during one of the hate phases that my husband and I got together with a group of equally awkward and frustrated friends to form the Thursday Group—an unofficial Lent course that went on to last for three years.

The book we used at first was a BRF title, *Oh God, Why?* by Gerard Hughes (highly recommended—I feel absurdly exalted to have my name on the same label), which encouraged us not only to read the Bible but to be completely honest about our reactions.

It was great. We learnt a lot—maybe more about ourselves than about God. We wallowed in the luxury of dropping those masks that church seems inevitably, if not intentionally, to invite. And I discovered that if I found actually sitting down and reading the Bible a struggle, my friends were finding it even more so. And the more I looked around, the more I found people who called themselves Christians (often fervently so), or who were genuinely searching for spiritual answers, but had either tried reading the Bible and given up, or had never really tried.

That bothered me. But that alone would not have prompted me to write a book. What did prompt me was being asked to write some of those traditional daily reading notes that BRF and other organizations produce.

Now I enjoy writing. And since I've learnt a fair bit about the Christian faith over the years, I felt humbly confident that I did have a few pearls of wisdom to offer. But I was uncomfortable. Although I was perfectly capable of producing thought-provoking gems as required, I felt a bit of a fraud. For a start, I don't use daily reading notes myself. I haven't done for years. I did when I first became a Christian and for quite a while afterwards, and found them very helpful. But after a time their allure began to fade.

Whether I felt it was cheating, or whether I just don't like being told what to think, I'm not sure, but I became more and more convinced that a packaged and predigested thought for the day wasn't aiding my spiritual growth. It felt like still being on a diet of junior mushed carrots and chocolate tapioca in adolescence.

And as the writing bug bit me and I began to learn a bit here and there about literature, I became more and more convinced that two-minute, snack-sized nibbles were not, in most cases, the way the Bible's authors intended their work to be read.

Now I'm not against daily reading notes *per se*. Many people find them an informative and manageable way to get into the Bible, and if so, that's fine. But statistics tell me that I am not alone in my discontent. Sales of traditional daily reading notes have plummeted in the last ten years and of those who do still read them, 80 per cent are over forty (Scripture Union research into readership of *Daily Bread*, 1998).

And neither am I alone in my struggle to read the Bible for myself. Further statistics tell us that although 75 per cent of the adult population of the UK own a Bible, 64 per cent never read it. Even among church-goers the proportion is not much higher. In a survey carried out by Bible Society in 1997, 18 per cent of adult churchgoers said they had never read the Bible in their lives, a further 14 per cent said they had not read it in the last year, and a further 23 per cent read it no more than a handful of times a year. So why?

## What's gone wrong?

Churches, on the whole, don't encourage their flock to think for themselves. Perhaps, like me, you have listened to erudite sermons which constantly refer to the original Greek or Hebrew, or tell you amazing historical facts that you would never have known just by looking at the Bible in the pew. It's great. It's fascinating. It brings it all to life. But perhaps, like me, you have been left feeling, 'It's all very well for them. How could I ever find out stuff like that?' Perhaps, long after the actual message of the sermon has been forgotten, you have been left with the subliminal one: 'The Bible is good for you, but in order to understand it fully, you need an expert to explain it to you.'

Perhaps you have listened to eloquent preachers who take a simple text and build on it a huge edifice of inspiring thoughts and demanding conclusions. Perhaps you have muttered, 'How did they get *that* from *that*?' or, more shocking still, 'I don't agree.' Perhaps, like me, you have longed to put your hand up and ask a question or, even more daringly, venture an opinion.

## Who am I?

You will probably have realized by now that I am not a minister of religion. I've never preached a sermon. I'm not a biblical scholar. I haven't got a degree in theology. In fact, I haven't got a degree at all, or even A' Levels. (I did study photography at art school, and I've been devouring books and adult education ever since, but that's another story.)

Perhaps I now have you asking along with me: who am I to write this book? In answer, I'm clinging to a theme I find threaded through the Bible from beginning to end: God constantly takes weak people and turns their weaknesses into strengths.

Perhaps my bolshiness, my refusal simply to accept what I am told, has its good side. God knows, it has got me into hot water often enough, but it has also many times sent me back to my Bible asking, 'Does it *really* say that?' And as I've dug around, I've become convinced that, complex and difficult as it often is, the Bible is not just a book for scholars. It is *about* ordinary people and *for* ordinary people and is still accessible *to* them— even now, nearly two millennia after it was completed.

For me, the Bible has proved to be what both the Psalms and Jesus claimed it to be—a solid rock on which to stand amidst a world of shifting sand. I cannot prove that it will continue to be so to the post-modernist, relativist, anti-authority, cynical, sceptical generation that is coming up behind me. I believe it could be. But I have a nagging conviction that, if that is to be the case, reading it needs a radically different approach. I don't claim to have seen in full what that approach should be, but I've had a few fuzzy glimpses.

A wiser author than I has proclaimed that writers 'do not write because they see, but in order to see more clearly' (Nigel Forde, *The*

*Lantern and the Looking Glass*, SPCK, p. 26). In writing this book, I'm hoping to turn those glimpses into at least part of a clearer picture. And I'm hoping that, if nothing else, it will say to you, 'If she can read the Bible and get something out of it, then so can I.'

## A NOTE ON GENDER

I do not believe that God is male. I believe God is transcendent, the ground of our being, the life-force, far greater than any human could ever comprehend or express, encompassing both the masculine and the feminine, and definitely not an old man with a beard. However, I do believe that God, the highest life-form, is person. If so, the limitations of the English language give me only two choices—to describe God as 'he' or 'she'. The Bible comes down unequivocally on the side of 'he' and so, despite its limitations, for this book I have decided to do likewise.

I have to acknowledge that the Bible is almost entirely male in its cast of characters. There are a few key females, but not many. Clearly Jesus broke through a lot of taboos and traditions in his respectful and open treatment of women, and there are signs that, despite Paul's apparent misogyny, the early Church was beginning to do the same. But as far as we know, all the Bible's writers were male, pretty well all the prophets were male and all the early Church leaders were male. I have therefore used the male pronoun rather more than I might otherwise do.

The Bible is a product of its time, and thankfully times have changed. In our generation, there are an increasing number of women writers, leaders and even prophets of outstanding spiritual calibre. Even within its own framework, there is no doubt that where the Bible speaks of God's relationship with 'man', it means with all 'humankind'. We can joyfully and unequivocally infer that God's love, God's gifts and God's calling are for all, regardless of gender.

## Where are we going?

This book is a guided tour. It is the sort of journey you might take if you did not know a country and wanted to get an overview, before returning to visit it on your own. I am not, however, the sort of guide, holding aloft a furled umbrella, who herds you round from site to site, delivering a barrage of historical, geographical and sociological information at each one. Rather, I will tip you out at each stop, give you a map and some handy bits of information and retire to let you explore for yourself.

It is true that there are other ways to get to know a place better—study every guidebook and travelogue, learn the language, do lots of background reading, concentrate on one tiny area at a time—but what I am suggesting here is that you simply take a wander, soaking up the atmosphere. If you like the place, if your curiosity is aroused, there will be plenty of time to return better equipped. But if you try to take in too much too soon, you may wish you had simply taken a beach holiday!

To put it more plainly: this book is not a Bible handbook—that is, it does not set out to fill you in on the history, geography, linguistics and culture of biblical times. Nor is it a commentary, providing explanation on each verse, chapter or even each book. Both these types of resource are valuable, and there are excellent examples around (see the Recommended Further Reading list on page 272). But what I am trying to do here is to help you simply to take the Bible at face value and read it for yourself—to deliver you to a destination and point the way in.

I have done this in three main ways.

In the rest of this first section, we look at Bible reading in general. The next two chapters take on some of the issues that are likely to be thrown up as soon as you open its pages. Chapter 4 looks at the long journey from its first beginnings to the anthology you have on your bookshelf.

Part Two looks at the widely differing types of literature in the Bible and suggests different ways of approaching each. You may notice that the way I have grouped them is quite different from the normal ways in which the Bible books are categorized. For example, Psalms and Proverbs are usually grouped together as Wisdom literature, but since psalms are primarily cries to God and proverbs are predominantly advice for living, it seemed to me that they should be approached in fundamentally different ways. So I have grouped books according to how we experience them as literature, rather than how they have traditionally been defined.

Part Three looks at different methods of approaching a text, from the intuitive and imaginative to the logical and systematic—each equipping you with a different tool to dig for meaning.

Each part is divided into chapters, each with an introduction to the subject (and in many cases an introduction to the Bible book in question), plus some exercises—a passage and a set of questions—to help you explore for yourself. Some of the questions are specific to the particular passage, others are more general in order to set up principles of what to look for. There are no right or wrong answers to most of these questions. Indeed, some may prove too difficult to answer at all. If so, no problem. The questions are simply there to stimulate your thinking.

When it comes to Bible passages, I have chosen neither the most difficult, nor the most comforting or easy. They are neither the most familiar, nor the most obscure, but a little bit of both and some in between.

Throughout this book, I have also scattered little asides of various sorts. Some are quotes from well-known or interesting people, alive and dead, on what the Bible means to them, how they read it, and what their favourite passages might be. Some take a quick detour and explore difficult, confusing or controversial topics that the chapter throws up.

And so, returning to our guided tour analogy, some parts of the Bible are places you need to visit simply to understand the territory. They may not be areas you would choose to return to very often, but you need to have been there to understand the lie of the land. Others you will immediately take to: they will be places to dwell in, to return to again and again. But if you want to understand the terrain through which you are travelling, you do need to visit them all. Lovely as it might be to spend a trip to Britain entirely in the Cotswolds and the Lake District, it hardly equips you to understand what it means to be British. For that you will need to visit London, Cornwall, Wales, the Suffolk Wolds, the Scottish Highlands, Liverpool, Birmingham, Northern Ireland and a whole lot in between.

So this trip requires effort. Not only does it cover a lot of ground, it also requires you to get out of the coach and walk around. Or in this context, just reading what this book has to say about the Bible will tell you so much—but not much. If you really want to see what's there, there is no alternative but to put in a certain amount of time and energy and explore it for yourself. And that takes time. Not a great deal, but some—perhaps a minimum of half an hour of concentrated attention per week.

You may prefer to travel alone or with companions. Although the exercises were written primarily for individuals, they will also work for group studies. Try them and see what works for you.

# What you need for the trip

For this journey, I am suggesting you travel light. Obviously you will need a Bible, and if you don't already have one, or are considering investing in another one, there are some comments on different versions in Chapter 4. Beyond that, there is only one essential piece of equipment I would like to recommend—a notebook.

A Bible reader without a notebook is like a tourist without a camera. OK, so I'm a writer; I *like* writing stuff down. But I would venture to suggest that pretty well everyone will benefit from putting down on paper (or screen, if so inclined) their ideas, questions and conclusions as they read. There is no better way to formulate your thoughts.

There is another reason why I recommend a notebook. I possess a truly lousy memory! If I feel God might be speaking to me through a passage, I want to make sure I remember. I want to mull it over, evaluate it, return in a few months and see what, if anything, came to pass.

There is one further piece of equipment that I recommend and that is a concordance. If you can only buy one book to help with your Bible reading, this would be it. A concordance is simply a great big index. It lists every word in the Bible, together with the places where it appears. Of course, some references will prove trivial and teach you nothing. But on the whole, if you want to check out a theme or an idea, or simply search for something you half-remember, the concordance is the best tool you can find. (Of course, if you are part of the wired generation, there are other ways of doing this via the Internet or on CD-Rom. See Chapter 13 for more detail.) You do not need a concordance, on- or off-line, to work through this book. Where that sort of exercise appears, I have given you a list of references. But if you wish to continue to use these techniques to explore on your own, it is invaluable.

This book is not intended to turn you into a spiritual whizz-kid, nor a biblical scholar. It may leave you with more questions than answers. If so, good, for that might just be the beginning of a lifelong journey of discovery.

# Finding out for yourself

*Even if you don't necessarily believe in Jesus as the central character of the Bible, I think the Bible is important because of its stories. The aspects of human nature that they show are so important for us to see, because it's so easy to be disconnected from our past and to feel that because of the time we're living in— everything is available, information is accessible, you can travel the world so easily, you can shop without ever leaving your seat—the things that happened in the past are somehow irrelevant. Yet what you see when you read the Bible is that human nature and the desires of the heart, and the things that affect people and hurt people and inspire people and destroy people, haven't changed. Basic human characteristics are the same, and if the questions that those characteristics throw up are the same, then the answers are the same. The way we apply them may have to change, but the answers don't.*

*I've also found that the Bible makes me ask a whole lot more questions. It breaks down a lot of preconceptions. I've often taken what I believe to be biblical from what people say. They say the Bible says this and Christians do that—and you read it and it doesn't say anything of the sort! When you read it for yourself, you find half the stuff you criticized the Bible for isn't even in there. It ends up like criticizing David Bowie for not being Lauryn Hill. You know, wrong gender, wrong generation, wrong type of music—apart from that, you've got a point! It gets like that with the Bible sometimes: people criticize it for being something it never purports to be. You can hear a lot, but until you read it for yourself you never really know. Reading it was my way of finding out for myself.*

DAVID GRANT (SINGER, SONGWRITER, TV PRESENTER, ACTOR, CURRENTLY MEMBER OF 'UNITED COLOURS OF SOUND')

# Two

# The Bible: why and how to read it

The Bible is both strangely alien and strangely familiar.

It is alien because it is ancient—very ancient. Its first stories were told around campfires by Bronze Age families living in goatskin tents. Its first writings were gathered when wandering, warring tribespeople were just beginning to experiment with becoming fragile nation states. As the ink was drying on its final words, the Romans were still trying to subdue the barbarian Britons and hadn't even started on the woad-covered Celts.

It is familiar because the English-speaking world has been steeped in it for 1,700 years. Phrases like 'an eye for an eye', 'vanity of vanities', 'the valley of the shadow', 'walking on water', are part of our collective language bank. Our library of mental images includes arks and rainbows, scapegoats and burning bushes, cross-shaped wooden gibbets and pavements of gold. Our literature from Shakespeare to Joyce to Douglas Coupland is riddled with references to it. So is our art—from Rembrandt to Dali to Hirst. We can picture Charlton Heston parting the Red Sea, and Jason Donovan in his technicolored dreamcoat.

So even if you believe God is dead and religion is the opiate of the people, if you have any interest at all in the culture you are part of, you owe it to yourself to read the Bible.

And of course there is that other cultural argument—that even had the Bible not been the root from which Western prose, poetry, art, architecture, law and social customs have sprung, it is still very good literature in its own right. (This argument, however, usually balks at anything other than the 'original' King James Version.)

These are good arguments for the culturally inclined, but what of the rest of us philistines? (Another biblical allusion there, incidentally.) Well, you don't have to be a scholar to see that if a body of writing has survived for twenty centuries and been a 'bestseller' in all of them, it must say something pretty important about the human condition. Even in today's supposedly post-Christian world, more than 958 million people profess to live by its teachings (Christian Research), not to mention the nearly fourteen million Jewish people who base their identity and values on the Old Testament (Jewish Central Enquiry Desk).

All these arguments would suggest that even if your Bible's flimsy, gold-edged paper and tiny print induce a certain amount of panic, it's still worth having a go.

---

## WHY READ THE BIBLE?

- It is ancient wisdom that has survived because it has something to say about the human condition.
- It is great literature and the basis of Western culture.
- It is still credited by millions today as their inspiration.
- It just might have something to say to you.

---

## How not to read the Bible (1)

The trouble with literature that has been around this long is that it has gathered to itself a huge number of accretions. Traditions and assumptions cling to it like barnacles on the hull of an old boat. Often it is almost impossible to see the original design.

I come from an evangelical church tradition and some of the assumptions I have grown up with are these:

- You *ought* to read the Bible every day.
- You *ought* to get 'divine inspiration' every time you read it.
- You *ought* to find something deeply relevant to your situation in every bit of it.
- If someone tells you anything about it from a pulpit, you *ought* to accept it as true.

But as time has gone on, I have discovered that religious 'ought-ism' can sometimes become a stifling handicap.

There's nothing wrong with regular and frequent Bible reading. Moses clearly advocates a life steeped in God's words in every way possible (Deuteronomy 6:6–9). Jesus, his disciples and the New Testament writers clearly knew their scriptures deeply and intimately. But nowhere do Moses, Jesus, the prophets or the apostles command that scripture must be read, without fail, every single day.

Common sense tells us that anything that is worth doing—exercise, time to rest, keeping abreast of current affairs—is often best done by building into our lives a routine that includes them. So we go to the gym once a week, we take a holiday once a year, we read the Sunday papers or watch the news at 9 pm. A routine, be it daily, weekly, monthly or annually, is worth cultivating. But it has to be something that works for you.

I've tried getting out my Rosemary Conley *Bums and Tums* exercise video every morning. I've tried reading *The Guardian* every day. It doesn't work. Not only do I fail, but I feel so bad about myself that I start eating chocolate and reading *Hello!* magazine to compensate. Eventually, trial and error has taught me that I can manage to go for a swim once or twice a week. I can read the papers at weekends. And in the same way, trial and error has eventually taught me how Bible reading works best for me.

As a freelance writer married to a freelance TV sound-recordist, with a house frequented by grown-up children, lodgers and visitors from all parts of the globe, my particular lifestyle has almost no routine. For me, reading my Bible on an *ad hoc* basis—a short passage most weeks, a longer study once every few months—is the way that works best. (I do, however, find it essential to pray every day.)

I don't know what works for you. And I certainly don't want to tell you. Where Bible reading is concerned, my clarion cry is: Scrape off the barnacles! Throw out the rule book—whichever church tradition wrote it. It's meant to be a help, not a burden—do what works for you.

## HOW NOT TO READ THE BIBLE (1)

- You don't *need* to read it every day.
- You don't *need* to get some inspired thought every time.
- You don't *need* to take on board everything everyone tells you about it.

# How not to read the Bible (2)

I wonder if you have noticed that I have not, so far, referred to the Bible as a book. It looks like a book, but it is not. It is a library—a bound anthology gathering together a whole range of books written centuries apart, by totally different authors with wildly different worldviews in a wide variety of literary styles. It is as if Charlotte Brontë were gathered in the same volume as Chaucer, the collected poems of Seamus Heaney, the diaries of Alan Clark and *A Brief History of Time*. And then we are exhorted to read all of it in the same way, in the same sized chunks, with the same expectations. No wonder we are so often disappointed—and confused.

Some of what we are reading is in poetic, metaphoric language intended to convey a mood. Other parts are logically laid-out arguments intended to expound a theory. Still others are stories. Even these are not the same. Some stories are clearly allegories, some are steeped in symbolic imagery, some feature heroic role-models. But many are nothing of the sort. They are just common-or-garden chronicles of ordinary people caught up in extraordinary events: 'This happened and then this happened and guess what happened next…'

And, exactly as we would not expect to read a whole poetry book, or a whole encyclopedia at a sitting, but might well take in a feature article, a short story, or even a novel, so the Bible's writings are intended to be taken in different sized chunks.

Just to make it even more complicated, not only are we looking at widely different literary styles, we are also looking at widely different theologies. All these authors believed in the One God—named 'Yahweh' by Moses, 'Our Father' by Jesus. They all believed that this God was deeply and directly involved in human affairs. (There are, you may be surprised to learn, two Bible books—Song of Songs and Esther—that do not mention God at all. However, even the writers of these, it is reasonable to conclude, believed in God at work behind the scenes.)

But there the similarity ends. The writer of Ecclesiastes clearly doesn't believe in life after death. Revelation is full of nothing else. The Judges believed that if God didn't punish their enemies, they were fully entitled to do it for him. Jesus came along and told us to love them and forgive them seventy times seven. James saw the new ways of Jesus as so compatible with the old Jewish ways that he wrote as if nothing had changed. Paul wrote as if everything had.

We can't even see the Bible as a steady progression from primitive beliefs about God to more enlightened ones. There is a development that is clearly discernable. But it is not that simple. Some of the earlier books contain wondrous insights that later ones lack. When you travel from the clarity and simplicity of Jesus to Paul's convoluted arguments and the wild images of Revelation, you could be forgiven for thinking that things are going downhill.

You might guess from my comments that had I to compile an anthology of Holy Writ, I might have done it differently. So, I would guess, might you. But the strange thing about this awkward, uneven collection—for all its varied styles and views, its odd inclusions and tantalizing omissions—is that underlying it all is a surprising cohesion. It is rather like those pictures made of little blobs that, when stared at long enough, suddenly reveal a completely different image.

Of course, nothing is more irritating than those people in the know, who claim they can see something amazing when you can see nothing at all. 'It's a stag,' they cry, 'on a mountain. Surely you can see it? Come closer. No, further away. Sort of let your eyes go fuzzy. Just keep looking at it. You will see it. You will.'

I'm afraid I am about to be just as irritating and claim an underlying picture beneath the blobby fragments of the Bible. And I am asking of you the same frustrating method—that you take time to look, simultaneously staring hard and letting it drift fuzzily beneath your gaze.

But just to give a few clues, I will tell you the picture that I, and others wiser than I, have seen there.

---

## HOW NOT TO READ THE BIBLE (2)

- The Bible is not a book but a library.
- It has a variety of literary styles which cannot be approached in the same way.
- It has a plurality of views which cannot be straitjacketed into one theology.
- It has an understanding of God which changes and develops but is not an even progression.

---

## What to look for—recurring themes

The Bible itself, because it is not a book but a library, does not have a beginning, a middle and an end. But the story that it builds up does. It tells of a recurring theme—one that can be seen on a cosmic level, on a national level, on the level of every human life, and within every human life and relationship as a repeating pattern.

To try to make sense of it, let me start at the lowest level—the repeating pattern. This could be described as 'Equilibrium–Conflict–Resolution', or perhaps 'Home–Journey–Destination'. Anyone who has studied ancient myths or Hollywood screenwriting will recognize that what I am talking about is the basic pattern of story. Story, in a million different forms, goes something like this.

The hero is going about his or her everyday life—until, that is, something out of the ordinary happens. They are catapulted out of safety, out of the familiar. This catalyst-event makes life difficult for them, compels them to take risks, sends them on a journey. And at the end of the journey they have arrived at a new destination. They are a stronger, wiser person. The new home is better than the old.

The hero could be Abraham, Odysseus, Ruth, the apostle Peter, Bilbo Baggins, Luke Skywalker, Bambi, or Dorothy in *The Wizard of Oz*. The principles are the same. And these stories are classics that remain with us because they are about what it means to be human (yes, even *Bambi*).

The human life was intended to be an adventure. It was intended to be difficult and risky. We were intended to grow. We could equally relabel this repeating pattern 'Safety–Risk–Growth'.

The repeating theme of the Bible, and the vital difference it brings to the human story, is that we were never intended to make the journey alone. 'Follow me,' says Jesus, in the archetypal call to adventure. 'Go and make disciples of all nations… and I am with you always.'

'Go,' God told Moses from the burning bush. 'I will send you to Pharaoh to bring my people out of Egypt… I will be with you.'

'Leave your country, your kindred and your father's house,' God told Abraham. 'I will make of you a great nation and I will bless you.'

Of course, most of us will never make epic geographic journeys. My life, on the surface, is deeply unadventurous. I was almost shocked to realize recently that when I travel by train from my current home into central London, I pass the place I was born, the place I went to school, the place I went to college and the place I spent most of my adult life, all within the space of fifteen minutes. I was shocked because on the inside, my life feels like a tremendous journey.

The journey I am talking about is a psychological and spiritual one. It is one that all of us, whether we like it or not, have to make. All us have to go on the journey from childhood to adulthood, from taking on the values of our parents to finding out what our own values will be. And that journey for each of us is an epic.

It feels, however, not like one but an endless series of journeys, or adventures. We could relabel them as 'Orientation–Disorientation–Reorientation' or again as 'Order–Disorder–Reorder'. No sooner do we feel ourselves to be safely settled in one pattern of living than something else comes along to disturb it and send us on a new journey of exploration. For me, these journeys have been as big as marriage, having children or pursuing my dream of being a writer; as small as talking to a stranger, upholstering a sofa, performing street theatre or climbing Helvellyn.

Some of my modest adventures have ended in disaster. Most—despite being exhausting, painful, tiring, scary or tedious at the time—have ended well. Almost all of them, in retrospect, have made me a tougher, deeper and, dare I say it, wiser person. Would they have turned out so well if I had not made most of the journey with God? I can't prove it, but I believe without a doubt that they would not.

This is not to say that most of my life has been lived in a world of happy-ever-after. Far from it. And why should it be? That is certainly not what the Bible promises. The Bible is deeply realistic. This is something that its writers do have in common: they understand that most of life is lived in the middle zone of Conflict, Disorder or Disorientation. Take the Psalms—some of them are songs of delight, many are cries of despair. Most move freely from one extreme to the other. The Bible is like this because life is like this.

My life may look on the surface to be the epitome of safe, settled equilibrium, but it rarely feels like that. Mostly I am in a turbulent, disruptive state of dealing with bills, deadlines, rejection slips, ill health, wayward children, ageing parents, demanding friends, faulty technology and my inability ever to complete the tasks I set myself. The list could go on, but you get the idea. Your list may be slightly different, but the feelings, I bet, are the same.

The Bible, although not set in 21st-century Britain, is delightfully crammed with just this sort of personal trivia. But through it all, as well as tracing the recurring theme through the lives of individuals, it gives us a cosmic overview.

## What to look for—the big picture

On this universal level, the theme that emerges could again be described as: 'Equilibrium–Conflict–Resolution', or perhaps as 'Health–Disease–Cure', or the more traditional church terms of 'Creation–Fall–Redemption'.

To see this pattern, we have to look first at the Bible's opening chapters—the Genesis account of life's beginnings. What the first chapter of Genesis shows is a picture of equilibrium. God made the world and the world was good. It paints a picture of a man and a woman in harmony with each other and with God, at home in an idyllic garden. (Bear with me here; I am not going to examine until later just how literally or mythically we should take these words, nor comment on the rights and wrongs of the protagonists' actions.) But by the next chapter, it has all gone pear-shaped. The man and woman are arguing with each other and with God, and swiftly find themselves outside the garden with no possibility of return. The man is condemned to wresting food from the harsh, prickly wilderness and the woman is condemned to the pain of childbirth and the ignominy of being the second sex.

The big picture it paints—whether you use the theologians' language of sin, death and the devil or the more scientific language of disorder, decay and disease—is this: the world is full of goodness, but it has also an inherent tendency to go to the bad.

So far, the Bible is not telling us anything we could not observe for ourselves, but it is in the final third of the recurring theme that the difference lies. For this we have to jump from the beginning of the Old Testament to the middle of the New. We have to look to the death and resurrection of Jesus Christ and the dawning realization of his followers that here was not just a classic tragedy of one man against the system, or even a martyr story of one man dying for the good of the people. Here, in this one man Jesus, was a cosmic story of God becoming human to bring humans back to God. Here was a story of *redemption*. Here was a possibility of cure.

And lest you suspect that the idea of a redeemer is no more than a good spin put on bad circumstances by a committee of disciples, over and over again throughout the Bible comes the same refrain.

'I know that my Redeemer lives,' cries Job in the midst of his torment.

'The Lord drew me out of the miry bog,' sings the psalmist, 'and set my feet upon a rock.'

'Even though you intended to do harm to me,' says Joseph to his brothers, 'God intended it for good...'

'The law of the Spirit of life in Christ Jesus,' exults Paul, who never met him in the flesh, 'has set us free from the law of sin and death.'

And right at the end, in that most baffling of books, Revelation, is the amazing assertion that not just individuals, but the whole of earth and heaven will one day be reordered, restored and renewed. 'See,' says God, in a dramatic vision of the end of time, 'I am making all things new.'

And throughout the Bible we find the same theme. It is there on the cosmic level, on the scale of nations, tribes, families and individuals. The Bible sees God deeply involved in the world he created, constantly taking humanity's bad decisions, bad actions and bad decisions and—when and where those humans turn to him for help—redeeming them and turning them to good.

Where scientists talk of nature's capacity to rebalance and evolve, sociologists and economists talk of society's capacity to rebalance itself, and self-help enthusiasts talk of serendipity, the Bible talks of 'grace'.

And this is perhaps where the Bible differs from the scientists and self-helpers. It talks about redemption and resolution as a recurring pattern, but *not* an inevitable one. Its big picture is uncompromising— the two absolutes of good and evil do exist. Humans can choose to do right or wrong and those choices have consequences.

And here is where we return to that idea of the Bible as telling a story with a beginning, a middle and an end. It builds a picture of our origins —Big Bang, evolution, genetics and all—designed by God and not by chance. It builds a picture of every human being, whatever side of the blanket they were conceived, as being individually formed and known by God and made in his image. It also builds a picture of a world that will end in a bang rather than a whimper, and an ending in which individuals are more likely to face a judgment than to slip into oblivion.

That little sub-clause I sneaked in, 'when and where those humans turn to him for help', is another recurring theme. It is sometimes called 'repentance', sometimes 'humility'; sometimes it resembles nothing more than desperation. But it is vitally important. Because another of the Bible's most recurring themes is that it requires a reaction. It is not just about how life used to be, or even how it is. It is much more about, 'What are you going to do about it?'

In this section I have arrogantly dared to suggest to you what the Bible is all about. I have probably become as annoying as the people who see a stag at bay in a collection of little blobs. So don't take my word for it. You can't, anyway. You will only ever see what you see for yourself. But in claiming that the Bible has these overarching themes, I am touching on another vexed question. Who put them there? Is the Bible divinely inspired and, if so, what on earth do we mean by it?

---

## WHAT TO LOOK FOR

Beginning–Middle–End
Equilibrium–Conflict–Resolution
Home–Journey–Destination
Safety–Risk–Growth
Orientation–Disorientation–Reorientation
Order–Disorder–Reorder
Creation–Fall–Redemption

---

# Endorsements from history

*Just as those at sea, who have been carried away from the direction of the harbour they are making for, regain the right course by the clear sign of some beacon or mountain peak, so the Scripture guides those adrift on the sea of life back to the harbour of God's will.*

GREGORY OF NYSSA (335–94), EARLY CHURCH FATHER

*In the Scriptures be the fat pastures of the soul.*

THOMAS CRANMER (1489–1556), COMPILER OF THE PRAYER BOOK

*I have sometimes seen more in a line of the Bible than I could well tell how to stand under, yet at another time the whole Bible hath been to me as dry as a stick.*

JOHN BUNYAN (1628–88), AUTHOR OF *THE PILGRIM'S PROGRESS*

*I must confess to you that the majesty of the Scriptures astonishes me, the holiness of the evangelists speaks to my heart and has such striking characters of truth and is, moreover, so perfectly inimitable, that if it had been the invention of men, the inventors would be greater than the greatest heroes.*

JEAN-JACQUES ROUSSEAU (1712–78), PHILOSOPHER AND NOVELIST

*The Bible is an inexhaustible fountain of all truths. The existence of the Bible is the greatest blessing which humanity has ever experienced.*

IMMANUEL KANT (1724–1804), PHILOSOPHER

*I have found in the Bible words for my inmost thoughts, songs for my joy, utterance from my hidden griefs and pleadings for my shame and feebleness.*

SAMUEL TAYLOR COLERIDGE (1772–1834), POET AND LITERARY CRITIC

*In all my perplexities and distresses the Bible has never failed to give me light and strength.*

ROBERT E. LEE (1807–1870), US CONFEDERATE ARMY GENERAL

*The New Testament is the best book the world has ever known or will know.*

CHARLES DICKENS (1812–70), AUTHOR

*A man may learn from his Bible to be a more thorough gentleman than if he had been brought up in all the drawing-rooms in London.*

CHARLES KINGSLEY (1819–75), AUTHOR

*The Bible is the one book to which any thoughtful man may go with any honest question of life or destiny and find the answer of God by honest searching.*
JOHN RUSKIN (1819–1900), ART AND SOCIAL CRITIC

*When you have read the Bible you will know that it is the word of God, because you will have found it the key to your own heart, your own happiness, your own duty.*
WOODROW WILSON (1856–1924), US PRESIDENT

*A thorough knowledge of the Bible is worth more than a college education.*
THEODORE ROOSEVELT (1858–1919), US PRESIDENT

## And one who got it wrong:

*Another century and there will not be a Bible upon earth.*
VOLTAIRE (1694–1778), WRITER AND PHILOSOPHER

# Three

# The Bible: tricky issues

## Questions of truth and authority

### Opposing claims

If you are a fundamentalist preacher talking about the Bible, you will say something like this: although humans actually wielded the quills or styluses, it was God who wrote the Bible. Therefore every bit of it is inspired and therefore by logical conclusion it is infallible. Every bit of it—six-day creation, tree of knowledge, belly of the whale and all the rest—is literal fact.

If you are a liberal theologian, you have probably long since thrown out any thought of the Old Testament being factual. You probably also see the miracles, the virgin birth, and even, as one Anglican bishop recently acknowledged, the resurrection, as symbols rather than actual events. As to who wrote the Bible, your prime interest lies in debate on the identity of the human authors, who, of course, can't possibly be who they were claimed to be.

If you are a post-modern philosopher talking about the Bible or indeed any book, you will speak of the 'death of the author'. You will claim that readers create their own meanings regardless of the author's intention. You will point out that words never possess fixed meanings, that to every word you read you will bring a whole host of subconscious associations, that yours will be quite different from mine and, of course, wildly different from those of an author who wrote three thousand years ago. When an author writes 'dog' they may be picturing a ravening wolfhound, and when you read it you are seeing a poodle. What you think you read is as much a product of the images within your own head as the ideas the author brought to the page. Any text (and by implication any idea, because ideas can only be conveyed in language) is therefore always shifting, unstable and open to question. And since unstable, unfixed words can only ever be defined by more unstable, unfixed words, how can any written word ever claim any fixed authority?

I would guess you are not a fundamentalist preacher, liberal theologian or post-modern philosopher and have probably never studied the outpourings of any of them. Nevertheless, each of these conflicting views has probably filtered down to you in one way or another to make it much more difficult as you open your Bible.

## Original intention

Perhaps the first question to ask is what the biblical authors themselves thought of what they were writing. When you look at many of the prophets, it is obvious.

Jeremiah, recording the vision which provoked his calling, makes it clear that it was by God's appointment. 'Now, I have put my words in your mouth,' says God. 'The word of the Lord came to me...' 'The Lord said to me...' 'Thus says the Lord...' repeats Jeremiah over and over again. The fact that it proved to be a long and rather thankless task is further evidence that it was hardly self-appointed.

'Your word,' says the writer of Psalm 119, 'is a lamp to my feet and a light to my path.' He was talking about 'the Law', the first five books of the Bible, mostly history and quite literally a statute book of laws— hardly what most of us would describe as 'inspirational'. But to this writer, clearly, it was the word of God.

The Gospel writers evidently believed that Jesus' words were divinely inspired, and recorded that Jesus himself believed the same: 'The word that you hear is not mine, but is from the Father who sent me.'

Not only that, but John begins his Gospel with the mega-statement that in Jesus 'the Word became flesh'. He is borrowing a Greek concept: the *logos*. The big idea, or basic principle behind the whole universe, he is claiming, was embodied in Christ—a thought that implies that all other words and ideas had their origin in him also.

Perhaps Paul sums it all up best when he writes to Timothy, his young trainee, that 'all Scripture is God-breathed' (2 Timothy 3:16, NIV). Note: this is translated as 'inspired by God' in many versions, but the original Greek word is literally made up of two parts meaning 'God' and 'breathed'.

Now, to say that something is 'God-breathed' is not quite the same as saying that it is infallible or all literal fact. So what is it saying?

## Open to truth

Strangely enough, when we go back to our fundamentalists, liberals and post-modernists, we can see that each of them in their different way has grasped a little of what this means.

The fundamentalists have grasped one vital aspect—it is all inspired by God. The problem here is that they often go too far and give the impression that the authors surrendered their brains and gave their hands over to automatic writing. That leads them on to an assumption that if God dictated it, it cannot possibly have any mistakes or contradictions. Unfortunately there are plenty of sceptics who have successfully proved that idea wrong.

In fact, you can even find a whole website devoted to debunking the Bible and listing its contradictions—seventy or so, it claims (see www.erols.com/cygnus/home.html). Now some of those contradictions, I would suggest, are not contradictory at all, but the two opposing ends of a paradox, something I will come on to later. Some of them are the normal confusion of detail you would find in any collection of reports by different witnesses, and some, yes, are mistakes. The mistakes are, however, surprisingly few, and mostly pretty trivial. (We may encounter a few of them later as we go along.)

The other problem with the 'God dictated it' approach is that along with infallibility, it tends to make a giant mental leap and assume that therefore all of the Bible must be *fact*.

This is where the liberals have a lot to teach us, because they understand that truth is not the same as fact; that great truths can often best be learnt from stories, metaphors and symbols—something Jesus also understood when he taught in parables. The problem with this 'metaphorical' approach is that it is a short step from deciding that *some* of the Bible is not *intended* to be taken literally, to deciding that *none* of it *need* be.

So where do you draw the line? If some of the Bible is factual and some is not, how do you decide which is which? The first way to tackle this problem is to try to see whether or not the authors intended it to be read as fact, and the best way to decide that is to understand what sort of literature it is—something we will pursue in further chapters.

Unfortunately for the Mr Spocks among us, this approach leaves some brain-stretchingly non-logical and non-reasonable things on the factual side—but then perhaps that's what faith is all about.

So what do the post-modern philosophers have to teach us about this idea of scripture as 'God-breathed'? Well, I don't claim to be an expert on this, but what the post-modernists seem to be saying is that any act of reading is a sort of interactive exchange between the reader and the page. The author has put on the page his/her ideas and images and the reader brings to them his/her experiences, so that, even with the same text, each act of reading is a unique act.

So what if each act of reading was not a two-way one but a three-way one? What if, when someone sat down to read the Bible, they asked God to inspire them, and he did? What if each act of reading the Bible became a unique, divinely inspired experience? For we have been talking about the images that words draw from our subconscious, and who other than God knows what is in our subconscious and has the capability to draw from it? If that is so, then reading the Bible could indeed be a 'God-breathed' experience.

If we pursue this idea of the 'God-breathed' act of reading, then we could say that God could breathe into any act of reading any book. Well, as far as I am concerned, that is true. God can and often does teach me from all sorts of literature, be it *Captain Corelli's Mandolin*, *Zen and the Art of Motorcycle Maintenance* or *The Selfish Gene*.

But if that is so, what is different about the Bible? It's a question I have asked myself many times. I can't prove it, but I remain convinced: there is a difference. What is it? I can only assume that with the Bible, a very special sort of 'God-breathedness' comes at both ends of the exchange—the act of writing and the act of reading both brought alive by the Spirit of God.

You may be ahead of me here and have glimpsed a snag. If, as I claim, every reading of the Bible is a unique act, then isn't it going to provoke endlessly differing views on almost every subject? After all, the Bible has been notorious over the centuries as a bigot's handbook. If you try hard enough, you can find a verse to justify almost anything you please, from slavery to spiritualism, homosexuality to homophobia, racism to revolution. Surely if you take this approach, then any thought of the Bible having authority goes right out of the window?

Well, maybe, in the strict 'party line' sense that many churchgoers have become accustomed to, it does. Religious leaders down the centuries have understood that 'knowledge is power' and that a flock who all accept the same dogma are an awful lot easier to lead. Priests in the fourteenth century recoiled in horror from the new-fangled printing press that would allow their parishioners to read the Bible for themselves in their own tongue. Perhaps their main fear, though, was not that the people might discover that the Bible had no authority, but that they might find it did.

There is a difference between an authority which sits like a heavy weight on its subjects, controlling and confining them, and one that is generously shared, enabling and enobling people to become more than they ever dreamed. Sadly, much religion has been of the former sort. The Bible, however, is more to do with the latter.

As it turns out, maybe the medieval priests need not have worried. Fortunately for religious leaders down the centuries, most of us, their flock, are a lazy lot, only too happy to have someone to tell us what to believe. But the priests were right to be concerned. The Bible is an explosive collection of writings, and explosives need to be handled with care. But there *are* safeguards, and before partying with the bangers and rockets, it's a good idea to run through what those safety procedures are.

---

## QUESTIONS OF TRUTH AND AUTHORITY

- The fundamentalist weakness: everything must be infallible.
- The liberal weakness: nothing need be literal fact.
- The post-modern weakness: words are shifting and unstable, so no text has any authority of its own.
- What the biblical authors believed: they were recording what God said.
- Paul's model: 'all scripture is God-breathed'.
- The fundamentalist strength: God inspired the whole Bible.
- The liberal strength: truth is not the same as fact.
- The post-modern strength: reading is a two-way (and maybe three-way) exchange.

---

# Problems of interpretation

## Texts in context

'A text without a context is a pretext.' Perhaps this is the most important bit of Bible safety drill that any of us needs to learn. And perhaps this is why reading the Bible for yourself is so much safer than getting it secondhand from a preacher.

I'm not against sermons, *per se*. I'm enormously grateful for what they've have taught me over the years. (I've dozed through a few stinkers, too.) But a sermon, be it ten minutes or forty, can really only concentrate on one small passage, one or two texts, three or four points. (You would think that the forty-minuters would get in more points than the ten-minuters, but in my experience they rarely do. They just repeat the same ones an awful lot.)

You can learn a great deal from sermons. But they are edited highlights. You are getting the goals, the fouls and the penalties, but not the whole match. If you didn't know any better, that could give you a very odd idea of what football is about. And so it is with only getting your Bible knowledge from sermons. At best, you are only getting a tiny bit of the picture. At worst, you are getting a gross distortion of what the whole thing is about.

A verse taken alone can be like a candle illuminating a pitch-dark pathway. It can be a comfort, a way of knowing where you are. It may even allow you to read the map or glimpse the signposts. But it can never show you the whole terrain. It may allow you to see a stream, a beautiful flower, a rocky outcrop. There will be mountains that you just won't know are there, resting places you will pass by, views you will never see. And if you are navigating by candlelight alone, it is terribly easy to take the wrong path.

Reading a whole passage or a whole book, and relating one biblical writer to another, is like seeing the scene in daylight. You are no less able to see the wonderful details, but there's an awful lot more out there. But before I work my mixed metaphors to death, I am going to move on.

## Reason or intuition

If the first safeguard is to ensure the scope of what you read, the second is to examine the manner in which you do so.

I wonder if you have heard of, or have done, one of those personality tests they call Myers-Briggs. (If you haven't, I'd highly recommend it.) As with blobby pictures, people in the know on this can be rather infuriating. They start conversations with, 'Well, of course, I'm an INTP...' or, 'Speaking as an ESFJ...'

For those not in the know, the Myers-Briggs test, by asking a hundred or so questions, discovers where you stand on a scale between each of four pairs of opposing characteristics: Extrovert/Introvert, Sensing/iNtuitive, Thinking/Feeling and Judging/Perceiving. The first and last pair need not concern us here, but it is worth looking briefly at the two in the middle.

The Sensing/Intuitive scale evaluates the way we perceive or acquire information. If you are predominantly 'Sensing', then you are the sort of person who deals with what your eyes and ears tell you. You like facts and figures—information that is measurable and practical and precise. 'Intuitive' types, on the other hand, prefer to look for the meanings behind what they see and hear, the relationships between different ideas and events. They are always looking beyond, searching for the pattern behind the facts. They perceive the world through imagination and inspiration.

The Thinking/Feeling scale looks at how we process the information we acquire. Thinkers prefer logic and reason. They form their opinions by analysing and weighing the evidence. They pride themselves on being objective and pragmatic. Feelers, on the other hand, have no compunction about being either subjective or illogical. They form conclusions based on what is important to them at the time. They focus on what they care about, on the values they espouse (not necessarily the same thing as basing decisions on their emotions).

Of course, on both of these scales, most of us are neither one extreme nor the other but somewhere between the two. But for each of us, one or the other characteristic will emerge predominant. And just as it can help if we understand our predominant method of understanding the world (and why others sometimes come at things so differently), so we also need to develop and learn to use the non-dominant side of our nature.

As you read through this book, you will probably prefer some suggested approaches to Bible reading over others. Some will like the meditative, imaginative techniques. Others will go for the more analytical, logical methods. And if you don't already know your personality type, this may give you some clues.

(It doesn't follow, incidentally, that just because you are a Sensing person you are also a Thinker, nor that Intuitive types are also Feelers. You can be a Sensing Feeler or an Intuitive Thinker.)

There's nothing wrong with coming at the Bible through intuition or feeling, nor with approaching it via facts, figures and analysis. But to discover its full breadth and depth, you need to work with a full armoury of understanding. You may need to develop those skills of perceiving and processing information that, by nature, you prefer to leave dormant. And nowhere is this full complement of skills more needed than when you approach what the Bible seems to be infuriatingly full of—contradiction and paradox.

## Contradiction or paradox

*Paradox: 'a seemingly absurd though perhaps actually well-founded statement; a self-contradictory or essentially absurd statement; a person or thing conflicting with preconceived notions of what is reasonable or possible.'*
OXFORD ENGLISH DICTIONARY

When it comes to Bible reading, understanding paradox is an essential tool. It is vital because the Bible, and especially Jesus' teaching, is full of these absurd, ambiguous, mysterious and apparently contradictory statements. 'The first will be last,' says Jesus (Matthew 20:16). 'Those who want to save their life will lose it... Blessed are those who mourn... the meek will inherit the earth' (Matthew 16:25; 5:4–5).

Those who followed after him soon got the idea. 'Whenever you face trials...' says James, 'consider it nothing but joy' (James 1:2). 'Whenever I am weak,' says Paul, 'then I am strong' (2 Corinthians 12:10).

Sometimes in their efforts to understand what this new Christian faith was about, however, they appeared to contradict each other. 'What good is it, my brothers and sisters, if you say you have faith, but do not have works? Can faith save you?' asks James (2:14). 'For by grace you have been saved through faith—and this is not your own doing; it is the gift of God—not the result of works, so that no one may boast,' claims Paul (Ephesians 2:8–9).

These are extracts from letters designed to correct believers who were in danger of falling into error. This is the problem of paradox—lean too far one way or the other and you are likely to topple.

Christianity is not about faith *versus* works, although plenty of people over the years have lined up on either side, but about faith *and* works. Paul and James are essentially agreed on what is important—the order of things. Faith comes first, putting people back into relationship with God. But if this doesn't bear fruit in practical ways, it is doubtful whether faith was ever there. So paradox is not about either/or but both/and. It is all a matter of balance.

Here I must add a proviso, suggested to me by a friend who hates the word 'balance'. To her, it conjures up a picture of religion at its worst. 'Balance' is what good, solid, pew-warming Anglicans love to invoke. It is an antidote to that most feared of states—fanaticism. Worship exuberantly, give up everything to go on a mission, start shouting about justice—these sorts of things are dangerous. They rock the ecclesiastical boat. We must be *balanced* about these things. This sort of balance is about keeping everyone happy, about never going too far in any one direction, about being sensible and safe and settled. And on this reckoning, Jesus was dangerously unbalanced!

The sort of balance that Jesus had in mind is rather more like crossing the Niagara Falls on a tightrope. It is about tension. It is about risk. It is not about taking on a little bit of faith and a little bit of action. It is about walking the wire carrying huge bundles of each at either end of an extremely long pole.

It is not about alternately standing tall as a 'child of God' and grovelling as a miserable sinner. It is about being both fully confident of your status in Christ and fully aware of your failings before God.

It is not about either waiting passively for God to direct you, or making up your own mind. It is about both listening to God and taking decisions yourself.

I have never learnt to walk along wire, but I can confidently assert that you are unlikely to master the tightrope without a good deal of falling off—which is why, for beginners, the wire is suspended only six inches off the ground.

Being able to recognize and understand paradox is an essential for extracting the full meaning from the Bible and learning to live by it. But don't worry if you find yourself constantly falling off on one contradictory side or the other. Living a paradox, like walking a tightrope, takes practice.

# Contradiction or paradox—how to tell the difference

Below are some apparent contradictions identified on the website I mentioned earlier, devoted to debunking the Bible. It is worth taking some time to see if they are really as contradictory as they first appear, and what are the clues to help us decide.

- *With justice you shall judge your neighbour (Leviticus 19:15).*
- *Do not judge, so that you may not be judged (Matthew 7:1).*

The clue here is context. Leviticus was talking about the setting up of a system of justice, while Jesus was talking about the ethics of personal conduct which go far beyond a legal system. Jesus points out that the person who judges will be judged in the same way, but Leviticus also assumes it.

- *Thou shalt not kill (Exodus 20:13).*
- *Thus says the Lord, the God of Israel, 'Put your sword on your side, each of you! ...each of you kill your brother...' (Exodus 32:27).*

The clue here lies in seeking out the original meaning of the words. Anyone sharp-eyed and knowledgeable might notice that 'Thou shalt not kill' comes from the older King James Version of the Bible. Most modern ones, including the New Revised Standard Version which I am most often using, render it as 'You shall not murder.' And this, of course, is how the ancient Israelites understood it. In their eyes God had no problem with warfare against ungodly enemies or, as in this case, putting down pagan insurrection with slaughter. Now we may think differently, and that is another issue to resolve, but the point is, the Bible is not contradicting *itself*.

- *Happy are those who fear the Lord... Wealth and riches are in their houses (Psalm 112:1, 3).*
- *It is easier for a camel to go through the eye of a needle than for someone who is rich to enter the kingdom of God (Matthew 19:24).*

The Old Testament is full of statements like the one from Psalm 112. Those who live justly and wisely will be blessed with material possessions. It is a statement of cause and effect. Not that wicked people never make big money, or that good people never go under; but if you work hard, live prudently, treat your employees well—live by God's principles, in other words—by and large, you usually end up living quite comfortably.

So why does Jesus contradict it so shockingly? The clue again lies in context. First, it is important to note that two different dynamics are working here. The Psalm talks of someone who, by living in God's way, gradually accumulates wealth. The man to whom Jesus addressed his words is described in one Gospel as a ruler, in another as a young man. It is a fair guess from these two descriptions that Jesus was talking to an aristocrat, someone with inherited wealth—someone who had no understanding of what it was like to be without, someone who had never had to trust God out of desperation.

Second, a look at other teachings provides an explanation. Jesus was unequivocal in his assertion that 'you cannot love God and money'. Paul backed him up: 'For the love of money is a root of all kinds of evil'. The psalmist is actually saying the same thing—loving God comes first. He is anticipating Jesus' promise, 'Strive first for the kingdom of God and his righteousness, and all these things [food, drink, clothes] will be given to you as well.' So here we find the principle that drives through the contradictions. Wealth *per se* is not wrong, but if it is a driving force, or an addiction in your life, boy, are you in trouble!

That doesn't quite solve the problem, though. We could summarize the Bible's teaching as follows:

- If you live rightly, you may well be given wealth. Therefore wealth must be good.
- If you have wealth, you will probably come to depend on it. Therefore wealth is evil.

And that leads us right back to paradox.

## Credulity or doubt

Reading the Bible can often make you feel like Alice through the Looking Glass—being asked to believe 'six impossible things before breakfast'.

The Christian faith is just that—*faith*. That means it must involve a leap beyond reason. It must involve an act of trust—of consenting to being led blind. But there is a difference between accepting what you cannot understand and pretending to believe something that in your heart of hearts you just can't take on board. Faith is about trusting in a person rather than assenting to a set of statements. (And, of course, we are already back in paradox territory here.)

So I am not asking you to go through the Bible screwing up your eyes and willing yourself to believe something that just seems downright impossible to you. It may just be possible to convince your religious mentors that you believe implicitly anything that is thrown at you, but deep down you will never convince yourself. If reading the Bible means trying to live a lie, then the Bible will soon go back undusted on to the shelf.

What I am asking you to do is exactly the same as you do when you watch a play or read any other story—to suspend your disbelief. What this means is that for the period of time you are reading or watching you willingly enter into the story's world. You see things as those characters, as this author, sees them.

The poet Nigel Forde, talking about literature in general, explains it thus:

*We must... suspend (suspend not obliterate) our prejudices, convictions and our sincerely held opinions in order that the work may speak. This may sound like a renunciation of responsibility and integrity, but it isn't; the same thing happens when we are arguing with a friend, at least, it happens if we are genuinely arguing and not merely taking up a position of intractable obstinacy. We listen carefully, we don't assume the conclusion, we do not interrupt; in fact we suspend our judgment until we have heard the evidence, until the case under consideration has been put. Only in this way can any mental or spiritual development take place.*

THE LANTERN AND THE LOOKING GLASS, SPCK, P. 138

Even though you have never lived as a nomad, or have never seen an angel in your own life, you consent to imagine what it would have been like to invite mysterious heavenly strangers into your tent. Even though you find it impossible to believe that five loaves and two fishes could feed five thousand people, you consent to listen with an open mind to someone who claims to have seen it happen.

Whether your disbelief will be conquered, I cannot say. But I will claim that it matters far less than you might think.

We may never know whether the mysterious strangers were just travellers from the Orient who just happened along at the right time. We may never know whether the bread mysteriously multiplied itself or whether a small boy's offering shamed others into sharing their resources. And it doesn't much matter. The world is full of things we can't understand. Amazing things do happen. What matters is that we are open to mystery, that we dare to believe that God might be involved in the here and now. If we do, the lessons from these stories can be powerful and far-reaching, even to sceptics like you and me.

---

## PROBLEMS OF INTERPRETATION

- A text without a context is a pretext.
- Intuition and reason—working with both tools.
- Paradox—truth often lies in the tension between apparent contradictions.
- You don't need to believe 'six impossible things before breakfast'.
- You do need to suspend (not obliterate) your disbelief.

---

# Discovering the personal in the perplexing

*There is one very puzzling parable in the Bible, at least to me. Actually, there is more than one that perplexes, but then parables are meant to be full of meanings and I can't claim to catch them all.*

*Well, this one is about the farmer who hired some people to work on his land early one morning. As the day went on, he hired a few more, and some right in the last hours of the day. Then when it came to pay them, he gave each of them the same amount, no matter how many hours they had worked. When the early birds grumbled at this, the farmer replied that he had paid them exactly what had been agreed and that if he chose to pay the same to the others that was due to the kindness of his heart and was no cause for them to complain.*

*When I first heard this story, I felt that Jesus was condoning injustice and arbitrary pay policies. Then I learnt that the parable was about the generosity of God's love. But parables at their best carry personal messages, and the message for me in this story is about the destructiveness of envy.*

*Some hold that envy is the spur to economic growth, and I guess that much of advertising is based on this belief. Dissatisfied souls try harder. It doesn't work that way with me. I want to pull down the others rather than climb up to them, just like the complaining labourers in the story, and when I can't, I growl and grumble about the unfairness of life until self-righteous misery envelops me.*

*So I have now resolved some things. I will try not to begrudge others their good luck in life but will wish them well with it. I will stop wondering about what might have been if I too had got in on those shares, if I had not sold the house five years ago or left that job. I will not yearn for the grass on the other side of the fence, which might be greener but seldom is, for I know, in my heart, that it is easier to walk down life's path if you look straight ahead and not over your shoulder at other people. It is certainly less depressing.*

CHARLES HANDY (MANAGEMENT CONSULTANT AND BESTSELLING AUTHOR), FROM
*THOUGHTS FOR THE DAY*, ARROW BOOKS, PP. 86–87

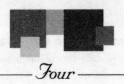

# Four

# The Bible: useful information

So, here you are with this volume in your hand, leather-bound, column after column of small print, proclaiming itself to be 'Holy'. But who put it together? Who decided what went in and what stayed out? What journey took it from a miscellany of scrolls, written and preserved across the Middle East, to this collection of writings in your living-room?

The history of the Bible, as far as we know it, goes something like this.

## The making of the Old Testament

It began 2,622 years ago. A workman sifting through rubbish in a dusty back room of the neglected Temple found a scroll. He took it to Hilkiah, the high priest. Hilkiah took it to Shaphan, the king's secretary. Shaphan took it to the king (2 Kings 22—23).

Josiah was one of Judah's better kings, authorizing the restoration of the Temple after half a century of the most pagan rule Jerusalem had ever seen. What he read in the scroll shocked him so much that he tore his robes, sent for priests and prophets to advise him on its significance, and then gathered the whole of his kingdom together for the scroll to be read aloud to them too.

What the workman had found was probably the major part of Deuteronomy, and what the king discovered in it was that long ago God had made a binding agreement with the Jewish people, one which they had now horrifically broken. Josiah instigated a programme of reform, sweeping away the pagan idols that had become part of everyday life, and the scroll became the first piece of writing to be seen as Holy Scripture.

Who wrote the scroll and who put it there, we do not know. What we do know is that it was part of a larger body of writing known as the Torah (Law) or Pentateuch ('five volumes'), the first five books of our present Bible. The material it contained dated back some six hundred years previously, to the time of Moses (estimated at around 1250BC), although it was probably only written in this form during the reign of King Solomon (971–931BC).

Why *then*? Because by Solomon's time, Israel had become a bona fide nation, stable, settled and powerful. It had a strong walled city, Jerusalem, and in the middle of it a great and marvellous temple to the one God, Yahweh. And as part of this flowering of nationhood, it wanted to chart its beginnings. It wanted to gather its history, both religious and secular, and so the many traditions which had been faithfully told from generation to generation began to be gathered and written.

As things turned out, Solomon's golden age was short-lived. The kingdom split into two, the Temple fell into disrepair and the people found it convenient or expedient to worship other gods. The scrolls of the law were hidden away, kept safe in the hope of better times.

Over the couple of centuries following Josiah's dramatic find, gradually these writings were rediscovered and edited. The process is unclear, but what we do know is that by about four hundred years before Jesus, the 'Book of the Law' was seen by the Jewish people as sacred, the cornerstone of their faith and identity.

The next chunk of scripture to be gathered was what the Jews called the Prophets. The 'Former Prophets'—the books of Joshua, Judges, Samuel and Kings—tell of events covering a span from roughly 1200 to 560BC and are not so much the writings of prophets as a history of their activities. The 'Latter Prophets'—Isaiah, Jeremiah, Ezekiel and the dozen from Hosea onwards—cover a period between the eighth and the fourth centuries BC, and centre on the prophetic words themselves.

It was during the time when the Judean nation was in exile that prophetic writing first became popular. If the Law had been the product of a golden age in Jewish history, the prophets came to prominence in its darker days. Not that they had not spoken their message before then. But nobody wants to hear a message of doom when times are good. Now, transported from their homeland by the mighty Babylonian empire, the nation could no longer escape the prophets' message. The people yearned for return, and the prophets, for all their warnings of the dire consequences of disobeying God, offered hope. They promised that God would restore his people. They spoke of better days to come.

And come they did. In 538BC, the Jewish people were freed and began to trickle back to Palestine. Around 400BC, the priest-scribe Ezra finalized the gathering of the Law and probably began to gather the prophetic writings together as well. By about 200BC, they too had become known as Holy Scripture.

A pattern is emerging here. No one (with the possible exception of Moses and the tablets of stone) set out to write Holy Scripture. No book was written and immediately decreed sacrosanct. The Old Testament did not spring into being ready-made. It is the distillation of centuries of gathering, reading, telling, pondering, sifting and editing. So much so that, once gathered, its claim to holiness has hardly been questioned at all, and then only regarding three books.

It was this same sifting process that brought the rest of the Old Testament books into the canon. ('Canon' is the word for those books which Judaism and then Christianity in its turn have considered 'official' and authoritative.) The Jews called these remaining books 'the Writings', a pretty unimaginative name for a hotch-potch collection which includes stories, poetry, wisdom, history and prophecy with a touch of apocalypse. Their origins cover as wide a timespan as the other scriptures and just a little bit more, as Daniel was probably written around 165BC. (This explains why Daniel was not included in the 'official' prophets, since this list was finalized around 200BC.)

The reasons for including 'the Writings' were various, but mostly to do with their use in worship. The Psalms were the Jewish hymn book, so well loved that no one argued with their claim. Five books—Esther, Ruth, Lamentations, Ecclesiastes and Song of Songs—were associated with particular Jewish festivals and read aloud at them each year. Chronicles, Job, Ezra, Nehemiah and Daniel also had a special place because they were read aloud at the Day of Atonement.

Three books were disputed at various times: the Song of Songs, because it was a sensual love poem which had no spiritual content unless seen as an allegory; Ecclesiastes, because of its weary pessimism; and Esther, because God doesn't get a mention.

Eventually, not until AD90 did a council of Jewish rabbis get together at Jamnia, near Jaffa, and lay down that the list of Holy Scripture was now settled, with none to be added and none to be taken away.

But if it was ever doubted how seriously the Jewish people took the holiness of their scriptures and how deeply they touched their lives, we need only look at the New Testament. Jesus, the disciples, the scribes, the Pharisees, the apostle Paul and the Gospel writers—all of them refer, directly and indirectly, over and over again to scriptures as their authority. They were steeped in its language, its imagery and its ideology. It was the plumbline by which every new claim, every new idea, must be measured. So convinced were they of their scriptures as the word of God that they could not conceive of any new revelation that was not related in some way to the old. Jesus knew and referred often (but sometimes obliquely) to these connections. Later his followers searched for them, found them and began to understand.

So, however thrilled the first Christians were by their new faith, they never lost their immense love and respect for the old. And that, essentially, gives today's Christians reason to love and respect it too.

---

## THE MAKING OF THE OLD TESTAMENT

- It took a period of six hundred years, from the eighth to the second centuries BC, to be written.
- It took from 622BC to AD90 to be compiled, a process of just over seven hundred years.
- It is composed of three main sections: the Law, the Prophets and the Writings (although in our Old Testament, the Prophets and Writings are interspersed).

---

# The making of the New Testament

The same pattern that we observed in the making of the Old Testament holds true for the New. No one believed themselves to be writing Holy Scripture at the time. The process by which these books came to be seen as holy took several centuries and the combined wisdom and experience of many Christians. As William Barclay points out, 'It was not the New Testament which produced the Church; it was the Church which produced the New Testament' (*William Barclay Introduces the Bible*, ed. John Rogerson, BRF).

It was Paul's letters that were the first to be written—real personal letters to newly formed churches needing advice and encouragement. Only later, when those men and women who had known Jesus personally were growing old and in danger of dying out, were the Gospels and Acts written. And maybe it was not until the churches began to read copies of Acts that they realized just what an important piece of history those letters were.

Of course, it was not only Paul who wrote letters. Some were written by Jesus' disciples Peter and John, others by Jesus' brothers James and Jude. The authenticity of these letters was, of course, disputed, particularly 2 Peter which is now generally thought to have been written much later, around AD120. The authorship and destination of the letter to the Hebrews remains a mystery, although it was originally attributed to Paul. Even more mysterious is that strange final apocalyptic book of Revelation, attributed to John, but unlike his Gospel and letters in style.

It was not until AD367 that the first mention is to be found of the New Testament in its present form. That was in an Easter letter to his flock from Bishop Athanasius of Alexandria, who decided to list the books which he considered valuable for Christians to read.

Soon afterwards, in AD382, a council headed by Damasus, Bishop of Rome, laid down the same list of books as canon, or Holy Scripture, affirming the canon of the Old Testament at the same time. A few years later, councils in Africa, at Carthage and Hippo, affirmed these lists for the Western Church.

Why *then*? Well, probably for the same reason that saw the setting down of the Law—its religion had become part of the establishment. The Church had won its freedom in AD312 when the Roman Emperor Constantine was converted. (He had dreamed of Christ the night before a battle and, marching out with the cross on his standard, had won a mighty victory.) There had already been several councils bringing Church leaders together to standardize beliefs and outlaw heresy. Now it was time to clarify the sources for those beliefs and create Christianity's Holy Scripture.

The decision over what to include in the New Testament had not been without debate. In the second century, two leaders on the woolly fringes of Christianity had posed opposite threats. In AD140, a wealthy ship-owner called Marcion tried to promote the view that only Luke's Gospel and Paul's letters were valid. In AD172, a young enthusiast named Montanus started to prophesy, claiming his words as direct from the Holy Spirit.

To stop these as being contenders for the Church's sacred writings, Church leaders decreed that only books by the apostles were valid for inclusion. Of course, this led to disputes about authenticity and value. Various lists were made over a couple of centuries. The first we have evidence of, known as the Muratorian Canon, was complied in AD170; two great Church scholars, Origen and Eusebius, also investigated the various writings in circulation and drew their conclusions.

Those books disputed at one time or another, but finally included, were James, Jude, 2 Peter, 2 and 3 John, Hebrews and Revelation. Other candidates that were eventually discarded and have now disappeared from view were books such as The Shepherd of Hermas, the Letter of Barnabas, the Gospel of the Hebrews and the Acts of Peter.

And so finally, by this same sifting process, the New Testament was formed—and has stood the test of time for over 1,600 years.

---

## THE MAKING OF THE NEW TESTAMENT

- It was written in Greek between about AD45 and 120.
- The first mention of an 'official' list of Christian writings is in AD170.
- Various other Christian writings were considered for inclusion but then omitted.
- Some books—Hebrews, James, Jude, 2 Peter, 2 and 3 John and Revelation—were disputed but eventually included.
- The first mention of the New Testament in its present form is in AD367 and this became standard in the West shortly afterwards.

---

# The Apocrypha—the bits that got left out

I say 'left out', because the Protestant Bible, the one I am familiar with, does not usually include them. The Roman Catholic Bible, however, does, and it is worth understanding how this divide came about.

The first reason is time—they came too late. As I explained earlier, the Old Testament canon was considered 'closed' somewhere around 200BC. The apocryphal writings date from around 200BC to AD70.

The second reason is language. The books of the Apocrypha first made their appearance in the Septuagint, the Greek version of the Old Testament begun towards the end of the third century BC at the behest of Ptolemy, ruler of Alexandria. (The Septuaguint, incidentally, is so called because seventy translators were involved in its creation. It is said that all seventy, working independently, arrived at exactly the same translation.) The apocryphal writings, however, have never been part of the Hebrew scriptures.

When the early Church came to consider these writings, this led to some interesting divides. Leaders like Tertullian and Augustine, who knew only Greek, tended to assume them to be scripture. Scholars who knew the original Hebrew, most notably Origen and Jerome, did not consider them to have the same status. Even so, Jerome, who translated the Bible around AD 400 into what became the Vulgate, the standard Latin version, included them because of the weight of popular opinion in their favour.

What is interesting, however, is that although the writers of the New Testament were all Greek speakers, none of them refers to any material from the Apocrypha.

In general, the status the early Church gave these books—one that still stands today—was that they were valuable to be read in private for 'example of life and instruction of manners' but that they were not to be read in public worship or used for the establishment of Church doctrine.

It was Martin Luther's translation of the Bible into German, published in 1534, which first pulled the apocryphal writings out from the Old Testament and gave them a separate section of their own. (Luther had a low opinion of some parts, considering Baruch trivial and becoming so frustrated with 2 Esdras that he gave up translating it and threw it in the River Elbe.)

Gradually in the years that followed, as hostility between Catholics and Protestants grew, the Apocrypha began to be seen by Protestants as essentially Catholic and therefore suspicious, a justification for beliefs they considered an anathema.

When John Bunyan discovered that a verse through which God had spoken to him was part of the Apocrypha, he was at first deeply disturbed. However, being a thoughtful man, he later decided that 'though it was not in those texts we call Holy and Canonical, yet... it was my duty to take the comfort of it; and I bless God for that word, for it was God to me' (*Grace Abounding to the Chief of Sinners*).

Others were less open-minded and gradually the Apocrypha began to be omitted from Protestant Bibles altogether. Even the very word 'Apocrypha' began to change. Its original Greek meaning of 'words which are secret and hidden' came to mean 'of doubtful authority' or 'fictitious'.

So what is it that Protestants are missing? It is an interesting miscellany.

## Additions to existing Old Testament books

The Additions to the Book of Esther seeks to remedy the perceived problem of Esther as it stands, adding mentions of God and of prayer that are lacking in the original.

The Prayer of Azariah and the Song of the Three Young Men, Susanna and Bel and the Dragon are all additions to the book of Daniel.

The Prayer of Manesseh refers to the evil king, grandfather of Josiah, whose reign had set up so much idolatry and caused so much bloodshed in Judah. The book of Chronicles records that late in his reign Manesseh was captured and taken as a prisoner to Babylon. There he repented and on his return to Judah tried to undo some of the worst excesses of his reign. This purports to be the prayer of his repentance.

1 Esdras corresponds directly to 2 Chronicles, Ezra and Nehemiah and contains only a small amount of additional material.

Baruch purports to be written by Baruch, the secretary of Jeremiah. The Letter of Jeremiah, sometimes attached to Baruch, is a scathing attack on idol-worship.

## Wisdom literature

The Wisdom of Solomon, although attributed to the king whose name above all others personifies wisdom, was written around the time of Christ. Whatever its origins, it contains some great advice for good living.

Ecclesiasticus is perhaps the best-loved apocryphal book and the one that many would most like to see included in scripture. It contains advice after the manner of Proverbs.

## Stories

Judith is a bloodthirsty little number featuring a heroine who seduces an Assyrian general, makes him blind drunk and then chops off his head.

Tobit is a somewhat gentler tale of an old blind peasant, his son, their dog and an encounter with an angel.

## History

1 and 2 Maccabees is an account of historical events between the two Testaments, the tale of a fight for freedom from foreign influences and control that took place between 175 and 134BC.

## Apocalyptic

2 Esdras is writing in the spirit of Revelation, around the same era and rather more obscure.

---

## THE MAKING OF THE APOCRYPHA

- It was written between around 200BC and AD70.
- It contains historical material that fills the gap between the Old and New Testaments, plus some great stories and Wisdom literature.
- It was included in the Septuagint, the Greek Old Testament, but not in the original Hebrew version, and is not accepted as scripture by modern Judaism.
- Martin Luther was the first person to classify it as a separate section in his German translation.
- Protestants came to see it as allied with Catholicism and therefore suspect. Gradually it was omitted from Protestant Bibles.
- The general view of the Apocrypha, by Catholics and Protestants alike, is that it is subsidiary to the main canon and not to be used for the making of doctrine or for reading in public worship, but that it contains material that is valuable and helpful.

---

# Copies and translations

If you were lucky enough to own one of the first copies of Luke's Gospel, you would probably be holding in your hand a scroll containing a nine-metre length of papyrus wrapped around two wooden rollers. The papyrus came in small sheets which were then stuck together. Each sheet cost around a working-man's daily wage and there were about forty-five of them to a scroll. Copying was also expensive, perhaps around thirty days' worth of a working-man's wages for the whole of

Luke. Imagine—a fifth of your annual salary for just one Gospel.

Scrolls were soon overtaken by the codex, a form similar to our books, but it was to be a further thirteen centuries before the invention of printing enabled the Bible to be gathered as one book and to be made widely and cheaply available.

(Writing this, it has struck me just how extraordinary it is that Christianity not only existed but flourished for sixteen centuries without ordinary people being able to read the scriptures for themselves; and for only five centuries with that privilege. The first conclusion is that it *is* a privilege and one that we should not take for granted. The second is that perhaps we need not get too hung up about personal Bible reading— God may not be quite so dependent on it as some people have claimed! But back to the history.)

The first Bible to appear in English was printed by William Tyndale, whose New Testament was published in 1525. Other versions followed quickly, and it was only a century later, in 1611, that what is still to many people the definitive version, the King James Bible, was published. Much loved for the beauty of its language, the King James Version held sway for generations and is still hotly defended in some quarters.

It is worth noting two things, however. Scholarship and the resources and skills of translators have moved on dramatically since then, and the KJV is certainly much less accurate than more modern translations. Also, as Oliver Barclay points out, however much some people might love language that is solemn, dignified and archaic, that is not the style of language in which much of the original was written. The Old Testament, it is true, is composed largely in classical Hebrew. But the New Testament is written not in classical but in colloquial Greek, the everyday language of the man and woman on the street.

Shock, horror—it was more *Daily Mail* than Booker Prize!

When it comes to translating, it is also worth pointing out that Hebrew in particular is notoriously difficult. For a start, it has no vowels and no punctuation. And translating any ancient language is a complex task. Some words are describing things that simply no longer exist. Others have changed dramatically in their usage over the years. We need only look at words like 'gay', 'wicked' and 'cool' in our generation to see how words can change, and even sometimes reverse their meaning, in the space of just a few decades, let alone several millennia.

So we need the best resources of contemporary translation to help us, and there are certainly plenty on offer. It was not until the beginning of this century that a mushrooming of different Bible translations began—at least forty-five versions in English alone.

What everyone would like is a translation that is easily understandable, an accurate rendition of the original, and beautiful in its use of language—but it may be that these three criteria are mutually exclusive. You may have to make a choice based on which of these qualities is most important to you. If you have the opportunity to own and compare several versions, you will probably find it helpful, especially for study purposes.

One thing to note: some Bible versions—the Living Bible, for example, or *The Message*—are described not as translations but as paraphrases. These can be brilliant for getting the overall sense of a passage, but do not claim to be an accurate rendering of the original and should be used with caution when the aim is to study in detail.

It would be impossible here to list all the translations on offer, and certainly not to evaluate them. A survey done by Bible Society in 1997 revealed that of those people who did read the Bible, 25 per cent preferred the Good News Bible, 17 per cent favoured the New International Version, 15 per cent still read the Authorized Version, 9 per cent read the New English Bible, and 8 per cent the New King James Version.

Clearly, each translation has its pros and cons and no one version has an unanswerable claim to be the best buy. The important thing is to find one that suits you. There is also a lot to be said for having a choice available. One thing is certain, however—if God is God, he is perfectly able to speak to you through whichever translation you choose.

---

## DIFFERENT TRANSLATIONS

For beauty of language:
> *Authorized (King James) Version* (1611). The one still most often quoted and assimilated into our culture. If you like Shakespeare, you'll love this.

For accessibility:
> *Good News Bible* (second edn, 1994). A simple English translation, very popular and probably the easiest introduction for a new Bible reader.

*Contemporary English Version* (1997). Especially designed for reading aloud; also includes some pages of explanation for new readers.

*The Message* (1993–95). A paraphrase by Eugene Peterson, colloquial and inclined to Americanisms, but very popular.

For accuracy:

*Revised Standard Version* (1952). An update of the King James, popular for many years, perhaps now eclipsed by the NIV. Throughout this book I am quoting from the New Revised Standard Version, an update completed in anglicized form in 1995.

*New International Version* (1978). A good, balanced compromise between the three needs of accuracy, fluency and accessibility.

# Choosing what works for you

*For those thinking of buying a Bible, I'd say: don't just think the Bible is like the one you see in the drawer in the hotel room, or the one that you read when you were at school. The Message is a great way of reading the Bible in a contemporary version. I would suggest having a contemporary version like The Message or the Living Bible in one hand and the NIV in the other. And a Study Bible is invaluable, for reading a bit of the background. In this day and age, with computer programs, there's masses there to help you understand it better. Don't expect to just read one Bible and understand everything from it, because you won't.*
ROSEMARY CONLEY (EXERCISE AND DIET GURU AND BESTSELLING AUTHOR OF *THE HIP AND THIGH DIET*)

*I think the main thing is to find a version of the Bible with which you're comfortable. For example, I can't stand modern versions that translate 'through a glass darkly' as 'we see dim reflections in a mirror'. It profoundly offends me. On the other hand, I'm sure that for people who are not terribly familiar with the language of the Authorized Version, that sort of straightforward translation is actually helpful. So the first tip I would give is, find the version that sits most easily with you. Find a version that you can cope with and which you find pleasant and easy and doesn't grate. I think that is a much neglected feature in all of this.*
ANN WIDDECOMBE (CONSERVATIVE MP)

*I've found it's important to find the translation you can identify with most easily. For instance, I know that a lot of people go for the King James because of the poetic nature of the language, and yet it wasn't until I'd studied Shakespeare that I understood half of what it was saying. It had wonderful phrases, they sounded great, but it didn't mean anything—they didn't speak that way in Hackney where I grew up!*

*I find having a Bible with a little column in the middle that explains things and puts them in cultural context is very helpful, because what things meant in the Middle East in the first century can be very different to how they appear to us in the twenty-first century.*

*I alternate between the NIV, for accuracy, and The Message for its wonderful use of today's language (despite the Americanisms). I also use something called the Jewish New Testament, which puts things in context and reminds me that the New Testament is still essentially Jewish.*
DAVID GRANT (SINGER, SONGWRITER, TV PRESENTER, ACTOR, CURRENTLY MEMBER OF 'UNITED COLOURS OF SOUND')

# Part Two
# TYPES OF LITERATURE

# Eye-witness accounts: stories from personal experience

### The hinge of history

Why start a book in the middle, or, to be more precise, some 900 pages from the beginning?

Well, perhaps the fact that it then leaves approximately 260 pages to go, rather than 1160, is no bad thing. But that is not the real reason. First of all, the Bible is not, as we have already established, a book, but a library. And secondly, in Christian terms, the Gospels are where the whole adventure starts.

For a long time I had a mental picture of the Bible as a journey across a vast plain of history. Granted, there were a couple of boring and barren depressions, round about Leviticus and Ezekiel, and a deep, impenetrable forest when it came to Revelation. But on the whole it was a trip across pretty level terrain. I mistakenly deduced this idea, I think, from that oft-repeated verse about all scripture being inspired (or God-breathed). All scripture, I therefore figured, must be roughly equal, a deduction subconsciously reinforced by the pattern of frequency with which various texts fuelled the sermon. (For some reason, although Jesus was often referred to, in the sermons of my memory at least, the Gospels seemed to figure less than the Old Testament or the letters.)

My mental picture of the Bible is now very different—a long, slow ascent from a deep valley through an ever higher mountain range to the spectacular pinnacle that is the arrival of Christ in human form. Then comes a descent into the more mundane landscape that is the Church. This is terrain with its own peaks and troughs, never as high as that great watershed, but consistently higher than the pre-Christ landscape. Only the very beginning of this later territory finds its way into the Bible, the rest is still being travelled. My picture is different because my view of Christianity is different. It is no longer a religion based on a book, but on a person. The book is precious, and, yes, it *is* God-breathed, but only in so far as it points me to this person.

The Gospels, as the principal source of information on this person, are the Bible's watershed (or threshold—the metaphor is different but the principle is the same). They are the pinnacle from which what went before and what comes after must be viewed. Everything else leads towards or away from this central point and it is from this central point that all other territory must be evaluated.

Nearly two thousand years of the greatest world religion are centred around these Gospel accounts (rather scrappy by today's biographical standards) of three years in the life of one person.

This life, as the new millennium has constantly reminded us, is for Christians the very hinge of history. It is certainly the hinge of this collection of sacred writings, and the threshold between one journey of discovery about God and the next. It is the start of a new, mind-blowing concept which has been described in roughly the following words: the Divine become human so that you might learn from a human being how a human might be divine—and it gives a radically changed perception of God. The awe-inspiring, all-powerful sovereign is suddenly revealed to be a loving, forgiving daddy as well.

But before grappling with ideas of cosmic proportions, let us begin in a much more down-to-earth way, by looking through the eyes of his contemporaries at one enigmatic and perplexing man and at the rather faltering and experimental activities of his followers.

## The unlikely Messiah

'The best-kept secret of Christianity'—that is how some people have referred to the Jesus of the Gospels. M. Scott Peck, a psychiatrist and bestselling author of *The Road Less Travelled*, who did not come to Christian faith until his forties, quotes this definition and comments, 'I was absolutely thunderstruck by the extraordinary *reality* of the man I found in the Gospels' (*Further Along the Road Less Travelled*, Simon & Schuster, p. 160).

I, in turn, am quoting these remarks because they are mirrored in my own experience. I had been a Christian for many years, but it was not until I had reached my forties, for once alone and with time to spare, house-sitting for some friends in France, that I jettisoned my presuppositions and sat down to read the Gospels with fresh eyes.

I was blown away by what I discovered—by the remarkable character that Jesus actually was. I found a man who was sometimes puzzling, sometimes abrasive, sometimes gentle, sometimes angry—and certainly never predictable!

He often spoke in paradox and taught as much by what he did as by what he said. He never made things easy, for his followers or for himself, and seemed deliberately to throw away what chances he had to court popularity. He mixed with a motley collection of characters and it was clear that no one came away from an encounter with Jesus and remained quite the same. And neither did I. I am not sure what was so different—it was not that I had never read the Gospels before. But perhaps before then, Jesus had always been more of an idea than a person. Now I was discovering a real human being—someone intriguing, someone that I rather liked.

I also liked the fact that he was portrayed in narratives that were naïvely devoid of 'spin'. With their contradictions, omissions and ragged edges, they had all the hallmarks of real, honest, eye-witness accounts.

## The gospel truth?

And here I hit a problem. Biblical scholars, of whom there seem to have been an interminable number over the ages, are in broad agreement: the Gospels were written at several decades remove from the actual events. Estimates vary wildly but the broad consensus on timing seems to be as follows.

The first New Testament writings were Paul's letters, starting with Thessalonians at around AD50–51.

Mark, the first of what are known as the Synoptic Gospels (the three accounts that are closest to each other), is generally thought to have been written between AD61 and 70. Matthew and Luke, it is usually agreed, followed on and drew from Mark. The latest and rather more individual account is the Gospel of John, often dated between AD85 and 95.

There have been those who suggested much later dates, well outside the lifetime of the apostles. But helped by the evidence of the Dead Sea Scrolls, the pendulum of academic opinion seems to be swinging the other way, with dating of the Gospels now being revised by some to as early as AD40.

The detailed and inconclusive meanderings of scholarship need concern us no further. What did concern me for some time, however, was this: why were such remarkable events not written up then and there? Was their significance not grasped at the time? Or, more worryingly, was the resurrection and 'Son of God' interpretation of Jesus an accoutrement added years after the more prosaic reality? The Gospels read like immediate reports from people on the spot. If they were not, doesn't that throw doubt on the whole enterprise?

It was some years before I stumbled upon an answer that made sense to me. And again it illustrates my earlier claim that if you can understand the nature of the authors and the reasons for and circumstances of their writing, you will understand a great deal more of the text.

## The market-place storytellers

The Greek word 'gospel' means 'good news' and was originally used of imperial proclamations. It is not found in the plural, describing the four written accounts of the life of Jesus, until the second century. Before then there was only one gospel, the good news that was spreading rapidly around the Mediterranean world, carried in the only way that news could be carried to ordinary people in those days—by word of mouth.

It never occurred to the first disciples to write anything down. What would be the point? Their target audience—common folk rather than officialdom, individuals rather than organized groups—could not, by and large, read, and certainly had little access to 'books' or scrolls.

And anyway, that was not what their Master had told them to do. His final command had been, according to Matthew, to make disciples, to baptize and to teach. He himself had seen no need to write down his teachings. Why, then, should they?

They were, they felt sure, living in the 'end of the age' that Jesus had predicted. Things were urgent. They were speaking to their own generation, because that is all they thought there would be.

But as time wore on, it became apparent that the end of the age might not be in their lifetime. Some of the apocalyptic happenings that Jesus foretold were certainly fulfilled. In AD70 the Romans, tired of their most troublesome subjects, reduced the city of Jerusalem to rubble. With it was destroyed the Temple, the most holy Jewish site. From then on, Judaism was destined to be a religion without a home.

But the world did not end. The Temple went up in flames, but not the whole earth. Life went on and those people who had actually spoken, tramped the countryside and eaten meals with Jesus were getting ever older. There was a danger that their unique experience could die with them.

And so the Gospels came to be written—not as stories dredged from the haze of old men's memories and interpreted for the first time, but as tales that had been lived and relived, told and retold in the intervening years until they were thoroughly understood.

This goes some way to explaining their anecdotal style. These are folk-tales, a series of lively, pithy narratives, designed to be told in just the same way that Jesus told his stories, to a circle of listeners clustered in a market-place or huddled round a fire.

It also explains the absence of what we would consider 'proper' biographical detail and chronological accuracy. These are stories honed down to their essence, with any digression thrown out long since.

## The unsatisfactory authors?

Even when the accounts finally came to be written down, it is unlikely that their authors thought they were creating holy writ. They most probably compiled their writings in a codex—an up-to-date functional system, with leaves arranged quite like those of a modern book—rather than in a scroll which would have been perceived and venerated as a precious object in its own right. It was the first-century equivalent of a paperback rather than a leather-bound volume, and that is how they saw it. The scriptures to them were what we have now labelled the Old Testament. They can have had no perception that they were contributing to the New.

Oh, how we might wish they had! How many gaps they might have filled had they known; how much more detail and accuracy they might have provided. Two of the Gospel writers at least thought it valuable to tell of the remarkable infancy of their hero. This had precedents—Moses in his basket in the bulrushes, Isaac born when all thought of child-bearing was past and spared the sacrificial knife. The Greeks had a similar tradition: Plato, born four hundred years before Christ, was said to have had a miraculous birth and some claimed that Pythagoras was the son of the god Hermes.

But there were no psychologists to tell the biographers how vital their subject's formative years were; no history professors to insist on accurate dating and the importance of the precise order of events. We can now begin to understand why the relation of one incident to another can vary so drastically from one Gospel to the next, why sometimes the writer bothered to make it clear that one episode followed immediately from another, but in many others gave no indication whether hours, weeks or months had elapsed.

There was also no tradition of description in prose. Unless it is something vital to the story—Samson's long hair, Goliath's height—we know nothing whatsoever about the physical appearance of any biblical character. There is no scene-setting, no atmospheric asides that tell us whether it was hot, rainy, noisy or smelly; no mention of birdsong, or gnarled olive trees, or the sun low on the horizon. (Perhaps if present-day writers had to copy everything laboriously by hand, having first made their own paper and pens, we would discover a sudden absence of purple passages in their writing, too.)

How much more I would like to have been told. But could it be, I wonder, that the Gospel writers, in ignorance of the enormity of their task, were able to be more honest? They may have been less thorough than we would have liked, but were they also less inclined to embroider, to neaten the rough edges of reality, and tidy out of sight the inconvenient and unpopular radicalism of their hero?

As someone who has written for both government departments and religious organizations, I am aware how easily truthful promotional material can tip over into truth-economical propaganda. Did God in his wisdom ensure that we got something as authentic as possible?

And could it be that a wise God also knew how much more we could remember and understand if we were allowed to fill those gaps with our own imaginations? Was this a kind of first-century equivalent of 'the pictures are better on radio'?

## The unexpected audience

Jesus seemed in no doubt of his prime task. 'I was sent only to the lost sheep of Israel,' he stated when pestered for a miracle by a non-Jewish woman. (He gave her what she needed nevertheless, as he did a member of the Roman occupying forces, a Greek madman and a Samaritan whore.) But if he was certain that his life's work lay in the tiny province of Palestine, his death and resurrection changed all that. It soon became clear that his message could not be contained there.

By the time of the destruction of the Temple in AD70, there were already four or five times as many Jews outside Palestine as inside. More open-minded than their home-town cousins, these ex-pats had absorbed the rationality of Greek philosophy and the individual salvation of the Greco-Roman mystery cults. They had also given a glimpse of the solid rock of monotheism to their Gentile neighbours. Across the Roman world there were people ready for something new.

It was this wider readership that the four Gospel writers addressed, although each of them had a slightly different target audience in mind.


## The picture in parallel

So, then, four different Gospels, each drawn from eye-witness accounts by people who had been close to this man, who had eaten with him, travelled with him, watched how he lived and died and, they all agreed, how he came back to life once more. Like all eye-witness accounts, they differ (and occasionally contradict) in how they remember the details, in the incidents they select as being important and in the significance they draw from what they saw and heard.


# Books covered in this chapter

## Matthew

### Authorship

Matthew is assumed to be the same disciple whom Jesus called from his tax-collecting booth (Matthew 9:9). As the quisling employee of a hated occupying power, he would have been seen by Jewish tradition-ists as the lowest of the low and a betrayer of Judaism.

### Target readership

Each of the apostles believed that Jesus came to fulfil and transform the

Jewish scriptures, but for Matthew, writing for a Jewish audience, this relationship to the old order is of paramount importance and he quotes or alludes to it sixty-five times. Could it be that the quisling was determined to show how much he now valued the Jewish tradition?

## Themes

Matthew wanted to convince his traditionalist audience that Jesus was the Messiah, the great King prophesied centuries before. Hence he emphasized Jesus' birth, family tree and teaching on the 'Kingdom'. The Jews expected a political leader; Matthew needed to persuade them that the Messiah's reign was always intended to be a spiritual one.

He was anxious to reassure them that Jesus never intended a jot or tittle—'not one letter, not one stroke of a letter'—to be lost from the Law (Matthew 5:18). Here he seems to be at odds with Paul, who claimed that Christians were no longer under the Law, and even with his later portrayal of Jesus himself, who is seen almost spitting with fury at the pettiness of the Pharisees' regulations (Matthew 23). It is not as contradictory as it seems. It is the values of the Law that Jesus, Matthew and Paul wished to uphold, not their crippling and oppressive application.

# Mark

## Authorship

Mark is thought to be the John Mark mentioned in Acts, whose mother's home in Jerusalem was a regular meeting place for the early Church (Acts 12:12), and whose cousin Barnabas took him on missionary journeys with Paul (Acts 15:39; Colossians 4:10). He was also a close companion of Peter, who referred to him as a son (1 Peter 5:13).

## Target readership

Tradition has it that Mark wrote this Gospel while in Rome with Peter, intending it for a Roman audience. Certainly Mark feels it necessary to explain some Jewish customs to his readers.

This is the Gospel that shows its street-preaching origins most clearly. Couched in simple, direct language, it is clearly a Gospel for the 'common man'. Mark has virtually nothing good to say about officialdom—priests,

Roman officials or even the apostles themselves, who are portrayed as understanding little or nothing that Jesus told them.

## Themes

This Gospel has an unrelenting urgency about it. Mark's favourite adverb is one variously translated as 'straightway', 'at once', 'immediately'—a word that appears forty times, eleven in the first chapter alone. Chosen verbs include 'run', 'arise', 'shout' and 'amaze'.

Mark likes action. He tells us nothing of Jesus' origins, showing him bursting on to the scene as the expected Messiah, and gathering four disciples and performing three and more miracles by the end of chapter one. Mark gives us more of Jesus' actions—seventeen miracles—and less of his teaching—only four parables—than any other Gospel.

Even if we did not have any biographical clues, we could hazard a guess that this material originated from Peter. Peter, who was always keen to get on and do something; Peter, who spoke before he thought; Peter, who misunderstood so often, but did grasp the main plot before anyone else—that this really was the Son of God. (Curiously, though, the last we see of Peter in this Gospel is a man weeping after disowning his Master. It is left to others to tell us of Jesus' loving restitution and commission.)

# Luke and Acts

## Authorship

Although we cannot be certain, all the evidence points to Luke, the Greek doctor who accompanied Paul on his missionary journeys (Colossians 4:14; 2 Timothy 4:11). In Acts the author (who refers to his 'first book') occasionally drops into the first person, describing 'our' adventures.

Even without these clues, the style of the text would point to a non-Jew, a learned man with a wide vocabulary and a skilled use of words, familiar with both Greek and Jewish culture. Not only does he quote from the Greek version of the Old Testament, at times he mimics it. His Gospel rings with ancient phrases: 'and behold', 'before the face of', 'in the days of'. If Mark's trademark is 'straightway', then Luke's is 'and it came to pass'.

## Target readership

We can be certain of Luke's target readership, because he tells us. He is writing to 'most excellent Theophilus' (Luke 1:3; Acts 1:1). Unfortunately that is all we know. Exactly who Theophilus was and what was his interest in the matter can only be guessed. You don't have to be Sherlock Holmes, however, to deduce from the name and manner of address that this was a high-ranking Roman. Moreover, Luke's style and choice of words point to his audience as the intelligentsia of Roman society.

## Themes

Luke takes a longer view than the other Gospel writers. His narrative starts before the others, with the story of the birth of John the Baptist, and continues long after the others have ended, with the beginnings of the Christian Church. He begins by explaining that this is an account of 'the things that have been fulfilled'. He is aware that he is writing part of a much longer history, that flowed out of the Jewish past and its prophecies and into a Christian future that he can only dream of. Perhaps Luke, of all the Gospel writers, had the strongest glimpse that he stood on the threshold between one religious era and the next.

# John

## Authorship

For many years, scholars claimed, based on this Gospel's allusions to Greek thought and its marked difference from the other three, that it must have been written much later. The discovery of the Dead Sea Scrolls in 1947, however, changed all that. It became clear that these writings of the Essene community, dating from a century before Christ, contained remarkably similar concepts and language to John's. It is now commonly thought that John comes from a source as old as, though independent of, the other Gospel writers.

So, after all, it is possible once more to take at face value the traditional view that this Gospel was written by 'the disciple whom Jesus loved' (John 21:20)—John, the brother of James and fishing partner of Peter and Andrew. Some have queried how an ignorant fisherman could write such a learned document. They forget, perhaps, that this was a fisherman who lived across the lake from, and probably traded with, the Decapolis, a vast Greek conurbation where philosophical ideas were to be heard discussed in the market-place. And maybe they also forget that unlearned does not mean unintelligent. John would not be the last person to be lifted way beyond humble origins by an encounter with Jesus Christ.

## Target readership

In his poetic prologue, John's words carry echoes of both Greek philosophy and Jewish mysticism. John was writing for the thinkers, those who realized that if Jesus did rise from the dead, here was an event with huge philosophical consequences. He wanted to tell his readers not just what Jesus did and said, but what it all meant.

Tradition has it that John, commissioned by Jesus to look after his mother Mary, took her to Ephesus, where they lived for many years. If so, John would have found, in one of the most cosmopolitan and highly civilized cities around the Mediterranean, an audience thirsty for deep ideas.

## Themes

Luke may take the longer historical view, but John could claim to have the furthest view of all. He starts his story outside time altogether, stepping into the realm of metaphysics with his opening statement: 'In the beginning was the Word...'

John also has the sense of standing on a threshold, not between historical eras but between eternity and time. He is concerned with what *was* (what has always existed), and how it crossed over into *becoming* (an event in time and space). Before embarking on an account of the man Jesus, he hints at the huge implications of this very earthly life.

It has been said that if the first three 'Synoptic' Gospels are like photos of Jesus, John is more like a painted portrait. It is certainly very different. It picks out different incidents, centring on the time Jesus spent in Jerusalem, and different aspects of Jesus' teaching. It contains no parables, but records many metaphors by which Jesus described his mission—the great 'I am...' statements: the Door, the Way, the Bread of Life and so on. It is more reflective, giving glimpses of much lengthier discussions between Jesus and individuals.

# Ways of reading

## For sheer enjoyment

First, and most important of all, we can read these stories just to enjoy them, taking them on their own, at face value, in as small or as large chunks as we fancy, reading just for the fun of reading and letting them say to us what they will. As far as I am concerned, this is always the most precious way of reading and should never, ever, be abandoned or despised.

But when it comes to the Gospels, you may want, and will probably be urged, to re-read them. Fine for the first few times, but when it gets to the umpteenth, there comes a moment when (go on, admit it) the freshness has gone. Been there, done that, got the 'Jesus saves' T-shirt.

If so, now is the time to dig a little deeper, to start *studying* rather than just reading, an activity that need not be half as daunting as it sounds.

## The literary critic

The first method I would suggest for this second phase is to turn literary critic. One thing I have found out, as I started this process of delving, is that none of the Gospels is quite as random and ragged a collection of incidents as it might first appear. Through each of them runs a thread of themes and ideas, a carefully built-up picture with its own particular 'take' on who Jesus was and why he was so special. Method one, then, is to try 'unpicking the thread' of the author's intentions, and to discover just why he put together the book the way he did. It involves seeing how the different component parts relate to the whole.

A note here on the idea of 'sub-text'. In the best writing, as in life, there is often something being said that never appears in the words themselves. To take a simple example, someone says to you, 'You look smart today.' The sub-text could be, 'And about time too. You usually look a right mess', or, 'Who are you meeting who's so special?' or, 'How much did you spend on that?' These words are never said aloud, but can be 'read' nevertheless. Jesus, who not only understood what was going on under the surface of people's lives, but also had far bigger truths he wanted to communicate, almost always had a sub-text and it is worth searching for.

## The super-sleuth

The second way is to try your hand at detective work. Like all good investigators, you will need painstakingly to examine the different accounts of a particular incident and piece them together to see where they agree with or augment, contradict or complement each other, and whether an overall picture will eventually emerge. This involves seeing how each of the four parallel books relates to the others.

## The archaeologist

When you start digging around the Gospels to see how they built on what came before, you will quickly find foundations going right down through the Old Testament to the founding of the Jewish nation and beyond. The Gospel authors packed their writing with references to the Old Testament. The last five chapters of Mark, for example, contain 57 quotations from, and 160 allusions to, scripture as he knew it, plus an additional 60 places where an Old Testament influence can be detected. It was not just the apostles who were keen to stress how the new order stood in continuity with the old, Jesus himself did it clearly and repeatedly. This is why we can never understand the New Testament properly without referring back to the Old, and why it is worth playing amateur archaeologist. The Christian religion sits firmly on a Jewish substructure and we will never understand the shape of the edifice unless we examine what underpins it.

## The historian

The life, death and resurrection of Jesus were only the start of something new, and my final suggested method of study involves relating the Gospels to what came later. The most tricky part of this is looking at them in relationship to the writings of Paul, who sometimes seems to know an entirely different Jesus! However, this is a minefield I will attempt to cross later when we come on to the letters.

But before that we must return to the last eye-witness account, which we have so far largely ignored: Luke's presentation to Theophilus, episode two, the Acts of the Apostles. It chronicles how the disciples set out on this new, uncharted Way of Christ, how they found themselves going in new directions they never dreamed of (and occasionally up blind alleys), how they negotiated their differences and navigated dangers and not only survived but grew in the face of opposition.

Acts needs to be studied in relationship to the Gospels and also to the letters, which were written to and from the characters in its pages, and often contemporary with it. It also needs to be read in relationship to the further history of the Church right down the centuries to our own. The church we find on the pages of Acts is no more or less holy and infallible than the one down our street. Those pages will spring into life when we start seeing its characters not as distant saints but as complex, flawed human beings. That in turn may lead to the discovery that the complex, flawed members of your local church could also be saints.

But I digress. For now it is time to move on to something practical.

# Exercises

## The literary critic: understanding the passage as a piece of writing

### Jesus and the woman at the well (John 4:5–42)

Step 1: Ask God for understanding.

Step 2: Read the passage.

Step 3: Look at the context.
- What comes directly before and after?
- Is there an underlying theme?
- How do the teaching and happenings relate together?
- Are there any aspects of this passage which recur as hallmarks of this particular Gospel?

Step 4: Look closely at the text.
- Are there any images which are powerful and universal ones?
- Are there any issues raised which are universal to human experience?
- What are the ideas that the Gospel writer is trying to draw out of this passage?

Step 5: Look at the sub-text.
- Is there anything going on under the surface of what is actually being said?

STEP 6: How does this passage relate to your personal experience?
• How do the images, ideas and issues relate to you personally?

## The super-sleuth: relating
## different accounts to each other

**The woman anointing Jesus (Matthew 26:6–15; Mark 14:1–10; Luke 7:36–50; John 12:1–8)**
STEP 1: Ask God for creative insights.
STEP 2: Read the passages.
STEP 3: Make a note of factual differences and similarities.
• Use a grid pattern. Put the names of the Gospels at the top. Down the side, put: who? what? where? when? why? how? Then fill in for each Gospel.
STEP 4: Work out which parts complement each other and which, if any, contradict.
• Could these different accounts fit together to make a composite picture?
STEP 5: Explore the passages further.
• What were the motivations of the characters involved, including Jesus?
• How did the incident affect each of them?
• What themes or aspects of Jesus' character and teaching was each Gospel writer most concerned with?
STEP 6: How does this passage relate to your own experience?
• Which account and interpretation has the most relevance for you right now?

## The archaeologist: digging down into the foundations

**Family tree/temptations/Jesus in the synagogue (Luke 3:21—4:21)**
STEP 1: Ask God for understanding.
STEP 2: Read the passage.
STEP 3: Which obvious quotes or subtle allusions can you find to the Old Testament? (Allusions are words, images or events that refer to, hint at or echo something else.)

- Which names in the family tree do you recognize? What was the significance of these people?
- How many literal Old Testament quotes can you identify?
- Are there any other words or ideas with subtle echoes?

STEP 4: Refer back to origins.
- Look up the references for quotations. (For Luke 4:4, see Deuteronomy 8:3; Luke 4:8, see Deuteronomy 6:13; Luke 4:10–11, see Psalm 91:11–12; Luke 4:12, see Deuteronomy 6:16; Luke 4:18–19, see Isaiah 61:1–2.)
- Try to find the original source of allusions. (For Luke 4:1–2, see Deuteronomy 8:2–4; 9:9–11.)
- Try to understand the significance of these roots.

STEP 5: How and why is the Old Testament being used here?
- Is it referred to in order to subvert, change or reinforce tradition?
- Why does the author consider these roots important?

STEP 6: How does this passage relate to your own experience?
- What does it tell you about the importance of understanding your heritage?

## The historian: relating the Gospels to the ongoing story

### The coming of the Holy Spirit (Acts 2:1–18, 37–47; 3:1–10)

STEP 1: Ask God for the spirit of understanding.

STEP 2: Read the passage.

STEP 3: Trace it backwards.
- Was this event predicted or referred to by Jesus? (See Matthew 28:19; Luke 12:12; John 14:16–17, 26; John 20:22.)
- Did it happen as predicted?
- What were the surprise elements?

STEP 4: Trace it onwards.
- Did an event like this happen again? (Acts 10:44–48)
- What were the repercussions of this event? (Acts 15:5–11)
- What were the controversial issues that needed addressing? (1 Corinthians 12—14)

STEP 5: Trace it up to the present day.

- How does this event and the issues it presents relate to the modern-day Church?
- Have manifestations of the Holy Spirit changed and/or developed?
- Have they become corrupted, confused or institutionalized?

STEP 6: Relate the passage to your own experience.
- Do you have preconceived ideas about how God might work in your era and your circumstances?
- Have you lost any of the characteristics that the early Christians displayed?
- Have these issues (relating to the Holy Spirit) got confused, corrupted or institutionalized in your personal experience?

## Meeting the Christ of the Gospels

*When I did finally come to read the Gospels, I did so with a dozen years of experience of trying in my own small way to be a teacher or healer... With this experiential knowledge under my belt, I was absolutely thunderstruck by the extraordinary reality of the man I found in the Gospels. I discovered a man who was almost continually frustrated. His frustration leaps out of virtually every page: 'What do I have to say to you? How many times do I have to say it? What do I have to do to get through to you?' ... I discovered a man so incredibly real that no one could have made Him up.*

*It occurred to me then that if the Gospel writers had been into PR and embellishment, as I had assumed, they would have created the kind of Jesus three quarters of Christians still seem to be trying to create—what Lily [Scott Peck's wife] refers to as 'the wimpy Jesus'. He is portrayed with a sweet, unending smile on His face, patting little children on the head, just strolling the earth with this unflappable, unshakeable equanimity, because with His mellow-yellow Christ consciousness, He's got peace of mind. But the Jesus of the Gospels—who some suggest is the best-kept secret of Christianity—did not have much 'peace of mind' as we ordinarily think of peace of mind in the world's terms, and insofar as we can be His followers, perhaps we won't either. Perhaps that's not the point.*

M. SCOTT PECK (PSYCHIATRIST AND BESTSELLING AUTHOR), FROM *FURTHER ALONG THE ROAD LESS TRAVELLED*, P. 160

*The Christ that emerges from Mark, tramping through the haphazard events of his life, had a ringing intensity about him that I could not resist. Christ spoke to me through his isolation, through the burden of his death, through his rage at the mundane, through his sorrow...*

*The Gospel according to Mark has continued to inform my life as the root source of my spirituality, my religiousness... The essential humanness of Mark's Christ provides us with a blueprint for our own lives, so that we have something we can aspire to, rather than revere, that can lift us free of the mundanity of our existences, rather than affirming the notion that we are lowly and unworthy. Merely to praise Christ in his perfectness keeps us on our knees, with our heads pitifully bent. Clearly this is not what Christ had in mind. Christ came as a liberator. Christ understood that we humans were for ever held to the ground by the pull of gravity, our ordinariness, our mediocrity—and it was through his example that he gave our imaginations the freedom to rise and fly. In short, to be Christ-like.*

NICK CAVE (SINGER-SONGWRITER AND MUSICIAN), FROM *INTRODUCTION TO MARK*, CANONGATE, PP. XI–XII

# Six

# Myth: stories that make sense of the world

## Seminal stories

Link the words 'myth' and 'Bible' in the presence of some Christians and they will immediately freak out. So great is the fear of erosion of faith that even to float the idea of the mythical seems dangerous.

I would really prefer not to make anyone's hackles rise, but it seems to me a subject so important that I would be doing no one any favours to skirt round it. I do not think it is possible truly to understand this collection of writings called the Bible without fully understanding the concept of myth.

Before every evangelical writes me off as a heretic, let me explain what I mean. The problem this word poses is that it has at least two quite distinct meanings. One is the more popular: 'a figment: a commonly held belief that is untrue or without foundation' (Chambers).

But it is the other that we need to home in on: 'an ancient traditional story of gods or heroes, especially one offering an explanation of some fact or phenomenon: a story with a veiled meaning' (Chambers).

I am using the word 'myth' not in the sense of something untrue, but in the sense of a story that helps us make sense of the world. 'People need a story, an idea of why they are here and what they expect from life and the universe,' says Bernadette Vallely in *The Young Person's Guide to Mind, Body and Spirit*. 'We use these myths to tell us how to live, to learn morals and to stimulate our emotions' (Virago, p. 94).

But this idea of myth is not just for New Agers and post-modernists. It is an idea deeply embedded in the Bible. The ancient Hebrews understood something that contemporary theologians and philosophers are prone to forget: when it comes to the spiritual dimension of life, to concepts of value and meaning, most of us find it virtually impossible to think in abstract terms. We need concrete images. We need pictures. We need stories.

## Universal pictures

Myths are not just something from the ancient world. They are alive and well, in our newspapers, on our TVs, on our cinema screens. The obvious example is *Star Wars*. George Lucas consciously set out to follow the pattern of ancient myths when he sent young Luke Skywalker on a journey in a galaxy far, far away. Off he went, overcoming obstacles, fighting enemies, rescuing the princess, learning to use the Force, ultimately having to confront his own father and the possibility that he, Luke, could also be turned to the dark side. Yes, the effects were stunning, but it worked so well because it tapped into deep concepts, ideas that were important to us, that made sense of our journey.

Not all cinema myths are set in distant galaxies: *Pretty Woman*—the poor 'working girl' who finds her prince; *Forrest Gump*—the simple soul walking a path of naïve integrity through a cynical world; *Schindler's List*—the amoral womanizer becomes the compassionate rescuer. You may recognize in these stories the big patterns that I spoke of earlier: Home–Journey–Destination, Equilibrium–Conflict–Resolution, Safety–Risk–Growth. You will recognize the idea of flawed and vulnerable human beings daring to set out on a journey of discovery and triumphing against the odds.

Not all myths end happily: think of *Romeo and Juliet*, *Thelma and Louise*, *Hamlet*, *Of Mice and Men*. Sometimes the fatal flaws in our heroes and their world can only end in a corpse-strewn stage. We need stories of tragedy, because we know that life can be tragic.

And not all myths are fictional. The greatest myth of our time is undoubtedly that of Diana, Princess of Wales. Even Shakespeare could not have written a tragedy like this one. The flawed, vulnerable heroine struggling to find her identity in a failed marriage, a dysfunctional family and a hostile world—no one could have imagined quite how deeply one person's life story could penetrate a whole nation's psyche until that week in September 1997. That funeral day—London uncannily still, silent, and scented by endless piles of flowers; that eerie wail as the gun carriage first appeared through Kensington Palace gate; the wave of applause for Earl Spencer's speech that rippled from the crowd on the street right down through the Abbey—if ever there was evidence of the power of myth, it was then.

Anthony Clare, reviewing a crop of books on Diana, wrote this:

*In life, it could be said that Diana was a kind of Rorschach test in which all sorts of people read their own message, made their own interpretation, drew their own conclusions, took sides. Death has not stilled this process. [These books] reveal the extent to which so many insist on taking the agonised saga of Diana and Charles as a clinical case history to be examined and re-examined, so as to help them find out how it is to be properly human.*

'THE HUNTING OF DIANA', *THE SUNDAY TIMES*, 14 JUNE 1998

## Pages from God's casebook

'[A] case history to be examined and re-examined, so as to help [us] find out how it is to be properly human.' This, then, is the role and function of the myth, and whether it originates in fact or fiction is neither here nor there. The myths that last down the ages, the ones that capture a society's imagination, do so because they tell us what it means to be human. They help us to understand something true. When we enter their story, we start to explore the story of ourselves.

So, then, the Bible is full of myths. The story of Jesus is, in itself, a myth. It is perhaps the supreme myth—the story *par excellence* that helps us make sense of the world. But that does not mean it is fiction. In this sense, it is possible for a story to be quite literal, historical fact, and still to be a myth.

But it is also possible for characters who were never flesh and blood, a place that could never be identified on a map, events drawn totally from imagination, to embody truth, meaning and reality—perhaps more deeply than any 'real-life' drama. And in a way, it doesn't matter. Whether a story is fact or fiction is irrelevant, if it teaches us a truth we really need to hear.

Unfortunately, for many of us, when we approach the Bible it *does* matter. We want to know. The Age of Reason has so drummed into us the importance of scientific method, of verifiable information, of facts and figures, that we find it difficult to approach truth in any other way.

It certainly mattered far less in the ancient world. How could it not?

They had no photographic evidence, no live recordings, no graphs, no libraries full of other people's recorded observations, measurements or surveys. They had their senses, their memories and their imaginations. And we will have to understand and forgive them if the divide is sometimes rather blurred.

Some stories, particularly those that deal with the origins of life, are by definition pre-history. Others—Job, Jonah—make no pretence at being set in a historical framework. Sometimes incidents in the lives of characters who were clearly seen as historical—Moses, David, Elijah—stand out as being highly mythological in style. Some describe the character's early life. Others describe events that no one else could have witnessed.

No one doubts that Jesus was an actual historical figure, but even here, in the case of Jesus in the desert (the passage referred to in the last chapter), we have to face the problem that no one else was there to witness these events. Would Jesus really have recounted such bizarre events of such a deep personal nature to his disciples? Maybe he did—seeing the importance of sharing them.

But even were this story imagined, it rings entirely true to everything else the Gospels say about Jesus. Whether or not he met an actual personified devil over an actual forty-day span, whether or not he physically balanced on the pinnacle of the Temple, the events that followed show us that something very like this must have happened. As we watch Jesus progressing toward Jerusalem, we can see that single-mindedness such as this can only spring from deep internal struggle. Integrity like this must come from a deep awareness of self and a deep understanding of faith, discovered in this case by studying the scriptures. These things in turn demand time and solitude. This ability—to know yourself powerful and yet not to use that power for self-aggrandizement —does not come easily. There is no way Jesus could have been who he was if this process had not happened.

I wish I could define for you which parts of the Bible are historical and which are imaginative, but I cannot. Was Adam a real man? Was Noah? Was Abraham? Were the Magi? There is no way of knowing.

It will help to ask ourselves those questions I have already outlined. What type of literature is it? What was the author's intention? It will also help to realize that imagination does not mean conjuring up something out of nothing. When we imagine, what we are doing is calling up the images in our heads. And how do images get into our heads in the first place? They come from our experience. However repackaged and reprocessed they become, they are essentially memories.

Three of the stories used in the exercises that follow—the garden of Eden, the suffering of Job, and Jonah and the whale—were not, as far as I can tell by the nature of their writing, intended by their authors to be taken as historical fact.

The last story is from the life of David, someone obviously understood as a real historical character. But were these events real? The battle between a boy and a giant has an air of legend, although there is no reason to suppose it could not have happened. But again, it rings entirely true to the rest of the picture painted of David. He was responsible for turning a weak, unsettled collection of tribes into a strong nation with a fortified capital city. He was fearless in fighting and conquering surrounding enemies. Even if the duel with Goliath never happened, the story totally epitomizes the character and life of David.

All these stories are about experiences that every one of us will encounter in our own lives. Every one of us will one day encounter a 'giant' of fear, injustice or oppression. Every one of us will encounter a choice of walking out to fight, or keeping a low profile; of doing what we believe God to have told us, or running away. Each of us will face choices between power and honour, reward and integrity. Each of us will have to decide whether to cross boundaries, to stay within the moral code we have been given or to break it.

Myths come from real experiences of being human and resonate with our own. They put flesh and blood on our feelings; they sum up things we have seen and heard for ourselves.

# Books covered in this chapter

## Genesis

### Authorship

Genesis, the first of the five books of the Torah, is historically attributed to Moses. However, evidence suggests that its present form dates to a much later era. The fact that it speaks of an era 'before any king reigned over the Israelites' (Genesis 36:31) implies that it was written after one already had. Moses was not in a position to know that there would ever be a king of Israel! Scholarly opinion now tends to the view that it is an edited combination of work by three different writers or traditions—the Yahwist, the Elohist and the Priestly.

The Yahwist (so called because God is referred to as Yahweh) probably began writing in the courts of Solomon around 950BC. When, after Solomon's death, the Jewish nation split into two kingdoms, this became the Sacred History of Judea, the southern kingdom. The Yahwist is the most vivid storyteller, with tales full of imagery and irony, describing a sometimes very human God who lives on familiar terms with his created beings and sometimes bumps into them in everyday life.

The Elohistic account (because God is called Elohim) was compiled in the northern kingdom of Israel perhaps two centuries later. The stories here are less vivid, less concrete. They tell of a God more remote, more moral.

The Priestly writer is the editor who brought the two original accounts together. A dry writer, more concerned with figures and lists, he probably started his task around 550BC, at a time when both kingdoms lay in ruins and the Jewish people were exiled to Babylon. It was probably finally completed around the time of Ezra, when the fragile task of rebuilding a temple, a city and a nation had just begun.

I have talked of three strands of authorship, but of course that is only a very small part of the story. This book began life as tales told round a thousand flickering campfires, a thousand meal-times and bed-times and family gatherings over cups of wine. They are tales handed down from parent to child over at least fifty generations and probably many more.

## Literary form

Tempting as it may be to try to trace the original authorship of various parts of Genesis (compare the Elohist's account of the receding flood in Genesis 8:1–5 with the Yahwist's more picturesque description in verses 6–12 to get a flavour), it is a task that has been likened to 'unscrambling an omelette' and is about as unproductive an activity for the ordinary reader. Dry the anonymous Priestly writer may have been, but he was also a remarkably good editor. The Torah is, as *The Literary Guide to the Bible* points out, a 'very well-made omelette indeed' (eds. R. Alter and F. Kermode, Fontana, p. 25)

As you might expect of a book compiled from so many sources,

Genesis contains a wide range of literary styles. It frequently jumps from prose to poetry, so that little two- or three-line verses, like the following, pop up to punctuate the text.

*So God created humankind in his image,*
*  in the image of God he created them;*
*  male and female he created them.* (Genesis 1:27)

It can also leap from large chunks of story told in a single narrator's voice to passages of dialogue where the characters speak for themselves.

Interspersed throughout the book are genealogies—those long family trees once characterized by the old-fashioned word 'begetting'. These may seem dry to us, but they were of vital importance to the Jewish people for whom the Genesis themes of survival and continuity could never be taken for granted.

## Target readership

The word Genesis means 'origins' or 'beginnings', not surprising in a book that opens with the words 'In the beginning...' It is not just about the origins of life but also about the origins of the Jewish people. It was first written down for a people who had just become a nation, and later for a people in exile, brought face to face with other gods and other traditions and straining to hold on to an identity of their own. Later still, it was a vital part of rebuilding that identity, of defining that uniqueness that has always characterized the Jewish people. It was about what it means to be a chosen people, a people who, earlier than any others, learnt what it was to live in relationship with the one true God.

## Recurring themes

In Genesis, God lives in relationship with humanity right from the start. Right from page two, God makes it clear that he has invested a great deal of trust in the human race. Made in the image of God, men and women's noble destiny is no less than the taming and stewardship of the whole earth (Genesis 1:26–30). That trust is quickly violated, but (despite being tempted!—Genesis 6:7) God does not give up. The commission is repeated and with it a covenant or promise (Genesis 9:1–17): God will never again send a flood to destroy the earth.

This pattern of commission and covenant continues with Abraham.

Sent off on a journey to a destination he does not know, Abraham is given a promise: 'I will make of you a great nation' (Genesis 12:2). There is, of course, a minor obstacle: Abraham has no offspring. But this is overcome and the commissioning and covenanting continues down through the generations.

Genesis depicts a series of patriarch figures—Isaac, Jacob and Joseph—overcoming obstacles and oh so gradually building a people who understand just a little of who the one God is. It is a book written under no illusion that these are especially good people. Far from it: they are throughout as tricky, turbulent and troublesome as any people you will ever meet. That, perhaps, is what gives Genesis its charm.

---

## OTHER CREATION STORIES

Every society has its creation myths, with little in common apart from the recurring idea of man being made from the clay of the earth and of the dividing of heaven and earth. The creation stories the ancient Israelites might have known, and which therefore might have influenced their thinking, are those from Babylon. In a poem known as the Enuma Elish, Apsu the male god and Tiamat the female unite to produce a family of younger gods. Because they annoy her, Tiamat wants to kill them. In the battle that ensues, Marduk the god of Babylon kills Tiamat and forms her split corpse into the world. Another Babylonian poem, the Atrakhasis epic, describes how the gods were weary of their labour of tending the earth, and created humans to do the job instead. Exploring these and other myths is fascinating, but perhaps only serves to show why the Genesis account has lasted and become the basis for three major world religions, while others have simply faded away.

The other major creation stories with which Genesis is frequently compared are those drawn from contemporary science.

The debate between creationists and evolutionists has generated a great deal of aggression and misunderstanding and I do not intend to perpetuate it here. Let me just reiterate: the early chapters of Genesis are not history in the conventional sense, and they are not science. They are about 'Why?' not 'How?' and as such are not in conflict with Darwinism, the Big Bang or any other scientific theory. (It is worth remembering that any account of the origins of life is only and can only ever be a theory.)

Anyone who wants to argue about whether Adam and Eve really existed is barking up the wrong tree of knowledge. Adam in Hebrew means Mr Man; Eve means Mrs Life. They existed and they still exist— they are Everyman and Everywoman and their story, like all myths, should be read as such.

---

# Job

## Authorship

No one knows who wrote the book of Job or when it was written. What is clear is that the *story* of Job is an extremely ancient folk-tale, probably originating in the time of the patriarchs, and known throughout the Middle East. The earliest mention of the name 'Job' is found as early as the nineteenth century BC and there are versions of the story in Persian, Sumerian, Akkadian and Babylonian cultures. The book of Ezekiel refers to Job, along with Noah and Daniel, as a byword for righteousness (Ezekiel 14:14). We can deduce from this that Job was a well-known character to the sixth-century exiles in Babylon.

Further to that, since the story describes him as a wealthy sheik (his vast herds of cattle were the ancient equivalent of big money in off-shore accounts), it is a reasonable guess that there once was a real-life person called Job.

The beliefs expressed in the story also point to a time long before the exile. (God is not all-knowing: he has to ask Satan, depicted as one of his courtiers, what he is up to. There is no real belief in the afterlife, beyond the shadowy and mysterious Sheol or 'place of the departed'.)

It has been suggested, and the style of the book would seem to bear this out, that the first two chapters and the last chapter of Job, which are written in prose, are the original folk-tale, and the larger middle chunk, all written in poetry, is the work of a much later and more sophisticated author, perhaps around the time of the exile.

## Literary form

Most of Job, apart from its prologue and epilogue, takes the form of poetic dialogues between Job and his three 'comforters'—the splendidly named Eliphaz the Temanite, Bildad the Shuhite and Zophar the Naamathite—

exploring the reasons for Job's suffering. Although in the prologue the friends have the wisdom to remain silent, here they bombard the luckless Job with theories to explain his misfortune. He must have brought it upon himself, they claim, by some sort of wrongdoing.

When at last their arguments grind to a halt, another character, an angry young man named Elihu, takes up the theme, promising new arguments but in fact reiterating the old ones in even more repetitive and florid language.

Eventually, in chapter 38, God speaks. He does not, however, address the debate, but simply points to how much greater and far beyond their understanding he really is.

The style of all this poetic debate is repetitious and perhaps tedious to a contemporary ear. Louis de Bernières, in his introduction to *Job* in the Pocket Canon, comments, 'It has to be said that one gains very little new information from each speech, and anyone looking for snappy action and exciting new events would certainly be better off hiring a video' (Canongate, p. viii).

The language of Job's poetry, whilst crammed with vivid metaphor, is also at times quite obscure. Of all the books of the Bible, Job contains the words and phrases that have baffled translators the most. But it is worth persevering with. It is, as Louis de Bernières concedes, 'a long and beautiful poem about divine justice, rendered in the forms of narrative, dialogue, hymn, lament, proverb and oracle' (p. viii).

### Target readership

In that the book of Job tackles one of life's biggest questions—'Why do good people suffer?'—its readership is universal. Again, the theory of its being poetry of the exile makes sense: here were people struggling to remain faithful to a God who had apparently deserted them.

### Themes

It is curious that the word we have learnt to associate with Job is 'patience'. Throughout most of this book, Job is anything but. He rails at God. He refuses to accept blame. The 'defiance' of Job, as de Bernières suggests, could be a better description. That is perhaps the book's strength. It subverts what we have come to expect. It turns simplistic answers on their head.

Anyone looking for a clear answer to the problem of suffering will not find it here. The book certainly suggests that it is right to ask the questions and to explore them to their limits. But here, above all, we come face to face with mystery and paradox. Job is about silence in the face of things we do not understand. It demonstrates the futility of preaching to someone whose shoes we have not walked in. And the prologue points out that there is something going on in heaven that none of the earthly characters comprehends at all.

# Jonah

## Authorship

Although this book appears among the prophetic books, it is quite unlike the rest. They consist of speeches or writings from the person whose name the book carries. This is a story about a prophet, but with no indication as to who wrote it, and with only one recorded sentence of actual prophetic speech. The fact that it has to tell its readers that 'Nineveh was an exceedingly large city' (3:3) indicates that it was probably written after Nineveh, capital of Assyria (in modern Syria), was destroyed in 612BC.

## Literary form

Again unlike the other prophetic books, Jonah is not set in any specific era, indicating that it has no intention of presenting itself as a historical account. The prophet Jonah *was* a historical figure, however, also referred to in 2 Kings 14:25, which would place him around the mid-eighth century BC.

It is not necessarily the miraculous swallowing by the great fish that points to the book of Jonah being fictional—sperm whales and sharks big enough to swallow a human being have been known in the Mediterranean. However, the tone of the whole book and its absurdities—Jonah vomited up by the fish, the unlikely and immediate repentance of the city, Jonah's petulance at God's forgiveness—indicates not only that it was a piece of storytelling, but that it was meant to be satirical.

## Target readership

If this book was written, as seems likely, around the time when the Jews were finally freed from their captivity in Babylon, then its target readership had been 'swallowed up' for many years among another people group. Jeremiah uses a similar image of Babylon as a dragon spewing up what it had devoured (Jeremiah 51:44). More than that, it was the leader of another foreign empire, Cyrus of Persia, who had freed them. The idea that God might be working in and through the life of nations other than their own was a natural one for them to explore.

### Themes

Tarshish, Jonah's destination, was in Spain, the westernmost point of the then known world. To this story's original hearers it would have been the back-of-beyond, an almost mythical place of escape. The storm, like all natural disasters, would have been understood by them as the judgment of God, and it is quite likely that the Temple, by that time distant and destroyed, would represent to them a far-off memory of 'home' and safety. Jonah, deep in the womb-like darkness of the fish, longs to return to the 'womb' of religious safety. If he is to continue to engage with God, however, he must first undertake the hard task God has set him.

# 1 and 2 Samuel

### Authorship

Essentially two volumes of the same book, its material may have been drawn from the writings of Samuel himself and the prophets who followed him, as well as quoting from David's poems. The several references to the kingdom of Judah (e.g. 1 Samuel 27:6) show that it was compiled some time later than the events of which it tells, probably after the division of the kingdoms but before the exile, any time between approximately 937 and 587BC.

### Literary form

These books show the beginnings of a structured national history. The account of David and Goliath stands out for its mythical quality amid a mostly far more prosaic and 'warts-and-all' narrative. (For more on history in general, see Chapter 9 of this book.)

### Target readership

Written after the time of Solomon, when a single kingdom had become divided into Judah in the south and Israel in the north, the books of Samuel are a reminder of the cultural and national roots which both kingdoms shared—of what had become, in retrospect, a golden age.

### Themes
Politics and religion are indivisible in this account of the beginnings of the Jewish monarchy, which occurred around 1000BC. David is clearly the hero, but there is no attempt to gloss over his failings, or over the rivalries and intrigue of the ruling families. Wrongdoing, whether it be by priestly dynasties or royal ones, is forthrightly condemned by prophets prepared to take their lives in their hands.

# Ways of reading

## Let go of mental baggage
You may well have questions of the 'Did it really happen?' variety. By all means pursue them in study as far as possible, but don't let them detract from learning from the story itself.

Because these are such well-known stories, you may also carry the baggage of what other people have told you about their meaning. The story of the garden of Eden is about sin and the devil, isn't it? Well, maybe, but these words are never mentioned. Try to discard what you have been told and let the stories speak for themselves.

(A little aside here that is worth mentioning: a myth is not an allegory. In an allegory, each part of the story stands for something else. *The Pilgrim's Progress*, with Mr Worldly-Wiseman, Giant Despair, Doubting Castle, Vanity Fair and so on, is the most obvious example. Allusions of this sort will no doubt occur to you, but don't try to squeeze out allegorical meanings where none were put in.)

## Look for ways in which it resonates with your own experience
Myths are deceptively simple. They often have many layers of meaning, and may well have different echoes at different times in your life. Or they may mean nothing at all until you have been through a particular stage or circumstance.

The story of Abraham sacrificing Isaac seemed an impossibly difficult one to me as the mother of young children. As a parent of sons about to fly the nest and make their own way in the world, it began to have echoes. It's still not an easy story, but I now know in painful reality what it means to let go of your children and offer their future up to God.

## Let the story teach you about life

The story of Abraham and Isaac has become a picture I carry around in the back of my mind, reminding me to trust God for the lives of my sons. Other Bible stories work in similar ways. Pondered, absorbed, and tucked deep into the subconscious, they tell us that what we are going through is universal, that God is involved in the process, and that good outcomes are possible.

# Exercises

## The problem of limits (Genesis 2—3)

STEP 1:  Ask God to help you dwell with this story and tease out all the meaning it has for you.

STEP 2:  Read the passage.

STEP 3:  What mental baggage do you carry with you regarding this story?

- Has it been pitted against science, history or archaeology? If so, is there any evidence or logic that makes it invalid as a way of looking at the world?
- What interpretations of this story have you already been taught?
- Are there any assumptions or associations that you have picked up regarding this story?

STEP 4:  What echoes, if any, does this story have with your personal experience?

- Has there been an incident or period in your life when you were in a similar situation to Adam and Eve (restricted in a way you didn't understand or thought unfair)?
- Have you ever made a choice like Eve's? Were there any repercussions? Were they good or bad?

- Are there things about this story that you find difficult (confusing, unfair, uncomfortable)?

STEP 5: What does this story tell us about life?
- Is it about one moment in history or a story repeated in every generation?
- Does it give an explanation of sin, death and punishment, or simply describe the fact that they exist?
- Is the portrayal of God helpful or unhelpful and why?

STEP 6: How can this story help you make sense of your life?
- Does this story condemn you, excuse you or simply give a picture of how you are?
- Are there any aspects of your existence that this story helps you to understand better?


## The problem of pain (Job 1:1—4:7; 38:1–21; 42:1–17)

STEP 1: Ask God to give you understanding.

STEP 2: Read the passages.

STEP 3: What mental baggage do you carry with you concerning this story and its main theme?
- Are we intended to take this story, and especially Satan's part in the affair, as a literal explanation of how suffering occurs?
- What views have people tried to sell you as 'what the Bible says' on suffering?
- Have you also been sold completely conflicting theories?

STEP 4: What echoes, if any, does this story have with your personal experience?
- If you have suffered, have you tried to blame God, Satan, yourself or no one?
- Have others tried to give you advice or theories? Have they helped?
- Have you settled on battling or passive acceptance or a mix of the two?

STEP 5: What does this story tell us about life?
- Assuming you don't take the 'bargaining in heaven' literally, what principles, if any, can you draw from it to help you?
- What can we learn from Job's example?

- What can we learn from the example of Job's friends?
- Does this story strike you as 'fair'? Do you think it is intended to be?

STEP 6: How can this story help you make sense of your life?
- Does it give you answers, or challenge you to live without them?
- Does it help to read of others in circumstances as hard and perplexing as those you experience?
- Does it give you any pointers in your reactions to others who suffer?


## The urge to run away (Jonah 1:1—3:3)

STEP 1: Ask God to give you understanding.

STEP 2: Read the passage.

STEP 3: What mental baggage do you carry with you concerning this story and its main theme?
- Does the unlikelihood of the 'fish-swallowing' episode pose difficulties for you?
- How does this story appear different if you see it as a metaphor for adult experience, rather than as a fable for children?

STEP 4: What echoes, if any, does this story have with your personal experience?
- Have you ever wanted to run away as far as possible rather than face a difficult situation?
- Have you ever actually done so?
- Have you ever felt that you were running away from God?
- Have you ever felt depressed and, if so, what echoes did that experience have with Jonah's descent into the depths (and perhaps his previous desire to sleep)?

STEP 5: What does this story tell us about life?
- Is it possible truly to run away, either from life or from God?
- Is it valid to want to sometimes?
- Does running away lead to depression?
- What was the memory that provoked Jonah's desire to return from the depths?

STEP 6:   How can this story help you make sense of your life?
- Are there any difficult areas in your life that you are currently running away from?
- Are there tasks you are reluctant to undertake, for fear you might appear foolish?
- Are there any positive memories that could energize you to return and face things?

# Facing giants (1 Samuel 17)

STEP 1:   Ask God to help you take the story from childhood fable to adult challenge.

STEP 2:   Read the passage.

STEP 3:   What, if any, mental baggage do you carry about this story?
- Do you think the author intended it as accurate history, embroidered fantasy or somewhere between the two?
- Are there any aspects of this story that trouble you?

STEP 4:   What echoes, if any, does this story have with your own experience?
- Have you ever faced metaphorical 'giants'?
- Have you ever found seemingly insurmountable obstacles removed by some apparently tiny means?

STEP 5:   What does this story tell us about life?
- Does this story tell us about life as we'd like to think it could be or life as it really sometimes is?
- What can we learn from David's example?
- What can we learn from the negative example of Saul?

STEP 6:   How can this story help you make sense of your life?
- What are the 'giants' you are currently facing?
- What conventional wisdom prevents you from facing them?
- Is there any unnecessary caution that hampers you?

# Trusting where you don't understand

*My favourite Bible verses are not the ones that are read very often either in private or in church, except perhaps by me!*

*I often think that it's ironic that the book of Job, one of the least read books of the Bible, immediately precedes Psalms, which must be one of the most read.*

*To me, the story of Job is the most relevant book of the Old Testament regarding our lives today. It is so difficult to know whether we are being tested from above or attacked from below or, indeed, whether both forces are at work.*

*The first six verses of chapter 42 explain everything, in as much as God knows all the answers and understands everything. We will never know the answers to the unanswerable, so why waste time looking? All we need to do is put our trust in the Lord and he will guide us through.*

*To me, Job sums it all up perfectly in these verses, and it is Job who has become my soulmate in the Bible. I know I can never have the strength of faith he showed, but it is something I aspire to, as can everybody.*

*In simple terms, I don't know how to fly a plane and I don't particularly want to. However, I have every faith in the pilot and put my faith in him to get me to my destination. I also don't have even a millionth of God's understanding and knowledge of this world he created, or what his destiny is for us all. However, I have every faith in him as my pilot and put my trust in him to get me to my destination along the route he has chosen for me.*

*If you're unsure whether or not you're being attacked or tested, spend some time with Job and he'll sort you out.*

RICK WAKEMAN (ROCK MUSICIAN AND COMPOSER), QUOTED IN *THE BIBLE SPEAKS TO ME*, CHRIS GIDNEY, MARSHALL PICKERING, PP. 130–131

# Seven

# Instruction: building God-centred lives

## Framework of faith

When I was a young Christian, it was to the New Testament letters that I first turned. I had no taste for mystery and ambiguity in those days. I wanted a solid framework within which to explore my new and fragile faith. I wanted things explained. I wanted to be told what to do.

Perhaps it is simply a late, late adolescence, but now I am prone to find dos and don'ts restrictive and simplistic. Then, however, I wanted things cut and dried. I was, it seems, not alone (see 'Stages of spiritual journey' on page 98). For many people in the early stages of faith, it is this instruction, whether from church or book, which is the most helpful to their development.

The Bible has three main types of instructional literature. Two of the three are particularly concerned with the early stages of faith, because each of them—the Law and the letters—is deeply bound up in the founding of a new religion—Judaism and Christianity respectively.

The third, Proverbs, is rather different. It is more home-spun, less authoritarian advice, an anthology gathered from many different sources and having its roots in common sense rather than theology.

None of these books of instruction is for new believers only. Each of them, like all great scripture, can be read on many levels of under-standing. They also deal with many levels of society.

The Old Testament Law contains the framework for a whole emerging nation. It begins with the basics, the Ten Commandments, and from there deals with issues of justice, crime and punishment, hygiene, sexual taboos, religious ritual and festivals.

Proverbs does not deal with ethics at the national level. It is about the personal—about families and friendships and sexual temptation.

The New Testament letters are working at a different level again—that of newly formed communities who found themselves deeply at odds with the society that surrounded them. Not only were they struggling to live as believers in a pagan world, they were also struggling to grasp a whole new set of beliefs and to understand how they related to the old. The letters therefore contain advice for personal living, advice for community building, but also a great deal of explanation of just what those new beliefs were and how they worked out in practice.

## Load-bearing walls

Moving to a 200-year-old cottage that was once stables has proved an interesting experience for me and my husband. In the course of redecorating, we have occasionally needed to knock out a wall, or at least drill into one. Some, we have discovered, are 30cm of solid brick. Others are no more than plasterboard and batten. Once, we hacked into what seemed like one of the latter, only to discover an old outside wall, complete with window, hidden within. Once, we decided that a particular wall must be supporting the floor above, only to find that it stopped short by about 10cm. It was not load-bearing at all.

The reason for this diversion into DIY is to point out that in any edifice, some of it is an essential part of the structure, without which the whole might fall down. Other parts have been put in to allow the place to be used in a certain way. When the needs change, they can be knocked down with no damage to the overall building at all. The interesting part is discovering which are which.

And that is the interesting problem that confronts us when we start to read these passages of instruction. How do we decide which is a principle laid down for all time and which is a ruling which cultural changes render irrelevant?

It is good to know that God is concerned with the prosaic issues of everyday life, but the more down-to-earth and specific the instruction, the more it is likely to be advice for *that* society with *that* set of circumstances, which may or may not coincide with ours. The issue of meat offered to idols no longer concerns us. Laws about menstruation or eating pork, wise as they may have been for hygiene at the time, are no longer relevant in these days of tampons and refrigeration.

Nowhere is this more apparent in our generation than in issues of sexuality and gender. A large proportion of the Church has decided that women can now become leaders. Have they violated a vital biblical principle or simply realized that circumstances—educated women, free from endless pregnancies and domestic chores—are no longer the same? Can we draw a line between this issue and that of homosexuality? Many people mention them in the same breath. But are they different and, if so, how?

## Finding the principles

Much of the Old Testament law strikes 21st-century sophisticates as primitive and alien. We are liable to turn away in disgust. It *is* primitive. It *is* alien. It is, after all, anything up to thirty-four centuries old. Nevertheless, there are beneath the primitive elements some fascinating, and strangely timeless, principles which are worth examining.

### Sacrifice

Old Testament Law does not record a command from God to Moses to *set up* animal sacrifice (see Leviticus 1:2). Rather, these are regulations on a practice that already existed. It was common throughout the Near East, and indeed in primitive cultures worldwide.

It is as if humans instinctively sense there is something or someone 'beyond', with whom they crave a right relationship. But just as instinctive is the feeling of being too insignificant or too unclean to approach that someone. There is a need for some dramatic act to break through and allow our flawed humanness to approach the divine.

Ritual, as the fox says to the little prince in de Sainte-Exupéry's story, is a way of 'dressing up the heart'. We need our feelings of awe, gratitude, dedication or remorse to be marked by some outward demonstration. The obvious problem is that the 'dressing up' may take the place of any real heartfelt emotion. Ritual can divert or hinder our spiritual journey or it can help it along. Either way, the human need for it remains strong.

Slaughtering a bull, sprinkling its blood, removing its fat and burning the rest of the carcass does not immediately strike 21st-century minds as the best way to do it. Could it really have been what God wanted? Ultimately, maybe not, but to me it demonstrates yet again the message that is shot right through the Bible, that God is prepared to meet people where they are, however absurd and petty their needs and ideas, to take what they offer, to work with them and move them on. And in taking these practices, but purging them of their more barbarous, immoral and idolatrous connotations (outlawing human sacrifice not least), these laws not only made a great leap forward, but paved the way for better things.

## Blood

There is an awful lot of blood in the Old Testament Law (the word appears eighty times in Leviticus alone). Not only is blood the focal point of ritual sacrifice, the 'eating' of blood is also forbidden (Leviticus 17:10–14).

'We should get into the habit,' says Etienne Charpentier in *How to Read the Old Testament*, 'of replacing this word "blood" by its equivalent "the life which is offered"' (SCM Press, p. 69). The taboo on eating blood is not a culinary nicety, but a permanent reminder of respect for life. Similarly, the idea of a blood sacrifice arises out of the concept of 'life for life' (Deuteronomy 19:21)—the idea that a life needs to be given in order for justice to be done and for new life to emerge.

Capital punishment may be outlawed in much of our contemporary world, but you only have to count the number of killings on our TV screens to realize that it is an immensely deep-seated concept even now. And, says the New Testament, it is in answer to that deep human need that God gave his own Son Jesus, to be the definitive blood sacrifice, the only one we will ever need.

Incidentally, on the subject of capital punishment, it is worth making one small observation: you can't keep prisoners in a tent. If you committed an offence, whatever it was, you either got away with it or you were killed. Most often, Leviticus would seem to suggest, you were killed.

Even so, it is hard to relate to a God who commanded such harsh justice. I can only offer one line of argument in God's defence—it is impossible to have mercy without having first established justice. You cannot let someone off an offence if they do not know, first, that it is an offence, and second, that it is punishable. Leviticus teaches us that God is directly involved in justice (albeit justice that seems harsh to our ears). Thankfully the rest of the Bible resounds with the idea that God is also merciful. Time and again, and supremely in Jesus, God does not punish people as they deserve.

One area where the death penalty seems particularly undeserved is that of sexual offences (Leviticus 20:10–16). We need to remember that in a world where sex and procreation could not be divided, sexuality was held as a sacred trust—the handing on of life. These laws too spring at base from a respect for life.

The books of the law are certainly not the ones to turn to when you need help to get through the day. But in among the blood and fire and arcane ritual are some fascinating principles that have more to teach our contemporary world than you might ever suppose.

## Foundation stones

Delving into such difficult issues takes time. It is unwise to knock away a wall and then discover that it was holding up the building after all. That is why the slowness with which the Church deals with change, frustrating as it can be, is no bad thing. But it is not just the Church authorities that change these things. They in turn are influenced by the opinions of their flock and public opinion as a whole. That is why it is so important for each Christian to know what their faith's holy writings actually say and to understand the solid foundational principles which lie buried beneath cultural edicts.

There are, I believe, at least two rock-solid reference points. One is the Ten Commandments. Their language is archaic—few of us 'bow down to idols' or 'covet our neighbour's ox'—but the principles they embody are still sound. They are to be jettisoned, I am convinced, at our peril. And I suspect that while the Church argues about gay sex and women bishops and charismatic worship, the subtle erosion of these principles—the need for a day free from commercial pressure, the need to honour our older folk, the need for a marriage commitment once made to be kept, the need for truth and simple living and God-centred value systems—may in the end bring Western civilization tumbling down around our ears.

The other is the teaching of Jesus. As I read it over and over, it is one of the things that most convinces me that he is the Son of God. I marvel at how he taught in a way that was totally immersed in the everyday world of his audience and yet is timeless and culturally relevant in a way that no other scripture, old or new, quite seems to achieve. He makes it look easy.

It is no coincidence that both the apostles Peter and Paul refer to Jesus as the cornerstone—the stone which unites two walls at the base of a building. In other words, he is the most important foundation of all. (See Ephesians 2:20 and 1 Peter 2:6.)

## A flexible structure

Discovering M. Scott Peck's 'Stages of Faith' (see page 98) helped me to see that my scepticism was not such a bad thing as 'Stage Two' teaching had led me to believe. It also helped me see the genius of the Bible.

Scott Peck points out, 'One of the things that characterize all of the world's great religions is that they seem to have a capacity to speak to people in both Stage Two and Stage Four as if the very teachings of a given religion have two different translations' (*Further Along the Road Less Travelled*, p. 125). I don't know how true this is of other religions, but I have certainly found it true of Christianity and the Bible.

Scott Peck gives two examples:

*'The fear of the Lord is the beginning of wisdom': At Stage Two this is translated to mean, 'When you start fearing that big cop in the sky, you really wise up.' That's true. At Stage Four it is translated to mean, 'The awe of God shows you the way to enlightenment'...*

*'Jesus is my Saviour'... Among Stage Two people, that tends to be translated to mean that Jesus is a kind of fairy godmother who can rescue me when I get into trouble as long as I can remember to call upon His name. And that's true; He will do exactly that. Whereas in Stage Four, people read it to mean that Jesus, through his life and death, taught me the way that I myself must follow for my salvation. And that is also true.*

FURTHER ALONG THE ROAD LESS TRAVELLED, PP. 125–126

There is, or so it seems so to me, no inherent moral superiority in later stages of faith. A Stage Two person may be more loving, more generous, more single-minded than a Three or Four. Nevertheless, if everything within us is crying out to move on, we cannot refuse the journey. To stay within the institutional confines, stifling doubts and questions, for the sake of safety and not rocking the boat, is ultimately to stifle the Holy Spirit. We have to trust that God can bring us through, perhaps to the place of which the poet T.S. Eliot speaks:

*And the end of all our exploring*
*Will be to arrive where we started*
*And know the place for the first time.*
FOUR QUARTETS: LITTLE GIDDING

But, and this is a big but, however much I believe that going on a faith journey ultimately means living with paradox, mystery and ambiguity, I am not sure it is ever possible to dispense with the Stage Two framework. Much New Age and alternative religion appears to deal with the needs of Stage Three and Stage Four people but I suspect that, without the solid foundation of wisdom proved down the ages, it is flimsy and ephemeral. Either that, or it ends up creating its own institutions, not just flimsy but potentially dangerous structures based on human personalities.

That is why I believe that being willing to receive instruction is so important.

---

## STAGES OF SPIRITUAL JOURNEY

M. Scott Peck, in his book *Further Along the Road Less Travelled*, describes four stages of faith. (He points out that this is a simplistic version of a more complex model worked out by others, and also that there is no clear division between stages. 'People can have a foot in more than one camp or can bounce back and forth between stages.') The following is a paraphrase of his definitions:

**Stage One: Chaotic/Anti-social:** A stage of absent spirituality. People at this stage may appear loving but they are basically self-serving. They are governed by no outside principles.

**Stage Two: Formal/Institutional:** People in this stage enjoy the shelter of a spiritual home within some institutional framework. They welcome rules and rituals (although if they are in one of the newer churches, they may not see them as such) and readily accept edicts from authority figures. They like their religion cut and dried. Many church-goers remain in this stage throughout their lives.

**Stage Three: Sceptic/Individual:** Perhaps the fact that you have picked up this book means you belong to this category. These are people who are beginning to have problems with the authoritarian approach of

Stage Two. They may be rebellious. Nevertheless, they are probably ahead of Stage Two, rather than regressing. They may get stuck in this stage and never move on, but they are by nature truth-seekers, and if they persist they will eventually find a deeper spirituality.

**Stage Four: Mystical/Communal:** These are people who have come through to deeper, although probably more ambiguous, faith. They are comfortable with mystery and paradox, far less comfortable with the cut-and-dried approach of Stage Two, although they may also have discovered how close this new spirituality is to the institutional *credo* they were taught.

---

# Books covered in this chapter

## New Testament letters: Romans to Jude

### Type of literature

By New Testament times, there were almost as many Jews living outside Israel as in it. They lived as distinctive communities all round the Mediterranean world. One way in which this distinctiveness was kept alive was by community letters. Such newsletters, sent from the religious leaders in Jerusalem, informed the dispersed Jews about dates of festivals and decisions. Paul had requested and was carrying just such a letter when he was converted on the road to Damascus (Acts 9:2). No wonder he believed so passionately in the power of letter writing.

It was this tradition, rather than the writing of holy scripture, that the New Testament letter writers believed they were carrying on. And they, with better reason than I, were also doing what I acknowledged at the outset of this book: 'not writing because they see, but in order to see properly'. It was all so new, this Christianity—such an unexpected, astonishing and mind-blowing turn of events. No wonder, then, that they were still grappling with its vast implications, rather than drawing solid, time-honoured conclusions. No wonder that they occasionally contradicted themselves, sometimes were unnecessarily dogmatic, and sometimes missed whole aspects of this faith business that we wish they had covered. The wonder is more that they got so much right.

# Paul's letters: Romans to Philemon

## Authorship

The author Fay Weldon in her introduction to *Corinthians* in the Pocket Canon, comments, 'It is hard to *like* Paul the Apostle. One is not out of sympathy when Ananias the Chief Priest... remarks to the Roman authorities, "We have found him a pestilent fellow"' (Canongate, p. vii).

Reading Paul's letters, I find myself in agreement. Paul comes across as authoritarian, arrogant, sarcastic, a misogynist, a bit of a loner. He also, in fairness, comes across as someone who cares passionately about those to whom he writes, someone with a talent for trouble-shooting, with an incredibly supple mind, and someone who knows his own weaknesses, even if he is sometimes reluctant to admit them.

I do not think that Paul and I would have got on. Nevertheless, I am bound to admit that were it not for him, I would not be a Christian now. Pioneers are often difficult people and Paul was certainly a pioneer, driving the news of Christ through the Roman world like a dose of salts. 'Certainly all at the time,' continues Weldon, 'were in awe of this slippery, preaching, threatening, cajoling young man, always one step ahead of his enemies' (p. vii).

Even if we don't like Paul, we have to admire the sheer dedication and persistence of the man—and his huge achievement. He had awesome energy and commitment, spending his entire post-conversion life (when not detained in prison) travelling round the Mediterranean region and founding churches. And, of course, writing letters. Thirteen have survived to enter the New Testament. It seems likely that there were many more.

As Fay Weldon points out, 'Because we today don't much like Paul, it does not mean God was not speaking to him. The ways of the Creator are very strange. Our contemporary judgment, our political, emotional and spiritual correctnesses are not His' (p. xi). So it behoves us to suspend our prejudices and listen carefully to what Paul has to say. If God spoke *to* him then, he can also speak *through* him now.

## Target readership

Nine of Paul's letters—Romans to 2 Thessalonians—were written to fledgling Christian communities that he had either founded or met on his travels. Four—1 Timothy to Philemon—were written to individuals.

Because the book of Acts details his travels, there are enough clues to put reasonably accurate dates to most of the letters. (They are arranged in the New Testament purely in order of size.) Galatians is thought to be one of the earliest—around AD47, after Paul visited the region and before the Council of Jerusalem resolved the issues under discussion.

1 and 2 Thessalonians come close on its heels, written soon after Paul had visited the city and established a church. He had not long moved on to Athens when, anxious for news of his converts, he sent Timothy back to them. The first letter, full of relief and delight at their progress, was written after Timothy's return with good reports. The second, also dealing with questions raised by them, was sent just a few months later.

The letter to the Romans was written before Paul had fulfilled his dream to visit the city, around AD57. Just a few years later, he realized his ambition, although not quite as he expected—he came as a prisoner in chains. Several letters—Ephesians, Philippians, Colossians—were written from prison. Others—1 and 2 Timothy and Titus—written after the record of Acts runs out, imply that he had been released, although most likely he was later imprisoned again.

# 1 Peter

## Authorship

This is generally accepted as being written by Peter the fisherman and number one apostle. There is a marked similarity of style between this letter and Peter's speeches in Acts. He writes of himself as a 'witness of the sufferings of Christ' (1 Peter 5:1) and frequently refers with feeling to those sufferings.

## Target audience

The letter is written to a group of churches in today's central and northern Turkey, and was probably written from Rome. (See 1 Peter 5:13—Babylon was a common nickname for Rome.) It was clearly written with an expectation that persecution was on the way. It may be that it was written shortly after the great fire in Rome, AD64, which Nero was suspected to have begun. Shortly afterwards, Nero started persecuting Christians and tradition has it that Paul was martyred around this time. Peter perhaps wrote out of an experience of these events and an expectation that persecution of Christians would soon reach even the distant shores of Turkey.

For background information on other letters, see the Appendix.

## Old Testament Law: Exodus to Numbers

### Type of literature

The Jews called the first five books of the Bible the Torah—a word translated as 'Law', although 'instruction' would be more accurate. In practice, laws and instructions form only part of it. Having dealt with pre-history and the nation's earliest origins in Genesis, much of the rest—Exodus, Leviticus, Numbers, Deuteronomy—is the story of an epic journey that moves from deliverance from slavery through wanderings in the wilderness to the brink of the promised land. Throughout the account of this monumental adventure are scattered passages of detailed lawgiving—everything from the design of priests' garments to capital punishment to the making of vows.

It seems strange to us to move so abruptly from such dramatic narrative to such minutiae of instruction. But to the Jewish people, the two—the epic and the Law—were inextricably interwoven. It was both together that formed them into a nation. It was both together that made them realize that God cared for them in every aspect of their existence.

The one book within the Pentateuch which is practically all law and no adventure is Leviticus. Dealing as it does with such matters as ritual sacrifice, obsolete cleanliness regulations, sexual taboos and forgotten festivals, it is hardly suprising that it does not emerge in anyone's top ten of Bible favourites. 'Faced with such an unappetizing vein of gristle in the midst of the Pentateuch,' says David Damrosch in *The Literary Guide to the Bible* (p. 66), 'the natural reaction of most readers is simply to push it quietly off the plate.'

There is a lot in Leviticus that is hard to stomach. Nevertheless, in the context of its times it represents a giant leap forward. It comes as a shock to our modern minds to realize that before this wilderness lawgiving, religion did not necessarily have any link with morality. Religion was about fertility, about ritual, about placating capricious spirits. The Torah was first given in a world where child sacrifice, temple prostitution and superstition were rife.

This is the amazing genius of Judaism—that it understood first that there was one true God, and second that serving that God involved 'righteousness' in every aspect of life. It understood that how you treated people—your servants, your wives, the strangers in your midst—were not just social issues but religious ones too.

## Authorship

The little that is known about the editorship and authorship of the Torah that I described in the introduction to Genesis all applies here— historically attributed to Moses (around 1300BC) although probably only gathered in this form several centuries later. We cannot prove that these laws were all forged in the wilderness (and undoubtedly some were added and amended as time went along). But, to me at least, it seems unlikely that a foundation of such magnitude was created by a committee of lawyers meeting in dusty rooms. Moreover, these instructions read, in the main, like rules for a nomadic rather than a settled people.

# Proverbs

## Authorship

The book is attributed at the beginning to Solomon, a king so known for his wisdom that not only the queen of Sheba (1 Kings 10:1–13), but also 'people… from all the nations… from all the kings of the earth' (1 Kings 4:34) flocked to his court to listen to his words. This is not intended to mean that the whole book was written by Solomon, rather that it is wisdom after the manner of Solomon, the first and greatest wise man of all.

It is, in fact, compiled of nine different sections, only two of which (chs. 10—22:16 and 25—29) claim Solomon's authorship. Two others (ch. 30 and the opening of ch. 31) are the sayings of non-Israelites: Agur and King Lemuel, probably Arabians from Massa. Another two (22:17—24:22 and 24:23–34) are described as 'Sayings of the Wise'. The first of these sections bears a striking similarity to an ancient Egyptian text, *The Teaching of Amenemope*.

The first nine chapters and the epilogue on 'the wife of noble character' are anonymous, different in style from the rest, and possibly later additions. Proverbs itself tells us that it was still in the making at the time of Hezekiah, 250 years after Solomon in 700BC (25:1). There is no other evidence as to when it was written but, like most Old Testament literature, it seems to have been finally compiled after the exile. Many of its thought patterns and its writing style, however, would be quite at home in the world of Solomon.

## Type of literature

Proverbs is so different from the Law and the letters that I hesitated before putting them in the same chapter. But different as they are at the point of origin, all of them are, for the reader, instruction on how to live your life.

Proverbs is not 'Do this because the Lord says'; rather, it is 'Those who have gone before have learned that this sort of behaviour works and you would do well to listen to their advice'. It is not about grand issues of ethics or justice, worship or doctrine; rather, it is about those everyday details of character that actually matter somewhat more when you end up living alongside them. It is about people who are unbearably cheerful in the morning, about those who pick arguments, fail to discipline their children, or love to meddle in other people's business.

In Proverbs, the key word is not 'righteousness' but 'wisdom'. Its maxims arise from rationality, common sense and observation of how things are. God does not get that many mentions throughout Proverbs, and you might be tempted to think that this is mere human wisdom. But at the outset the book declares otherwise: 'The fear of the Lord is the beginning of knowledge' (1:7). 'For the Lord gives wisdom; from his mouth come knowledge and understanding' (2:6). 'Trust in the Lord with all your heart, and do not rely on your own insight' (3:5).

The bulk of Proverbs is a collection of brief, pithy sayings, nearly always in a striking two-part format. Many of these are 'but' statements, showing opposing ways of behaviour:

*A cheerful heart is a good medicine,*
  *but a downcast spirit dries up the bones (17:22).*

*Rash words are like sword thrusts,*
  *but the tongue of the wise brings healing (12:18).*

Some are 'and' statements, where the second part reinforces the first:

*A friend loves at all times,*
    *and kinsfolk are born to share adversity (17:17).*

Some use a vivid metaphor in the first part to describe an aspect of human behaviour in the second:

*Like a gold ring in a pig's snout*
    *is a beautiful woman without good sense (11:22).*

Just to make reading more interesting, or frustrating, the subjects leap with abandon from one topic to another. I was pleased to find one commentator recommending a reading method I had already worked out for myself—why not gather a handful of pens and highlight the different themes in different colours?

When it comes to Proverbs' thought patterns, we find no understanding here of a life beyond the grave. Proverbs deals entirely with the consequences of actions in the here and now. Neither is there any mention of God reclaiming or redirecting those who are on the wrong path. The wicked and foolish are on a collision course with disaster, says Proverbs. This is somewhat at odds with other Bible passages, where Jesus offers the most renegade a second chance, or God chooses some pretty foolish people for his heroes. But in this, as throughout the Bible, we are dealing with paradox. *Both* are true. Here is my two-part pithy statement on the subject:

*Humans have choices to live wisely or foolishly and those choices*
                                                *have consequences;*
*and God can change our direction and save us from the consequences*
                                                *of our choices.*

# Ways of reading

The Bible's instructional passages cover a great deal of ground in a very short time. They dart from subject to subject with startling abruptness. The first thing to note about this particular type of literature, therefore, is that it is constructed in very small units. It may work better to read a single verse and take time to explore that one, than to read a whole passage containing several topics in one chapter. In the main, we need to look closely at the detail, rather than standing back and trying to grasp a grand design. The exercises that follow give four suggested ways of exploring instruction.

## Following a line of theological argument

The daily choices we make are influenced deeply, subtly and perhaps surprisingly by what we believe God to be like.

Take a simple event, such as a family meal. If you understand the doctrine of the Trinity to mean that relationships lie at the very heart of God's nature, then taking time to sit down and converse with family and friends will be important to you. If, however, you believe God has high standards and expects his followers to make sacrifices, you may well dash through the meal in order to get out and do a soup run or run a children's club.

If you believe that all matter is essentially evil and that spirituality lies in denying the flesh, then your meal may be frugal, basic or plain. If, however, you believe that God gave us a beautiful world to enjoy to the full, you may take time making salmon with dill sauce followed by raspberry pavlova, and laying the table with flowers and candles.

(Don't forget, incidentally, that our ideas about God are not always conscious ones. I have been in a church where the message preached was that God loved everyone unconditionally, exactly as they were. The message we absorbed subconsciously, however, was that God was a hard taskmaster. No one ever said it, but the sheer busyness of the place, the endless exhortations to pray, fast, study, evangelize, care for our neighbours and so on, the never-ending requests for workers to do this or that, all reinforced that view. And guess which one proved the more powerful!)

And so it is sometimes necessary to work through the theological arguments step by step (and to grapple with paradox) in order to understand fully the different facets of God's personality and how they fit together.

## Finding the principles behind the practice

Do you know what gleaning is? Full marks in the 'useless knowledge' contest if you do. Even so, and even in the unlikely event that you own a cornfield, I doubt that its practice concerns you much. Neither does advice on how to deal with runaway slaves. And do you know why circumcision mattered so much or why women wore head-coverings?

Many practices advocated in the Old and New Testaments seem irrelevant to us today. A first reaction might be to turn the page. But that could be a loss. Even if the practice does not concern us, chances are that exploring the principle behind the practice might teach us a great deal.

(Incidentally, I love the idea that God commanded a symbol of faithfulness and holiness to be placed at such a crucial location on the male anatomy. Who says God hasn't got a sense of humour?)


## Exploring a topic

The Proverbs are a collection of sayings but they are not a catalogued one. The letters were written to respond to different people with different needs and not as systematic teaching. The books of the Law have some system but, even then, the same topic can receive several airings in different books.

This means that if you want to find out what the Bible (or even one biblical genre or author) has to say on a given topic, you will need to dart around from place to place. This type of study takes a topic and digs out the different references associated with it.


## Disentangling long-term principle from short-term culture

When we come to those commands that seem anachronistic or controversial to modern ears, there are some important questions to ask. These include:

- Why did the author think it was important?
- What were the cultural assumptions in place at that time?
- How are ours different?
- What, if anything, did Jesus say (or do) about the subject?
- How does it relate to our understanding of God's nature?

# Exercises

## Following a line of theological argument

### Being made right through faith (Romans 3)

STEP 1: Ask God for understanding.

STEP 2: Read the passage.

STEP 3: Wade through the argument till you find the main point about Jesus that Paul is trying to defend.
- Which verse or verses best sum this up?

STEP 4: What arguments against his main point is Paul trying to counter?
- What distortions and misunderstandings could easily and quite genuinely taint this main point?
- In what way would Paul's teaching have proved a threat to the existing religious establishment?

STEP 5: What cultural assumptions is Paul grappling with here?
- What is the bigger issue embodied behind the custom at stake (circumcision)?
- Is Paul trying to do away with previous customs or cultural divides, subvert them, change them or uphold them?

STEP 6: Focus on how Paul's main point could affect your life.
- Is this an easy bit of teaching for you to accept?
- What are the ways in which you distort it, misunderstand it or find it threatening?

## Finding the principles behind the practice

### The Sabbath year and the year of Jubilee (Leviticus 25)

STEP 1: Ask God to draw insight for you from 3000-year-old words.

STEP 2: Read the passage.

STEP 3: What principles are embedded in this legal framework?
- Do they all relate to justice and fairness or are other principles involved?
- Which are pragmatic and which are moral issues?

STEP 4: These laws are made for a culture vastly different from our own. Could any of the principles behind them be taken into our own laws to make a fairer or wiser society?

- What injustices do you see in our society because these principles have not been followed?

STEP 5: Does Jesus or any other Bible teacher have anything to say on this issue?
- Look at Exodus 20:8—the basics 'set in stone' from which all Judeo-Christian societies derive their law. Or do they? How far has this principle been eroded?
- Look at Mark 2:24—3:6. Is Jesus reinforcing the principle, subverting it, changing it, or just treating it with common sense?

STEP 6: Does this principle have anything to do with me?
- Is there any way I could fight to maintain these principles in society at large?
- Is there any way of maintaining these principles in my own personal life that would make it braver, saner, wiser?

## Exploring a topic

### Speech and conversation (Proverbs 17 and 27)

STEP 1: Ask God to help you listen.

STEP 2: Read the passages.

STEP 3: Draw out those verses which have anything to do with the topics. Note them down—do they divide under headings or categories?

STEP 4: Are there any principles, running themes or key words that emerge?
- Are these issues of morality or common sense (or can one even divide the two)?

STEP 5: Does Jesus' teaching or any other Bible teaching have anything to say on the subject?
- Look at Matthew 12:33–37.
- Can you think of any Gospel passage where Jesus' actions or reactions gave a good model on these topics?
- Look at James 3.

STEP 6: How does the teaching on this topic relate to your life?
- Pick one of the proverbs that is particularly pertinent to you right now. Write it out and stick it up somewhere, or commit it to memory.

# Disentangling long-term principle
# from short-term culture

## Wives, slaves and the principle of submission
## (1 Peter 2:13—3:9)

STEP 1: Ask God to help your understanding.

STEP 2: Read the passage.

STEP 3: Trace the major principle that runs through this passage.
- Why does the author think it is important?
- What benefits arise from it?
- From where does the principle come?

STEP 4: What assumptions are made in this passage based on the culture of the time?
- Which, if any, are seen as completely wrong by our culture?
- Which are seen as simply outmoded?
- Are there any ways in which changes in culture or contemporary thinking make the basic principle invalid?

STEP 5: Do Jesus' words or actions have any bearing on this principle or on these cultural assumptions?
- Look at Matthew 5:38–42 (going the extra mile) and Luke 23: 32–43 (the humiliation of the cross)—the principle embodied.
- Look at John 8:3–11 (the woman caught in adultery) and Mark 5:25–34 (the woman with menstrual problems)—the cultural assumptions challenged.

STEP 6: How does the principle behind this passage relate to your life?
- Would taking on any of these principles mean 'going against the flow' of assumptions around you?
- Can you see any personal benefit in taking on these principles for yourself?
- Can you see any benefit for the society around you in taking on these principles?

# Inspiration for spirited individuals

*My favourite passage has to be Ephesians 6:10–18, all about putting on God's armour to stand firm and fight off all of life's difficulties and temptations.*

*This is the piece of scripture I always turn to when feeling under attack and vulnerable. And at long last the penny's finally beginning to drop. I can do very little in my own strength and anything in God's! All I need to do is use every piece of God's armour for protection—and pray!*

*How brilliant it is to know that his support is always there!*

DIANE-LOUISE JORDAN (TV AND RADIO PRESENTER—MADE HER DEBUT ON *BLUE PETER*)


*2 Corinthians 1:19–20 is one of those passages that has stuck in my memory and become significant. It says, 'For the Son of God... was not "Yes" and "No"; but in him it is always "Yes" ... For this reason it is through him that we say the "Amen", to the glory of God.'*

*What I love about that is the total readiness of Jesus always to say 'Yes' to the Father. I don't see that as Jesus up there saying 'Yes' to the Father up there, but Jesus within me saying his 'Yes' within me to the Father who, in turn, is within him.*

SISTER WENDY BECKETT (NUN, ART HISTORIAN AND TV PERSONALITY)


*A verse that sums up what I believe is 2 Corinthians 4:13: 'We also believe, and so we speak.' A lot of people say that I should keep religion private, but I say, 'Oh no, quite the contrary.' If you have belief then you should speak. It is something I've always believed—though it's not always been an easy thing to do. I get a lot of criticism from people who say that religion is a private matter, that you don't have to bring it into the secular world, but I always remember that exhortation. If anyone asks why, I say, 'Because I believe it.'*

ANN WIDDECOMBE (CONSERVATIVE MP)

# Wisdom for busy days

When you're working on location, moving backward and forward, away from home for long periods, unable to attend church meetings and missing the stimulation of other people, then finding the inspiration to go away and read the Bible can be hard.

Something that has helped us a lot over the last year is an idea from an American preacher who visited our church some years ago. One thing he suggested was reading the chapter of Proverbs that fits that day of the month. That has proven to be really amazing—we found that God really planted something every day and you can actually find so many things that are quite applicable to your life. Often we would find that we would read a bit in the morning and it would come alive during the day. You'd say, 'Oh, yes, I remember that bit about being wise or prudent in that way.'

From the point of view of busy lives and busy schedules, you need something that is easy to get into. For me [Paterson], when I have to be up at 5.30 to be on set, to go to a place in the Bible that's easy to find, that doesn't depend on you remembering the bit before, is a huge help. It also means you can just take a pocket edition of Psalms and Proverbs, so you can have it with you wherever you are and read a Psalm as well if you have time.

PATERSON AND EMMANUELLE JOSEPH (PATERSON IS AN ACTOR, BEST KNOWN FOR HIS PARTS IN CASUALTY AND THE BEACH. EMMANUELLE, A TRANSLATOR AND HOMEMAKER, ACCOMPANIES HIM ON LOCATION WHERE POSSIBLE)

*Eight*

# Prayer poems: songs of hope and despair

The Bible is threaded through with poetry. Even in those books that are almost entirely prose, you will find sudden outbursts of verse. Some books—Song of Songs, Job, Proverbs, many of the prophets—are written almost entirely in poetic form. The comments that follow on this type of literature and ways of approaching it are true for all of them. But one Bible book above all stands out for its poetry, and it is on that book—the Psalms—that this chapter focuses. It stands out not only because of its beauty, nor for its 'no-holds-barred' honesty, but because it has a unique function. It is not just poetry but prayer—the pouring out of the heart's deepest feelings to God.

## Strict structure

'It is,' said C.S. Lewis, '…either a wonderful piece of luck or a wise provision of God's, that poetry which was to be turned into all languages should have as its chief formal characteristic one that does not disappear in translation' (*Reflections on the Psalms*, Fount, p. 12).

The psalms are not just outpourings of emotion. They are also poetry—structured and organized within the clear conventions of the time. Happily for us, those conventions do not depend on rhyme or on strict metre, both of which would be lost to us. Rather, Hebrew poetry works through a rhythmic two-part pattern, known as parallelism. It is a simple formula: the second part of the verse always carries the same thought as the first.

Sometimes it simply says the same thing twice in different words:

*Lift up your heads, O gates!*
*and be lifted up, O ancient doors! (Psalm 24:7).*

Sometimes, the second half of the verse mirrors or opposes the first:

*Some take pride in chariots, and some in horses,*
*but our pride is in the name of the Lord our God (Psalm 20:7).*

Sometimes the second half enlarges on the first, or draws a conclusion:

*Therefore let all who are faithful*
*offer prayer to you;*
*at a time of distress, the rush of mighty waters*
*shall not reach them (Psalm 32:6).*

Within this pattern there is also a rhythm, where a sentence with four or five stressed syllables is matched with a following sentence carrying the same beats:

*The **Lord** is my **light** and sal**va**tion;*
*  **whom** shall I **fear**?*
*The **Lord** is the **strong**hold of my **life**;*
*  of **whom** shall I be a**fraid**? (Psalm 27:1).*

Some other aspects of Hebrew poetry are lost to us completely. Psalm 119, for example, is composed in the form of a giant acrostic, with a section for each letter of the Hebrew alphabet, each section containing eight lines beginning with that same letter. It is a mark of the poet's skill and depth of passion for their subject matter—in this case, a delight in the word of God, what C.S. Lewis describes as 'a delight in having touched firmness' (*Reflections on the Psalms*, p. 55)—that even with the structural pattern lost, this psalm can still be beautiful and meaningful to 21st-century readers.

## Elastic imagery

One reason the psalms carry their life so well down the ages is that their imagery is so strong.

William Barclay explains: 'Among the Hebrews in biblical times, there were few—perhaps none—who thought, or could think, in abstract terms and abstract arguments. *They thought in pictures*' (*William Barclay Introduces the Bible*, p. 130).

This is so much the better for us, for in our image-soaked televisual age, we are once more accustomed, subconsciously at least, to doing our thinking in pictures. In fact, when approaching abstract ideas, it is almost impossible not to use concrete imagery. It is easy enough to describe a toothbrush, but try describing toothache without saying, 'It feels like...'

All cultures develop a set of image-words to describe abstract concepts. Here are some of ours:

*Happiness:* 'over the moon', 'walking on air'.
*Depression:* 'the pits', 'the blues'.
*Integrity:* 'straight as a die', 'rock-solid'.

Many are so much part of our language that we don't even notice they are images at all.

The great strength of these metaphors and especially the ones in the psalms is that they are elastic—they can be stretched to fit a million different circumstances. When the psalmist says, 'My soul thirsts...' I know exactly what he means. When God's word is described as 'a lamp to my feet and a light to my path' I understand, because my life has often felt like walking in the dark and often a word from the Bible or spoken by a friend has suddenly shown me where to go next.

You too have had experiences of thirst or darkness—everyone has. Were we to share the circumstances of those experiences—you, me, the psalmist and billions of people through history—we would find that they were wildly different (and perhaps, on the surface, embarrassingly ordinary). But that is the genius of poetry, and especially the psalms. It allows us to express the inexpressible, to say what we are unable to say in any other way.

## Obscure expressions

There was a chorus current in our church a few years ago which contained the mystifying words:

*Beautiful for situation,*
*The joy of the whole earth,*
*Is Mount Zion on the sides of the north,*
*The city of the great king.*

Week after week we sang it with gusto but, looking back, I wonder if any of us had any real concept of what we were singing about. We probably guessed that it came from a psalm (in fact, it was lifted—by one Robert Ewing—virtually intact from the King James translation of Psalm 48) but I doubt that anyone in the entire congregation knew what 'the sides of the north' actually were. Well, here is one advantage of researching a book—I've just found out. Or, to be accurate, I've discovered that it's pretty much a mistranslation.

The word causing the problem is 'Zaphon', which can be used either as 'north' or as the title of a mountain which was known as sacred. The two ideas are probably linked—'north' was apparently a traditional expression for 'God's royal seat' and could also be used to refer to 'heaven'.

Curiously, Zaphon itself was near the River Jordan, halfway between Galilee and the Dead Sea—in other words, not very far north at all. I suppose it is the equivalent of Cockneys talking of going 'up West'. The expression has little to do with geography—the West End being right in the centre of London—but a great deal to do with the nature of the trip, in this case, a glamorous night out on the town. In the same way, for Jews of a certain period, going 'up north' meant going somewhere to meet with God. (I still don't know how the 'sides' got there!)

So it is easy to see how a word, which on the surface has a clear literal meaning, can also carry many shades of associated meanings.

Zion, too, is just such a word. It wasn't just the Judean capital, the place where the Temple was founded and where worship services were held. It wasn't just the city founded by great King David and the Temple built by the great King Solomon. It didn't just refer back to the Jewish nation's golden age. More than that: it was home, heartland, a source of such strength and identity that the cry of longing, 'My soul longs, indeed it faints for the courts of the Lord' could hardly be overstated. This is not just the colonialist's nostalgia for warm beer and cricket on the village green. It is more even than that.

A friend of mine surprised me recently by describing a writers' group that both of us attend as being like a 'spiritual home'. It is a tiny group, half a dozen at the most; we meet in a cold, rather soulless room and she has only been two or three times. But I knew what she meant. It was the only place she had found with people who were totally of like mind, people who cared passionately for the same things she cared about. And because it was a Christian group, for the first time it allowed her to believe that God was passionately concerned in the same things too. It had become to her both a sanctuary and a release—not somewhere she needed to stay in for long periods of time, but somewhere she needed to visit, somewhere she needed to know existed.

Even if you know very little about the place the psalmists called Zion (and in a way, you don't need to know), perhaps you can identify with the longing for a spiritual home? And, I hope, with finding it.

## Embarrassing sentiments

There's one problem with the psalms. For the most part they contain beautiful imagery and high moral sentiments. And then they go and spoil it! Psalm 137, for example, begins with the wistful yearning of exiles for their homeland and ends with:

*Oh daughter Babylon...*
*Happy shall they be who take your little ones*
*    and dash them against the rock!*

Or Psalm 109:10–12:

*May his children wander about and beg;*
*    may they be driven out of the ruins they inhabit.*
*May the creditor seize all that he has...*
*May there be no one to do him a kindness,*
*    nor anyone to pity his orphaned children.*

Or how about Psalm 58:

*O God, break the teeth in their mouths...*
*Let them be like the snail that dissolves into slime;*
*    like the untimely birth that never sees the sun.*

It's such an embarrassment, this lust for destruction and revenge—if only they could have toned their language down just a little.

There is much in scripture that you and I might like to sanitize, and people have often tried. But the cry for vengeance cannot be excised from the psalms; it is much too closely intertwined with higher things.

But then, perhaps that is just as well, since no more can it be excised from human experience. Of course, in a 'civilized' society, we would never put it in such crass terms. And although they are no less than ever the 'collateral damage' of our modern-day conflicts (from divorce to economic rivalry to smart bombs), we would never claim any pleasure in harming innocent children.

But just because we would never say such things, it does not mean the feelings have disappeared. As Walter Brueggemann puts it, 'We must not be so romantic as to imagine we have outgrown the eagerness for retaliation' (*Praying the Psalms*, St Mary's Press, p. 58).

This capacity for hatred is a deep and integral part of being human. If we pretend otherwise, it will not make it so. And if the psalms make us face up to that darker side of ourselves, then it is no bad thing. But that still does not do away with the problem—that people who loved and understood God seemed to see no shame in such cruel and vindictive attitudes.

The first thing to note is that even if God allowed such things to be said, he made it quite clear that vengeance was not to be practised.

'You shall not hate in your heart anyone of your kin,' commands Leviticus 19:17–18. 'You shall not take vengeance or bear a grudge against any of your people, but you shall love your neighbour as yourself.'

Exodus does not even allow the secret satisfaction of revenge by omission: 'When you come upon your enemy's ox or donkey going astray, you shall bring it back' (23:4).

And even that apparent charter for revenge, 'an eye for an eye, a tooth for a tooth' (Leviticus 24:20), has more to do with limiting revenge than condoning it. It is about justice—rough justice, but still justice—that the person who harms will have harm done to him and that there it stops. The account is then closed. There is no excuse for ongoing feuds.

And the psalms themselves make clear that these enemies were not just people who happened to be disliked but people who had done great evil and got away with it. The opponent whose children the psalmist wished to be beggars was no innocent victim:

*For he did not remember to show kindness*
*but pursued the poor and needy*
*and the brokenhearted to their death.*
*He loved to curse...  (109:16–17).*

And it may not have been the fault of the daughters of Babylon, but the fathers and mothers had indeed been responsible for savage ethnic cleansing as they dragged whole families from their homes and their lands and into wretched exile.

As for those whose teeth the psalmist wanted broken, as a remedy for lying and image-conscious politicians, it is a tempting suggestion even now. And aren't there a few slimy power-brokers you too would be happy to see melt into obscurity?

I can't excuse all of the psalms' vengeance-seeking, but it does seem to have at least as much to do with a passionate concern for justice as it does with the pleasure of reprisals.

I have one other defence for these passages and it is the one that I believe most concerns us. In giving voice to their most evil thoughts, putting them out there hanging shockingly in the air, the psalmists were allowing their real selves to be seen where it most mattered—before God. And by saying these things *before* God, they were handing them over *to* God, and thereby defusing their power.

'Vengeance is transferred from the heart of the speaker to the heart of God,' explains Walter Brueggemann. 'This full rage and bitterness is yielded to God's wisdom and providential care...The yielding cannot be full and free unless the articulation and owning is first full and free. That submission to God is an act of faith and confidence. The speaker has no doubt that God will honour and take seriously the need for vengeance and will act upon that need... The rage is not removed. But it has been dramatically transformed by the double step of owning and yielding' (*Praying the Psalms*, p. 60).

# Book covered in this chapter

## Psalms

Unless you have been inoculated at an early age by a surfeit of chanting, you, like most Bible readers, will probably gravitate fairly quickly to the

Psalms. For a start, they are short and therefore approachable. Secondly, one or two at least are familiar. But above all they are intensely personal and real. The whole gamut of human emotion is found here—from chandelier-swinging 'God-intoxicated' praise to the deepest depths of despair; from a longing for purity to snarling, teeth-baring vengeance; from a celebration of trees and skies and mountains to flag-waving nationalism. These are the last sort of lyrics to be sung in a dreary, shuffling monotone.

## Target audience

But they *were* intended to be sung—the word 'psalms' can be translated 'songs accompanied with stringed instruments' (not to mention flutes, horns, trumpets, drums and cymbals). No Calvinist austerity here, and definitely no organs.

It may be that not all the Psalms were put to music, but certainly all were used in worship, for this is why this book was gathered—to be used as the combined hymn book and prayer book of the Jerusalem Temple.

## Type of literature

Entirely poetry, as outlined above.

## Authorship

Just as with most of the other Old Testament literature, so with Psalms— no one can pin down exact dates or authors, but they were almost certainly gathered over a period of several centuries. And as with the Wisdom of Solomon, so with the Psalms of David—the 'of' does not mean 'composed by' but 'after the manner of'. This suggests, of course, that there was a 'manner' to be imitated and that some psalms almost certainly came from the great king himself. No one knows, however, exactly which ones they were.

A few place themselves directly within David's history. Psalm 51, for instance, is identified as 'after David had gone in to Bathsheba'; Psalm 57, 'when he fled from Saul, in the cave'. In contrast, Psalm 137 jumps 450 years to 'the rivers of Babylon...' where the Israelites sat and hung up their harps in miserable exile.

## Themes

Those present-day worship leaders who encourage their flock into happy-clappy cheeriness may be surprised to learn that the largest proportion of psalms are not songs of joy, but cries of need. Maybe some of their congregation will be relieved.

Praise does come next, however, with just under a third in this category. The remaining third is divided between several different categories. One is that of pilgrim songs, such as Psalm 84, which express just how intensely the Temple had become a focus of Jewish hopes and dreams.

Some psalms are further examples of the tradition of wise sayings found in Proverbs. Psalm 1: 'Happy are those who do not follow the advice of the wicked...' is an obvious example.

Then there are psalms like 105 which retell Jewish history; psalms like 72, a Judaic version of 'God save the king'; and even a royal wedding song, Psalm 45.

The actual circumstances may be long gone, but the experiences that the psalms embody are universal. Like the old favourites in church hymn books, they were, in the words of Robert Alter in *The Literary Guide to the Bible*, already 'worn to a lovely smoothness by long usage' by the time they were gathered. Like carved pew-ends in ancient churches, they are good for many a long year yet.

# Ways of reading

## Taking things literarily, not literally

Metaphors breathe life into language (and that's a metaphor, too). Take these three descriptions:

*Dust in the air makes the sky change colour when the sun is low.*
*The sunset is beautiful and awe-inspiring.*
*'This majestic roof fretted with golden fire...'*

The first gives a (vaguely) scientific explanation of sunsets. The second tells you some of the feelings associated with sunsets. The third, spoken by Shakespeare's Hamlet, *shows* you the sunset.

Of course, the sky is not a fretted roof and Shakespeare did not think it was. He didn't think the golden streaks of cloud were actually flames. He just wanted to grab the audience's attention with an image that was vivid and unusual. He wanted to build up a picture of the sky as beautiful and awe-inspiring in order to contrast the way Hamlet—feeling rather low just then—felt about it: 'It appeareth nothing to me but a foul and pestilent congregation of vapours'.

This is the way poetry works. It *shows* you things rather than *telling* you. You can perhaps understand from this why taking the Bible literally does not work when it comes to the Psalms or indeed any of the Bible's many sections of poetry. Reading poetry is primarily a right-brain, intuitive activity, not a left-brain exercise of logic. Poetry is meant to be relished, not dissected.

So, it may seem an obvious statement, but the first task when reading the Bible's many stretches of poetry is simply to enjoy them. Reading aloud is always a good way to do this—perhaps best indulged in private (which is why I always keep books of poetry, psalms included, beside the loo; they are also just the right length—if you know what I mean).

## Unpacking imagery from a different world

Of course, the images the psalmists used were images from their world and not ours. Few of us will have watched a deer panting for water or a shepherd leading his flock. We are unlikely to have been in chains or thrown into a deep pit.

Sometimes it takes a little work to dig out a long-buried meaning (another metaphor there). At other times, a stretch of imagination may be needed to think yourself into the mindset of a Mediterranean peasant.

Some of the differences relate to geography. Take the simple matter of weather: when the psalmist sings, 'He covers the heavens with clouds, prepares rain for the earth...' (147:8) it is in the context of a parched, dusty landscape where even the wells sometimes run dry. When the church choir sings it on a drizzly February morning to a congregation who take for granted their baths, showers and hosepipes, the context is rather different. When the psalmist promises that 'the sun shall not strike you by day' (121:6) and rejoices that 'all people may take refuge in the shadow of your wings' (36:7), he is seeing a scorched land where the chicks will die if the mother hen does not stretch out her wings over them in the noonday heat. In our grey, northern climes, sun is blessing and rain is threat. In Israel, the reverse is often true and the Bible must be read accordingly.

Some of the psalms' other images meant so much to their earliest readers or listeners because of a shared history. Psalm 81, for example, has God reminding the congregation, 'I tested you at the waters of Meribah', a story of events in the wilderness several hundred years previously, but still a story that the listeners took as *their* story. This is why a basic knowledge of Jewish history is so important in understanding many other parts of the Bible, and where having a concordance or a Bible with cross-references will help. (For the record, you can read about Meribah in Exodus 17:1–7 and Numbers 20:1–13.)

## Expressing deep emotion

One of the great dangers of church life is the tendency to want to 'make things better'. 'We're all Christians—we should feel fine. We should be confident and serene, trusting God through every difficulty.' It is a short step from claiming that that is the way things should be, to a tacit agreement of cover-up whenever they are not.

'Buck up! Things aren't that bad.' I wonder if anyone said that to the psalmist who wrote:

*Every night I flood my bed with tears;*
  *I drench my couch with my weeping (Psalm 6:6).*

Of course, it's an exaggeration. Of course, he didn't literally hang his mattress out to dry every morning. But that is how it felt. And, of course, there's a time and place to say these things. We all know the bore to whom we dread asking the question 'How are you?' knowing we will be told in long, *angst*-ridden detail.

The wonder of the psalms is that they allow you to say exactly how you are, but at the right time and in the right place—before God. And the wonder of the psalms is their insistence that before God you can say absolutely anything.

'The speech of the Psalms is abrasive, revolutionary and dangerous,' says Old Testament expert, Walter Brueggemann. 'It announces that our common experience is not one of well-being and equilibrium, that life is not like that. Life is instead a churning, disruptive experience of dislocation and relocation... The Psalter is a collection of the eloquent, passionate songs and prayers of people who are at the desperate edges of their lives… There is no thought here that Israel must be on good behaviour in the presence of God' (*Praying the Psalms*, p. 17).

I hope you have the blessing of a community of fellow pilgrims with whom you can be honest. Experience tells me that such a thing is far less common within the church than might be hoped. But such places do exist (perhaps the 'Mount Zions' of our experience) and they are worth thirsting for, fighting for and seeking out, no matter how hard the journey.

But if you do not have such a place, at least you can take comfort in the company of the psalmists. They told God everything exactly as it was, and so can you.

## Cultivating celebration

Perhaps my melancholic nature is closer to those who cry out from the depths, but the psalms never let me forget that God can also be addressed from the giddy heights of joy. He is to be approached with dancing (Psalm 149:3 and 150:4), clapping (Psalm 47:1) shouting (Psalm 27:6) and feasting (Psalm 81:3).

If you, like me, are more inclined to gloom than exuberance, these psalms of praise and rejoicing still have a lot to offer. And what they offer is a challenge: to cultivate—even against the odds—a mindset of delight. This cultivation is to the psalmists a quite deliberate exercise. Time and again they look with wonder on the natural world; count their blessings; recount their history; and sing.

Sing, above all, say the psalmists, recognizing, perhaps, that singing is a gift given to lift our gaze from the mud to the stars. They recognize that no matter how poor or downtrodden, human lives are to be lived with celebration. They challenge us, whatever our circumstances, to open our eyes to God's faithfulness, confident that once we start looking, it will be there to be seen.

## Creating our own psalms

The Jewish people made songs and prayers using images from their own surroundings, memories from their own history and emotions lifted straight from their own experiences. Strangely, Christians, rather than taking the principle and using it within our own culture, have too often simply repeated or copied the originals, thereby wearing them down to a weak parody of their former selves.

This is where the idea of scripture as 'holy' is a false ideal, if it makes us think that speaking to God in the language of another age is inherently more valuable than speaking to him in our own.

The psalms of the Bible are beautiful and valuable, but neither the art of poetry nor the practice of honest prayer stopped with the Jewish exile. If the psalms teach us anything, they should teach us to address God in our own words, our own imagery and out of our own memories and experiences. For that is the power of the psalms—as real expressions of real people rooted in real places and real times.

# Exercises

## A cry from the depths (Psalm 88)

STEP 1:  Ask God to help you call to him in every situation.

STEP 2:  Read the passage.

STEP 3:  Read it again, slowly and aloud.

STEP 4:  Make a note of those 'image' words that build up the mood of the poem.

- Look for repetitions that intensify the mood.
- Look for images of environment that describe how it feels to be in such a place of despair.
- Look for images that express the emotion in bodily terms.

STEP 5:  How does the psalm relate to your experience?

- Are there times when you have felt/do feel as low as this?
- Which image expresses those feelings most precisely?
- Does it help to know that others have felt the same?
- Has anyone ever made you feel bad for expressing your feelings as honestly as this?

STEP 6:  How can the psalms help you in building a relationship with God?

- Can you tell God exactly how you feel without guilt kicking in? If you haven't up to now, let this psalm give you permission.
- Affirm your trust. This psalm is unusual. Most others move on from despair to trust (see Psalm 13). Try to move from

a cry for help to an affirmation of trust, even if through gritted teeth!

- Remember past rescues (see Psalm 40). Even if your own experience has been bleak or at best uneven, remember that others have been to the depths before you and been lifted out.

## A celebration of nature (Psalm 104)

STEP 1: Ask God to help you see your world more intensely.

STEP 2: Read the passage.

STEP 3: Read it again, slowly and aloud.

STEP 4: Make a note of those 'image' words that build up the mood of the poem.

- Are there any images that are unfamiliar in our world? Can you guess or work out what they are intended to convey?
- Think about the significance of 'water' imagery in a hot, dry country and allow your imagination to play on it.
- Observe how the sheer volume and diversity of imagery builds up the mood of the psalm.
- Look for the words that accentuate this sense of fullness and richness.

STEP 5: How does the psalm relate to your experience?

- Do you have, or have you had, times when the sheer wonder of the world bowls you over?
- Are they part of your everyday experience or do they tend to come at times when you get away from it all?
- How could you develop more of a sense of wonder and appreciation in your everyday life?

STEP 6: How can the psalms help you in building a relationship with God?

- Choose one aspect of nature expressed in this poem (light, water, animals, birds, the seasons, food) and take time to ponder how amazing it is.
- What does this psalm say about the ongoing involvement of God with his creation? Consider how God is involved with your immediate environment.

- How could you creatively express your praise to God in a way other than words or song?

## An act of contrition (Psalm 51)

This is an expression of repentance for a specific and spectacularly messy bit of sinning. The story can be found in 2 Samuel 11. It might help to glance at it now, but it is covered in more detail in the next chapter.

STEP 1: Ask God to help you say your own sorries.
STEP 2: Read the passage.
STEP 3: Read it again, slowly and aloud.
STEP 4: Make a note of those 'image' words that build up the mood of the poem.
- Look at the words used for wrongdoing and its results. In our contemporary world of tolerance for 'inappropriate behaviour', how do they sound to you?
- Which images describe methods of getting rid of something unclean or unwanted?
- Look at how the poem moves between the external and the internal.
STEP 5: How does the psalm relate to your experience?
- Have you ever felt this guilty and unclean?
- Did you acknowledge it or try to hide it away? (To see how David was finally made to face his own wrongdoing, read 2 Samuel 12:1–13.)
- The psalmist clearly believes in the possibility of being made clean and new. Do you?
STEP 6: How can the psalms give you an example in building a relationship with God?
- If you have done something that makes you feel unclean, what pointers does this poem give for dealing with it, both inwardly and outwardly?
- If you have done something that cannot now be put right (as in David's experience), is it possible to feel clean and right again? If so, how, and does it come easily?
- Even if you haven't done anything as spectacularly bad as

murder and adultery, does this poem have anything to say to you about the ups and downs of your life?

## A celebration in time and place (Psalm 135)

STEP 1: Ask God to help you make your own celebrations.

STEP 2: Read the passage.

STEP 3: Read it again, slowly and aloud.

STEP 4: Make a note of those images that build up the mood of the poem.

- This poem visits a series of 'scenes'. What are they, and how do you think they relate to the author?
- This psalm relies heavily on names. Even if you don't know the characters referred to, what feel does this use of names give to the poem? (Note: if you want to find out about the splendidly named Og, king of Bashan, you can find him in Deuteronomy 3. Don't dwell on the bloodthirstiness. We will examine that later.)
- The psalm begins and ends in the same place—the Jewish Temple at the heart of Jerusalem—and sounds very much as if it was sung there. For more on what this place meant to the psalm singers, read Psalm 122.

STEP 5: How does the psalm relate to your experience?

- Are there any 'scenes' which readily evoke in you a sense of the reality of God?
- Are there any memories of past events which stand as evidence of God's involvement in your life?
- Which place most readily symbolizes to you a sense of identity and belonging? Do you identify God with that place?

STEP 6: How can the psalms give you an example in building a relationship with God?

- The psalmists clearly saw no need to see God as distant, abstract or purely on a 'spiritual' dimension. Have you divorced God from the everyday realities of time and place?
- Is there a place you can use as a symbol of God's faithfulness and return to as a symbol of your faithfulness

to him? (It could be anywhere: a church, a retreat house, an attic, a hill or a park bench.)

- Are there events from your personal history that showed you God was rooting for you? Have you learnt to remind yourself of them at times of doubt?

## Recipe for success

*I love Psalm 112. For me it has always had a personal resonance. I'm inspired by its promises—'He will have no fear of bad news'—and challenged by its lifestyle demands—upright, gracious, compassionate, righteous. In the aggressively competitive business world I inhabit, it is a constant reminder of God's way. On the wall of my office is an old poster for Levi's jeans. It says, 'When the world zigs, zag'—a contemporary expression of the theme of Psalm 112!*

RICHARD EYRE (CHIEF EXECUTIVE, PEARSON TELEVISION, PREVIOUSLY CHIEF EXECUTIVE OF ITV)

## Comfort in failure

*The more I studied the Psalms, the more I found them an incomparable treasure-house of hope and encouragement. One of their most compelling messages is that there is nothing new under the sun in the human condition. King David himself appears to have had more than his share of dark sins and darker periods of despair, yet his total reliance on God always pulled him through, often with a refreshed and quietened soul.*

*My starting point in these readings was that great penitential cri de coeur, Psalm 51, which had been recommended by the Manhattan pastor. It became a turning point in my journey because of its clarion call to face up to guilt, repent and accept God's promise of receiving forgiveness through faith.*

JONATHAN AITKEN (EX-CABINET MINISTER, IMPRISONED FOR PERJURY), FROM *PRIDE AND PERJURY*, HARPERCOLLINS, P. 250

# Nine

# History: God and a recalcitrant people

## What makes history?

The first question for sceptics to face on this subject is whether most of these books can accurately be called history at all. After all, there is no firm evidence outside of the Bible that Abraham, Isaac, Joseph or even Moses ever existed.

Absence of evidence, however, is not evidence of absence. And the absence of evidence outside of the Bible does not mean that the evidence within the Bible is therefore to be discounted, especially when the disputed event took place over three thousand years ago.

Take that central event of all Jewish history—the Exodus. You might expect that the Egyptians would have told of it in their writings. But history tends to be told by the victors, and the Egyptians hardly emerge well from the encounter with their rebellious slaves.

Also, history only becomes history after the event. Now I know that sounds a ridiculously obvious statement, but what I mean is this: you are unlikely to know the significance of an event until years later.

One day sometime in 1968, a young man gave a young girl a lift home after coffee at a mutual friend's house. It was hardly a significant event. But since it led eventually to that young man becoming my husband, it became an event of great significance—not least to our sons! In the same way, who was to expect that the ragtag band of Hebrew slaves who disappeared into the wilderness would emerge years later as a nation responsible for a faith and a moral code that shaped half of the world for three millennia afterwards?

The Brand family is no great lineage, but even we have a history we tell ourselves about our origins. It's true that we've never found concrete evidence of the Huguenot ancestry that my father's side of the family is rumoured to have, nor of the forebear who was shipped to Australia for stealing a sheep, but both ideas are firmly embedded in our consciousness and must have come from somewhere.

Some memories have a more solid base. I have seen the house in Peckham where my maternal grandmother grew up in a family of twelve brothers and sisters with sing-songs round the piano and chickens in the back yard. I have heard direct from my father-in-law the tale of how he was evacuated from Dunkirk without his trousers, and how he and my mother-in-law went on their honeymoon on a punt down the Thames in the blackout.

All of these stories and many more make up the legacy we will hand down to our children's children. Since they are word of mouth, the stories of Peckham and Dunkirk will eventually seem as misty and mythical as my Protestant ancestors escaping persecution in France. But there is a history even more shadowy than this that my children's children will stand to gain. This is the unspoken history—memories of faith, disappointment, hard work, low expectations, duty, free thinking, a creative spark. None of these things has ever been articulated to me, but I see more and more that somehow I have absorbed them not just from my parents, but from a chain that could quite possibly go right back to those black-clad, silk-weaving Huguenots.

The memories of the Brand family have little significance for the world at large. That is where the Old Testament is different. These books are the family memories of a turbulent, complex and fascinating people who have had a far greater influence on world history than their numbers or economic power could ever justify. They are also the family memories of Jesus Christ—and you only have to count the number of times he refers to them, both directly and by allusion, to realize how formative they were.

Whether all these memories were exact and literal fact, dramatically reconstructed fact, or based on any sort of fact at all, we may never know. What is far more important is that they articulate the sort of history that is never normally told—the deep, hidden history of what makes people what they really are. Embedded in a cast of characters and a set of events, occasionally fantastical, but for the most part remarkably believable, is a much deeper story about what it means to be human.

It is about the deepest human choices, the deepest moral values, the constant underlying struggle between good and bad. Long before psychology was ever invented, it is a story of what goes on in the human psyche.

This depth comes from an astonishing premise: that the one Creator God—ground of being, life force, far beyond human knowledge—could and did interact in the lives of ordinary people, person to person, day to day, in epic and triviality alike.

## Whose history is it?

What makes this story so fascinating is that it is set at many different levels.

### God and individuals

At the first level, it is about God interacting with *individuals*. The Bible has many heroes (and a few heroines) and almost all of them are glaringly and irrevocably flawed. God certainly doesn't pick people of good reputation, good track record or good background to be his partners. Perhaps the only thing they all have in common is a sort of crazy courage and a willingness to take risks.

### God and families

At the second level, it is about God dealing with *families*—and highly dysfunctional ones at that. Their problems were more to do with polygamy than the sort of serial monogamy we are living with today, but the hurts, confusions and jealousies they provoked seem pretty much the same. The struggle of parents disappointed in their children, and children trying to shake free of their parents, seem universal to all generations and they are to be found here too.

### God and tribes

At the third level, it is about God dealing with neighbouring communities or *tribes*—and a bloodthirsty tribalism it is too. The Western world perhaps thought at the beginning of this century that tribalism belonged only to primitive peoples—in the African jungle or the South American rainforest—and that if those people could be 'educated' enough, it would die out. The recent history of Northern Ireland, the former Yugoslavia, even of English football supporters, tells otherwise. Tribalism—the need to protect boundaries, group identities and self-esteem—can lead to great evil, but it is an indelible part of being human.

The idea of God taking sides, backing one community against another, is a troublesome one and leaves many questions to answer (see 'Old Testament views of God', pages 143–147). But at least these stories—of God right in there, getting involved in such tribal struggles—remind us that there is no circumstance of life or level of society in which God does not care for the people involved.

And the books of the Pentateuch give a wide range of God's commands about fair and compassionate behaviour towards 'the alien living among you'. There may be wars between tribes, but never is racial prejudice towards an individual condoned.

## God and nations

At the next level, we find God involved with a *nation*. It began in the desert wanderings, where the ethics, rituals and laws on which a nation could be built were dramatically forged and gradually refined. The closeness of that involvement seemed to peak during the short while when Israel was one kingdom under David and Solomon—an era that seemed golden in retrospect but had its share of troubles at the time. But even when the one nation split into two, even when these two nations began to abandon their roots and absorb the pagan lifestyles around them, even when they became puppet states of powerful empires, even when they were finally destroyed and their peoples carried away to exile in foreign lands—even then God was still involved, if only to weep along with them. But it was not only weeping, it was also cajoling, condemning, bludgeoning, promising—like any parent, doing anything that would bring the errant child into mature adulthood. And eventually, it was about fulfilling those promises and bringing the people back into fragile nationhood once more.

## God and all peoples

It has to be admitted that the Old Testament is rather parochial. It was written *for* one people group *by* one people group, and gives the impression that God is interested in them alone. But scattered through this history, and increasingly as their horizons widen, is a realization that God is also working *internationally* and is there for all peoples and all nations. Some Old Testament books seem to have been written to say that alone. Ruth is the story of how a woman from another race became great-grandmother to the greatest king in Jewish history. Jonah is a tongue-in-cheek tale of how a prophet tried everything rather than fulfil God's command to preach in a foreign city—and about his annoyance when these pagans responded and God showed mercy!

Perhaps we have to wait for the New Testament for a fuller flowering of this international understanding. Indeed, perhaps God is still waiting, maybe for people such as us, at last to reveal how he cares *globally* for our whole diverse planet and peoples.

But that brings us back to where we began—with individuals. It is individuals who effect change, whether personally, communally, nationally or globally, and that is the Bible's biggest strength—its insistence that God can and does meet with the most unlikely and unsuitable individuals and help them to become what they want to become and do what he wants them to do.

## A history of the underdog

This is one reason why the Old Testament has had so many reverberations down the centuries. It is, at so many points, the story of God raising up the underdog.

It is the story of how God takes the children of a *dysfunctional* family—Isaac, Jacob, Joseph—and offers them the possibility of rising above their roots.

It is the story of how God takes *dominated* people, people of ethnic minority, people ground down by hard work—the Jewish slaves in the Egyptian brickyards—and offers them freedom, dignity and identity.

It is the story of how God takes *dispossessed* people—homeless people wandering in the wilderness, exiled to Babylon—and offers them a homeland and a place of their own.

It is also the story of how God takes immoral people, self-indulgent people, cruel people, cowardly people, and shakes them up, dusts them down and helps them clean up their act and get on with life in a new way.

## Exodus and exile

People living through a time of dislocation and disappointment are particularly prone to return to their roots in a search for meaning. It has been suggested that this explains the late 20th-century 'heritage' boom. Costume drama, country kitchens, stately homes and historical 'experiences' littering the tourist trails—all have been taken as a symptom of a post-modern yearning for roots and lost stability. It is a recent phenomenon: up to the middle of the 20th century, Western society was still governed by the predominant worldview of modernity. It still believed in the dream of 'progress' and the capacity of scientific, rational people to better themselves. It still believed in looking forward rather than looking back.

But two world wars, the atom bomb, overcrowded and impersonal cities and the failure of ever-increasing affluence to deliver the dream has changed all that. Despite, or perhaps because of, the racing changes in technology and sexual mores that we are living through, many people would rather look back than look forward.

So perhaps it is especially easy for us to see why, when the people of Israel were taken captive to Babylon in 587BC, they became so desperate to cling to their origins.

It is particularly easy to understand why it was at this time of exile that the Exodus became such a loved and retold tale. It told of people in a very similar situation to their own. It reminded them that God was in the business of deliverance then, some seven hundred years earlier, that he had kept them as a nation over the intervening centuries, and would not desert them now. It gave them hope. It also reminded them that this deliverance was not going to be an easy ride and that God might just be waiting until the people he needed were fully focused on him and fully willing to obey.

In the event, the people of Israel discovered that God never works the same way twice. The deliverance from exile was very different from the deliverance from Egypt. And when the Messiah, the great leader they came to expect, finally arrived in the shape of Jesus Christ of Nazareth, that was totally different too.

## A sense of flow

I have read the Bible over many years. I have consulted many other books on the Bible. I have looked at many of those diagrams and timelines that try to chart the flow of Old Testament history. And I confess that it is not until now, writing this book and going over the material again and again, that I have finally got into my head a reasonably clear overview of this historical flow. I confess this only to reassure you that if you find it difficult, you are not alone. The books of the Bible were not usually written at the time of the events, and are not necessarily assembled in the order of the events. They are sometimes parallel accounts of the same events from the point of view of two different nations or two different eras, and sometimes the same events viewed from the differing perspectives of prophets and historians.

So, for example, the moment when Josiah first discovered the scroll of the Law is described in both 2 Kings and 2 Chronicles and overlaps with the life and work of the prophets Jeremiah and Zephaniah (and probably Nahum and Habakkuk too, although they don't mention him). No wonder we're confused.

I have tried to outline the basics both in list and diagram, and I hope they help. Don't worry, however, if you still find yourself a little bemused.

Do try as you dip into the Old Testament to get a sense of the ebb and flow of events, rather than just a pick-and-mix of unrelated incidents. It is only as you begin to sense the bigger picture that you will be able to see fully those recurring themes I wrote of in Chapter Two:

Equilibrium–Conflict–Resolution
Home–Journey–Destination
Safety–Risk–Growth
Orientation–Disorientation–Reorientation
Creation–Fall–Redemption

Put another way, the pattern that can be found repeating itself down the Old Testament generations could be described as:

Stage 1: Living rightly according to God's principles
Stage 2: Getting lazy, cocksure and selfish
Stage 3: Drifting into wrong life patterns
Stage 4: Falling on hard times
Stage 5: Turning to God for help
Stage 6: Experiencing God's mercy and restoration
Stage 7/1: Living rightly according to God's principles again

# Old Testament history for beginners

## Pre-history

**Dates:**       Unknown
**Bible book:**   Genesis
**Characters:**   Adam and Eve, Cain and Abel, Noah
**Events:**       Expulsion from garden
                  Flood
                  Tower of Babel

Although the Jewish nation traces its ancestry back to these first characters, there is no sense that these are 'Jewish' characters and events. They are folk-tales shared in different forms by the various people groups who lived around the eastern Mediterranean.

## Patriarchs

**Dates:**       Somewhere between 2000 and 1500BC
**Bible book:**   Genesis
**Characters:**   Abraham and Sarah, Isaac, Jacob and Esau, Joseph
**Events:**       Journeying from Ur (present-day Iraq)
                  Settling in Canaan (present-day Israel)
                  Relocation to Egypt in time of famine

Abraham, the 'founding father' of Judaism, was an adventurer in both religion and geography, discovering not only a new territory, but the one God—Yahweh. The three generations that followed him were less towering figures, with their own family problems, but they stayed true to the one God. Jacob was renamed Israel and his sons became the forebears of the twelve tribes of Israel. Joseph's adventures led the whole Israelite clan to settle in Egypt at a time of famine.

The record then goes silent for around four hundred years. Somehow during that time the Israelites managed to retain their distinct identity and some vestige of their monotheistic beliefs. At some time, perhaps because of poverty, perhaps because of this very distinctiveness, they fell into slavery to the Egyptians.

# From Egypt to Canaan

**Dates:** Somewhere between 1300 and 1200BC
**Bible books:** Exodus, Leviticus, Numbers, Deuteronomy, Joshua
**Characters:** Moses, Aaron, Miriam, Joshua
**Events:** Escape from Egypt
Nomadic wandering in desert
Conquering and settlement of Canaan (present-day Israel)

It was during this period, particularly the relatively short nomadic existence as desert wanderers, that under the genius of Moses the nation of Israel was formed. Its monotheistic beliefs were formalized and so was its legal framework. Moses never reached the destination he sought, but it was left to Joshua, a military man, to effect the victory that gave them the land and to settle the twelve tribes in their allotted territories.

# Settling the land

**Dates:** From around 1250 to 1050BC
**Bible books:** Judges, Ruth, 1 Samuel
**Characters:** Deborah, Gideon, Samson, Ruth, Hannah, Samuel
**Events:** Establishment of leaders (mostly military)
known as Judges
Warfare with neighbouring tribes

The Israelites may have gained a foothold in the land they called their own, but it was a very tenuous one. A plethora of surrounding tribes—Midianites, Amalekites, Ammonites, Moabites Philistines—set out to contest their claims of ownership. Not only were they assailed by warfare, but by the temptation to forsake their strict monotheism in favour of a return to the varied forms of paganism that surrounded them. Leadership was somewhat random: every so often, people with strong talents and personality (but not necessarily moral stature) would arise and be given the title of Judge. Not surprisingly, with no clear structure to hold the tribes together, they were beset by internal fighting, in particular a dispute which began with a gang rape and set eleven tribes against the perpetrators, the tribe of Benjamin.

# The monarchy

**Dates:** 1040–933BC
**Bible books:** 1 and 2 Samuel, 1 Kings, 1 and 2 Chronicles
**Characters:** Samuel, Saul, David, Jonathan, Solomon
**Events:** Kingdom brought together under strong unifying control
Establishing of Jerusalem as capital
Building of Temple by Solomon

It was the prophet Samuel who, at the people's demand, first selected and established a king—Saul. It was not without misgivings, shared apparently by God, who warned that although the establishment of a monarchy was necessary, it brought with it the danger of the people worshipping the king rather than God himself. Saul proved to be less honourable and obedient to God than had been hoped, and it was Samuel again who sought out and annointed David as his successor. There followed a period of civil war between David and Saul, but David eventually succeeded to the throne and thus began what is always seen as Israel's golden age. He established Jerusalem as capital, but it was left to his son Solomon to build the Temple. Under Solomon, the kingdom grew in wealth and acclaim, but in doing so it gradually fell prey to foreign influences and abandoned the high moral ground of Judaism on which it was founded.

# Divided kingdoms

**Dates:** 935–587BC
**Bible books:** 1 and 2 Kings, 2 Chronicles
**Characters:** Rehoboam, Jeroboam, Elijah, Elisha, Hezekiah, Josiah
**Events:** Revolt led by Jeroboam against Rehoboam
divides kingdom
Northern kingdom, Israel, falls to Assyria in 721BC
Southern kingdom, Judah, falls to Babylonians in 597BC
People of Judah deported to Babylon around 587BC

Within two years of Solomon's death, the golden age was over. Solomon's taxations had already provoked the people and now they turned against his son Rehoboam. Jeroboam led the revolt and in 935BC he and his followers took the northern territory around Samaria and proclaimed it a separate kingdom, the true Israel. Rehoboam held on in

Jerusalem and established the smaller kingdom of Judah. There followed a see-sawing succession of bad and not-so-bad kings in both kingdoms, and a succession of prophets to challenge them.

In the northern kingdom, Elijah, Elisha, Amos and Hosea spoke out against the absorption of pagan practices that threatened to swamp Judaism. Eventually, however, Samaria, the capital, was captured by the Assyrians and gradually the people intermarried and assimilated the beliefs of their new rulers, until their distinctiveness was all but lost. This explains the scorn with which Samaritans were treated at the time of the Gospels.

In the southern kingdom, first Isaiah and Micah, and later Nahum, Habakkuk, Zephaniah and Jeremiah warned of the approaching menace from the Assyrian and later the Babylonian empires, and of the vulnerability of a nation that does not stay close to God.

Two kings, Hezekiah and Josiah, also stand out for their integrity and faithfulness to the Jewish religion. Even so, nothing could stop the onward sweep of the Babylonian empire, and in 597BC Jerusalem was captured by Nebuchadnezzar and the exile of the Jewish people began.

## Exile and return

**Dates:**        597–538BC
**Bible books:** Jeremiah, Daniel, Ezekiel, Ezra, Nehemiah, Esther
**Characters:**  The above, plus Shadrach, Meshach and Abednego,
                 Nebuchadnezzar, Belshazzar, Zerubbabel
**Events:**      Jerusalem captured in 597BC and successive
                             batches of captives taken to Babylon
                 Jerusalem destroyed in 587BC
                 Cyrus, king of Persia, conquers Babylon in 538BC
                 First wave of Jews under Zerubbabel return to
                             Jerusalem in 538BC
                 Second wave returns under Ezra in 458BC
                 Third wave returns under Nehemiah in 445BC

Jeremiah warned rightly that there was no resisting the Babylonians but also that the captivity would last less than a lifetime. He himself chose to remain in Judah along with a disempowered and dispossessed remnant of the people, while the rest were taken to Babylon (in modern Iraq).

The Jews' salvation came from an unlikely source—Cyrus, king of Persia (modern Iran), who overtook Babylon in a bloodless coup, and allowed them freedom of worship and the possibility to return to Jerusalem and rebuild the Temple. Zerubbabel spearheaded this return while the majority of the Jewish people remained in Babylon. Were it not for Esther, Jewish wife of the Persian King Xerxes, these remaining Jews might have been the victims of ethnic cleansing, but her cunning defeated the plot.

Eighty years after the first return to Jerusalem, Ezra, a priest and teacher, was allowed to return to Jerusalem with a party of 1,700 people to set up an official programme of reinstating the Jewish religion. Meanwhile, though, the rebuilding programme had stopped and it fell to Nehemiah, a Jewish official in the Persian court, to return and refortify Jerusalem by rebuilding its walls. And there the record ends.

## Between Testaments

**Dates:**        445BC to AD1
**Bible books:** None, other than Maccabees in the Apocrypha

The reformed Israel gradually grew in strength and in understanding of its faith, as the books that make up the Old Testament were compiled and their teachings disseminated. Along with this teaching came a belief that the great days of God's speaking were over. Scripture became a closed canon. History, however, continued, and the same pattern was no doubt discernable to those who had eyes to see, even though it was not recorded in the same way. Certainly, the same pattern of threat from outside empires continued. After the Persians it was the Greeks, led by Alexander and his general Ptolemy, who conquered the region (now named Palestine). Many Jews moved to Alexandria in Egypt, and Greek became the common language. The Seleucid dynasty from Syria were eventually handed power from the Greeks, until they in turn were eclipsed by the Romans, who gradually extended their grip and occupied Israel in 63BC.

Somehow, through all this domination and dispersion, the Jewish people held on to their identity, to the God of their father Abraham and the Law of their great prophet Moses and hoped for a deliverer, the Messiah who they believed would one day surely come.

## Top timeline (2000–1000 BC)

2000 — 1900 — 1800 — 1700 — 1600 — 1500 — 1400 — 1300 — 1200 — 1100 — 1000

PATRIARCHS – NOMADIC TRIBES
Abraham/Sarah   Isaac   Jacob/Esau   Joseph

SETTLEMENT IN EGYPT

SLAVERY IN EGYPT

EXODUS
Moses   Joshua

SETTLING THE LAND (JUDGES)
Deborah   Gideon   Samson   Ruth

EGYPT (MIDDLE KINGDOM)

HITTITE EMPIRE

AGE OF PHARAOHS

## Bottom timeline (1000–0 BC)

1000 — 900 — 800 — 700 — 600 — 500 — 400 — 300 — 200 — 100 — 0

MONARCHY
Saul   David   S'mon
Samuel   Nathan

—— DIVIDED KINGDOMS ——

NORTHERN KINGDOM (ISRAEL)
Jereboam   Ahab   Amos   Hosea
Elijah   Elisha

SOUTHERN KINGDOM (JUDAH)
Reheboam   Jehoshaphat   Uzziah   Hezekiah   Josiah
Isaiah   Jeremiah

EXILE
Daniel

RETURN
Zerubbabel
Ezra
Nehemiah

Esther

BETWEEN TESTAMENTS
Alexander the Great   Seleucids   Maccabees   Romans

EGYPT

ASSYRIAN EMPIRE

EGYPTIAN POWER WEAKENS

BABYLONIANS

PERSIANS

GREEKS

ROMANS

# Old Testament views of God

## Problem areas

Of the many problems that contemporary readers meet when reading the Bible, perhaps none is more challenging than the Old Testament portrayal of God. Critics of Judeo-Christian religion are quick to point the finger at the vengeful, fickle, bloodthirsty God of the Bible (and they do usually express it this way—the fact that the New Testament portrayal is somewhat different seems easily forgotten).

Many Christians are content to point to a New Testament Mr Nice Guy God and tidy the Old Testament Mr Nasty conveniently out of sight. This is a bad idea. First, because it probably means that their Bibles will end up gathering dust on a shelf. Second, because it is impossible to comprehend the New Testament fully without some understanding of the Old. And third, because the Mr Nasty Old Testament God will not disappear that easily. He will still be there lurking as a skeleton in the cupboard of our collective cultural memories. It's far better to take him out and face him.

God is, by definition, far greater, bigger, more complex and all-encompassing than any human being could ever hope to grasp. All views of God are limited, ours included. The Bible charts the very first glimmers of understanding that there might even *be* one God rather than a pantheon of warring local deities—a giant mental and spiritual leap which should never be underestimated. Of course, this understanding was limited. What is so remarkable is that it was there at all.

I don't want to explain all the problems away, and couldn't if I tried, but I do think there is far more to be learned from these earliest glimpses of the one God than might be supposed.

I suggest that the first step lies in trying to think our way into the mindset of these ancient people. That will mean identifying and perhaps trying to shake off the many other presuppositions about God that we have accumulated. It will also mean asking whether these early peoples had some valuable insights about God that our more sophisticated world has lost. Could it be that, just occasionally, the problem is in our limited vision and not theirs?

## An anthropomorphic God

One problem that sceptical readers encounter early on is that the Old Testament God is just too human. He is portrayed as strolling through the Garden of Eden (Genesis 3:8), as well as paying a surprise visit to Abraham and being willing to bargain with him (Genesis 18).

We rightly understand that many aspects of God can only be expressed in abstract terms: love, goodness, wholeness, life-force, ground of being. But you cannot relate to an abstraction. If God is love, then love can only be expressed in relationships and relationships can only be expressed between persons. And if the highest earthly life-form is human—persons—then why are we surprised when God, a far higher life-form, is expressed as personal rather than abstract?

Isn't that just exactly what Christianity is about—that the vastness of God was encapsulated in the person of Jesus Christ? It's difficult. It's mind-boggling. But could it be that for those who are unsophisticated enough to expect God to relate to them in direct, tangible and personal ways, God might just be gracious enough and humble enough to do so?

## A fickle God

What is God up to? He creates humans in Genesis 1 and by Genesis 6 he is so fed up he is thinking of wiping out the lot of them.

It is hardly surprising that early peoples looked at unpredictable weather patterns, especially freak events like floods, and concluded that they were directly ordered by some divine mind—if not the mind of a malefactor, then definitely of a trickster.

Of course, we are far more rational. Since then, scientific method has come along and we have been affected by the Age of Reason, with its conviction that the universe ran on predictable ordered lines, and that someday soon we would not only understand it all but be fully capable of harnessing its power. 'God does not play dice,' wrote Einstein as recently as 1926 (in a letter to Max Born).

But although science has made many great and exciting leaps forward, through relativity, quantum mechanics, chaos theory and an under-standing of DNA, these discoveries have only served to demonstrate that things are far more complicated than we thought. 'God not only plays dice,' the scientists have avowed, 'but he throws them in dark corners.'

This may seem a long way from God weeping over the evil of humankind and creating a flood to wipe out the evil. But just as we now know that the universe runs on lines far more complex and less predictable than we thought, perhaps we need also to regain the idea that God is not as predictable as we would like. As C.S. Lewis wrote of Aslan in the Narnia stories, 'He is not a *tame* lion.' We are right to avow that God must be good, and goodness cannot be merely fickle. But perhaps we need to regain a sense of God as 'wild', unpredictable and sometimes inexplicable.

'I will be gracious to whom I will be gracious, and will show mercy on whom I will show mercy,' says God to Moses (Exodus 33:19). Or in other words, 'Yes, I will be with you and care for you, but don't ever think you can own me.' Both the God of the Old Testament and the Jesus of the New are like this, and those who try to 'tame' them may be in for a shock.

## An angry God

Look up the word 'anger' in a Bible concordance and you will be struck by one very obvious fact: the Old Testament is crammed with references not to human anger, but to God's. Far from being a God of love, you would think this God was permanently boiling with fury.

Again, this flies in the face of our preconceptions—God should be loving and gentle and kind, not chucking thunderbolts from heaven at anyone who annoys him.

The people of the Old Testament lived in a harsh world, at the mercy of drought, disease and failing crops, so we should hardly be surprised that they expected God to be harsh. But perhaps that was not the only reason for this understanding of God's anger. Perhaps they also had a far greater understanding of a concept that our present age has lost.

'Sin' is a deeply unfashionable word these days. Instead, therapists talk of 'inappropriate behaviour'. Now I know that psychology has made great strides, and that human behaviour is far more complex than our forebears thought and that 'bad' behaviour often springs from nature and nurture over which a person has no choice. But it is a short step from that to asserting that you can never label anything good or evil; and from that to concluding that absolute values do not exist at all, and so nothing is really our fault and God should not blame us for anything at all.

I'm glad the Church now places more emphasis on God's love and forgiveness than on his anger. It is, after all, what Jesus came to teach.

But you cannot understand mercy unless you first believe in the possibility of blame, and you cannot understand forgiveness unless you first believe in the possibility of guilt. When we look around at what we humans do to our world and our fellows, we should not be surprised that God's anger sometimes boils over. Perhaps we should be more surprised that he is so often merciful. The Old Testament writers understood this too. Look up 'anger' in the concordance and you will also find a recurring theme: 'God is slow to anger and abounding in love.'

## A vengeful God

The Old Testament describes a God who not only feels anger, but acts on it. God takes vengeance, often swift and shocking, on those who disobey his commands.

Again, our image of God as a God of mercy is right and good, but it is sometimes easy to forget that in order to show mercy, you must first have a system of justice—and it is impossible to have justice without punishment. You can't understand a God of mercy unless you also understand a God of justice who has every right to dole out punishment for wrongdoing and is sometimes prepared to do so. I don't want to set God up as a Tory Home Secretary, but I suspect that the descriptive slogan 'Tough on crime, tough on the causes of crime' is a pretty accurate one when it comes to the Almighty. And I certainly don't want to label myself as a reactionary lady from the Shires, but maybe we should be careful not to use our faith to justify a sort of 'politically correct' softness that excuses everything. Far from elevating the importance of mercy, eventually that simply devalues it.

## A partisan God

Does God take sides?

The mental picture of the First World War that I have absorbed is something like this: two armies dug into the mud for months and years, slaughtering each other senselessly, the reason never clearly explained or long ago forgotten, each with the conviction that God was on their side.

I also have an aural memory echoing round my head as I write—Bob Dylan drawling angrily about 'God on our side'. With it come a whole host of visual images—children bombed with napalm, Vietnamese peasants shot and thrown in a ditch, US soldiers shocked and bewildered at what they were being asked to do.

When the twelve tribes of Israel marched into the land of Canaan and started to do battle with everyone around them, they did so in a world where everyone assumed that the gods took sides. That's what gods were—talismans and symbols of identity for your people and your tribe. Small wonder then that the nation of Israel, who had only recently discovered the one God who was far more than a bronze statue and could not be contained in the form of one, still carried with them this idea that God was on their side and against the rest.

In one sense they were right: God was on their side. God did care deeply and personally about them and that included caring about their territorial disputes, their need for a clear identity, their concern for justice and a land free from sordid pagan practices.

With our long experience of centuries of warfare in the name of religion, we now know that their conclusion—that if God was for them he must therefore be automatically against anyone else—was deeply wrong. But perhaps we should wonder whether they needed first to understand how much God cared for *them*—*their* family, *their* tribe, *their* nation—before they could even begin to comprehend a God who cares for *all* peoples and *all* nations.

And perhaps we should also question whether the opposite idea—of a God who stands coldly neutral, detached and unconcerned—has so much going for it either. If God does care so deeply and passionately for human beings and for justice, then is it so surprising if sometimes he does take sides?

I will finish this section where I started. There are descriptions of God in the Old Testament that I find unpleasant, unpalatable and uncivilized. I do not want to justify them. All I am doing here is pleading that we face these passages and grapple with them. Because the strange thing about these tales of blood and gore and vengeance is that embedded in them are often gems of stories about faith, courage, love, loyalty and mercy—and to reject the former is to miss out on what the latter have to teach.

# Books covered in this chapter

For Genesis and Numbers see Chapters 6 and 7. For 1 and 2 Samuel see Chapter 6.

# Nehemiah

## Authorship

The basis of this book is the personal memoirs of Nehemiah, a Jew who had risen to high office in the Babylonian court and who gave up the comfort and prestige of life in exile to return and build the ruined city of Jerusalem some time around 445BC. It was edited at a later date, probably by the same hand that compiled its companion volume Ezra, as well as 1 and 2 Chronicles, histories of much earlier events seen from the perspective of the returning exiles.

## Themes

The first wave of Jewish people had been suddenly and miraculously freed to return to their homeland some ninety years previously. Their priority was to rebuild the Temple. For Nehemiah, the most pressing need was the more prosaic but essential task of fortifying the city by rebuilding the walls. Faced with a heap of rubble, scorned and sometimes obstructed, armed only with determination and love, Nehemiah motivates the people into a phenomenal feat of construction.

But it is not only bricks and mortar: the structure of society must also be rebuilt and the foundations must be right. That is why the people were called together to listen to readings from the Book of the Law, why they gathered to fast and confess their sin, and why they made a binding agreement 'to walk in God's law, which was given by Moses' (Nehemiah 10:29).

For background information on other historical books, see Appendix A.

---

## HOW HISTORY WAS GATHERED—A QUICK RECAP

- The Old Testament evolved from stories told round campfires and meal-tables to a written history, often finally compiled long after the event.
- The establishing of the Jewish nation under David and Solomon led to a need for the people to chronicle their origins.
- It was traditional for books to be attributed to a historical figure—the Psalms of David, the Proverbs of Solomon, the Law of Moses—even

when much of the material in the book was not actually written by them.
- Much of the Old Testament was not finally written and compiled until during and after the exile to Babylon (587–538BC).
- Some of the historical books are parallel accounts of the same events: Exodus, Leviticus, Numbers and Deuteronomy all cover the era of Moses from different perspectives and with different emphases. 1 and 2 Chronicles are later accounts of the era originally covered by 2 Samuel and 1 and 2 Kings.

## HOW TO READ HISTORY

- At a sweep.
- As a serial story.
- Taking one character or one era at a time.
- Seeing how God kept faith with unlikely material, with 'good' people and 'bad' people, through good times and bad.
- Seeing how God's purposes evolved through a chequered history.

---

# Exercises

## God and a far-from-perfect family
### (Genesis 25:19–34, 27–33, 35—36:8; 37:1–4)

STEP 1: Ask God to help you step into these characters' shoes.

STEP 2: Read the passage, possibly at a sitting, although over a period of days is probably more realistic and more effective.

STEP 3: Look at the raw material.
- How would you describe Jacob's character?
- How would you describe Esau's character?
- Where did the sibling rivalry come from (25:28)?
- Which (if either) would you have said was the more promising material?
- What paybacks did Jacob receive for his early actions?

STEP 4: Look at Jacob's encounters with God (28:10–22; 32:22–32).
- Do you think Jacob had any sense of God's presence before the first encounter?

- Why then? Was Jacob more ready to believe and, if so, why?
- Did he become a changed man in any way?
- The second mysterious encounter was very different from the first. How would you interpret it? What do you think Jacob's struggle was about? Was there any significance in the timing?

STEP 5: Look at what they learned and how they changed.
- The story ends with reconciliation. How did Jacob's experiences help him toward this point?
- The viewpoint of the story and the build-up of assumptions after it might imply that God favoured Jacob over Esau. Is there any evidence of this?
- The beginning of Joseph's story gives a horrible hint of history repeating itself. How does the story of Jacob's marital relations shed light on the rivalries that followed?

STEP 6: How does this relate to your experiences?
- Have you ever felt undervalued as a child, by a parent or others?
- How have you come to terms with it? Or have you yet to do so?
- Both Jacob's encounters took place at night. Have you ever encountered God at night, whether asleep or awake?
- We see God involved here with a complex and dysfunctional set of family relationships (polygamous at that). What does that say about God's relationship with ordinary families in today's world?

## God and an unruly tribe (Numbers 14:1—21:9)

STEP 1: Ask God for understanding. (You're going to need it. We are about to enter one of the harshest, most primitive and most alienating of biblical eras.)

STEP 2: Read the passage, probably over a period of days.
- Feel free to skim-read the details of ritual in chapters 15 and 18, but try to take in a little of it.
- Expect more questions than answers.

STEP 3: Look at the raw material.
- Think yourself into the era and type of society we are

looking at. Think 3200 years ago. Think Bronze Age. Think fierce feuding nomads.

- Think yourself into the landscape. Think hostile semi-desert. Think heat. Think disease. Think famine.
- Try to imagine what ideas these people have of God.
- Try to imagine what experiences of God they have to fall back on.
- What sanctions does a primitive, nomadic society have against wrongdoers other than death?

STEP 4: Look at these people's encounter with God.
- Look at his 'vengeful' activity.
- How do these people understand the bad things that befall them? Do they attribute every natural disaster to God? Do they show any evidence of believing in a devil?
- Look at the things Moses tells them about God.
- Look at their encounter with religious ritual. What ideas are being reinforced behind the symbolism?
- Look at God's rescuing activity. Is it always linked to the miraculous? Could any of the miracles have had natural explanation? What are the people learning about cause and effect?

STEP 5: Look at what they are learning and how (if at all) they are changing.
- Are the vengeful acts of God arbitrary or are they teaching any lessons?
- Are the disasters that befall them teaching them anything about God? about survival technique? about cause and effect?
- In a world without books, what value do the religious rituals have? What pictures are they building about God and society?
- What have Moses' speeches taught them about God?
- What have the rescues and the miraculous happenings taught them?
- Have they changed much in this passage? If not, do you think their experience filtered down to later generations? Did it bring about ultimate change?

STEP 6: How does this saga relate to your experience?

- Have you ever experienced a period of harsh discipline or a steep learning curve? Did it break you or strengthen you (or both)?
- Have you ever been in a situation where your basic survival was in question? Did it make you turn to God in a different way?
- The Israelites had every reason for grumbling but it hindered them from receiving what God wanted to give. Is there any way in which negative attitudes are blocking your development?

## God and a charismatic king
### (1 Samuel 8; 2 Samuel 5—7, 11—12)

STEP 1: Ask God to help you understand unchanging human nature.

STEP 2: Read the passages over a period of days, perhaps in three separate chunks.
- The chapter in 1 Samuel is only background material. What does it have to say about the pros and cons of monarchy and God's view of it?
- For background information on the strange 'ark of the Lord' (no relation to Noah's), read Deuteronomy 10:1–5. What light does this shed on the awe and reverence displayed for the ox cart's cargo?

STEP 3: Look at the raw material.
- What were David's skills and abilities?
- What were his strengths as a personality?
- What were his weaknesses?

STEP 4: Look at David's encounters with God.
- See particularly 2 Samuel 5:19–25; 6:21–22; 7:1–29; 12:1–14.
- Putting aside for the moment any reservations you may have about God's involvement in warfare, what is the positive model that chapter 5 gives of David's relationship with God?
- Why was the role of Nathan the prophet so important?
- Do you feel that David's reverence for God was genuine? What evidence is there for this?

STEP 5: Look at what David and his nation learnt.

- Strange as the incident of Uzzah's death (6:6–11) seems to us, what did it teach David and his people about religious respect?
- The delightful opening to David's prayer (7:18–19) shows a man who cannot believe his luck and is surprised that God should promise so much. What does this show of his culture's expectations of God's involvement in their affairs, and how does it develop their understanding?
- What does the story of David and Bathsheba teach about the paradox of forgiveness and punishment? Do you think the consequences would have been different if David had not spoken the words in 12:13 (amplified in Psalm 51)?

STEP 6: How does this relate to your own experience?
- Have you ever tried bringing your day-to-day decisions and choices to God? If so, have answers come and in what way?
- Have you ever 'danced before the Lord'? Or in other words, has God ever become so important to you that every concern for your own dignity and appearance before others has ceased to matter? Why could such an act be important?
- Do you have a 'Nathan' in your life who will tell it as it is, good or bad, and to whom you are accountable? If not, should you have and could you take steps to find such a person?

## God and a return from exile (Nehemiah 1—6; 8—10)

STEP 1: Ask God to help your understanding.
STEP 2: Read the passages, perhaps two chapters at a time, with chapter 10 on its own.
STEP 3: Look at the raw material.
- What were Nehemiah's personal strengths?
- What were the strengths of the people?
- What were their weaknesses?
- What were the things they were most vulnerable to at this time?
STEP 4: Look at Nehemiah's and the people's encounter with God.
- Nehemiah is clearly a man of decisive action. Why, then,

did he take so much time weeping, fasting and praying before responding to the need (1:4)?

- Why do you think the people reacted with weeping to hearing the Law read (8:9)? (Remember that the Law, to the Jews, was not just the instruction and legal passages but included all the history of their people—that same history that is recited in 9:5–36.)
- What was the point of the public act of confession (9:1–3)? Can a ritual act like this ever be deeply genuine?
- The binding agreement (10:29–39) could seem like a charter for exclusivity and for setting up a demanding religious establishment. On the other hand, what do you think were the strengths and joys of living in such a close and God-centred community?

STEP 5: Look at what was learnt.

- Most of this story is taken up with a very practical and seemingly not very religious task—building walls. What lessons do you think the people were learning as they laboured?
- What do you think was the biggest lesson the people learnt from hearing the Law read to them?
- When in later years the people looked back on those days, what do you think they would tell their grandchildren were the things they learned most overall?

STEP 6: How does this relate to your own experience?

- Rebuilding the walls must have seemed an impossible task to Nehemiah as he surveyed them silently by moonlight. Have you ever been faced with a task as daunting? Is there anything this story can teach you about achieving the unthinkable?
- This story is driven by a powerful motivating force (4:6). Do you give your 'whole heart' to your daily work? If not, then what would you work wholeheartedly for?
- Sanballat and Tobiah never took arms against the people of Jerusalem; nevertheless they employed several powerful weapons (2:19; 4:1–2; 6:9–13, 19). Are there times in your life when you allow those sorts of weapons to stop you doing what you want to do?

# Telling the truth about a real world

*When I read the Old Testament, I read of battles and of people slaughtering each other, knocking the daylights out of each other. At the very same time, that was just what was happening outside the room in which I was kept [as a hostage]. Just down the road was the land we call the Holy Land. Jerusalem. Just a few miles away.*

*Then I realized that the Bible, more than anything else, gives us the truth about human nature very, very clearly; straight between the eyes, no messing. And the truth that one sees in the Bible is necessary. But truth by itself can be brutal and it can destroy; it can actually destroy people. And in the situation of constant isolation and constant examination, there is probably a limit as to how much truth you can take.*

*When you come to the New Testament, you realize that truth needs to be balanced with compassion. Where truth and compassion walk hand in hand, then there is a possibility of people growing up into their fullness as human beings.*

TERRY WAITE (ARCHBISHOP OF CANTERBURY'S SPECIAL ENVOY AND BEIRUT HOSTAGE), INTERVIEWED BY ALAN TITCHMARSH, *SWEET INSPIRATIONS*, HODDER & STOUGHTON, PP. 48–49

*The Bible is about hatred, lies, corruption, lust, broken promises, prostitution, murder, adultery, pride, rape, war, torture, deformity, military occupation, famine, unbelief, fratricide, voyeurism, ignorance, injustice, slavery, drunkenness, rebellion, incest, madness… the occult, revenge, conspiracy, abuse of power, betrayal, greed, envy, racial hatred and death.*

*Because of that, it is even more powerfully about love and truth and honesty, friendship, courage, childbirth, dancing, eating, drinking, laughter, simplicity, presents, repentance, endurance, chastity, faithfulness, trust, self-sacrifice, bread, wine, music, consolation, renewal, forgiveness, passion, beauty, justice, peace, humility, miracles, lilies, children, freedom, sleep, poetry, honey, gold, prayer and angels.*

NIGEL FORDE (PLAYWRIGHT AND RADIO PRESENTER), *THE LANTERN AND THE LOOKING GLASS*, P. 102

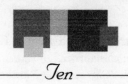

## *Ten*

# Social comment: God's perspective on current affairs

### What makes a prophet?

'A spokesman of deity, one who proclaims a divine message; …a foreteller' (Chambers).

These are the dictionary definitions of a prophet. Why, then, have I chosen to label this chapter on the prophetic books of the Bible as 'social comment'? It is not because I believe the dictionary definition is wrong when it comes to these writings, rather that these definitions of prophecy come to us piled with accretions of meaning that distort and obscure the original. They also only tell half the story.

### A spokesperson for God

The charismatic movement that has invaded the churches for the last forty or so years has done some exciting things. It has alerted people to the possibility that God might actually speak to them and through them. It has broken down barriers and made some normally very buttoned-down people willing to do some very wacky things (and as you will see, doing wacky things is very much the province of the prophet).

Unfortunately, humans being what they are, almost as soon as the Holy Spirit is set free to fly where he wills, he seems to get caged in convention again. The rather limited phenomenon many charismatics describe as 'prophecy' has been a victim of this.

Having been a sceptic hovering around charismatic churches for quite a while, one way I have noticed convention surfacing is in certain stock phrases, their purpose being to announce, 'What follows is a prophecy'. 'Thus says the Lord…' was popular for a while, although the current tendency is for introductions more like, 'The Lord's been telling me...' or 'The Lord's given me a picture...'

They are all very biblically correct—the Old Testament prophets frequently prefaced their words with 'The word of the Lord came to me...' or 'This is what the Lord says...' or 'The Lord showed me...' But along with the contemporary use of these phrases has often come an unspoken assumption that to be valid, the words have to have come into your head only seconds before. It is as if, to be a spokesperson for God, you have to be quite literally just a mouthpiece—for the words to be true prophecy they have to bypass your brain.

Now on the surface it does appear that, for the Old Testament prophets, receiving words from God was that direct and intuitive. But read a little more closely and you will discover something else. These were highly intelligent and perceptive people who not only listened carefully for what God was saying but also watched closely the developments in society around them. They knew how to read 'the signs of the times'. They were often more akin to social commentators, conceptual artists or political activists. Their writings are not just instant outpourings; more often they are highly formed poetry and well-structured prose. Their wacky acts were not outbursts of emotion but deliberate and costly public performances.

## A proclaimer of divine messages

Back in the contemporary Church, it is my experience that some of the statements that followed these 'Thus saith the Lord...' introductions have been profound, uncannily apt and life-changing. They have also sometimes been manipulative, or downright incorrect. But all too often they have been just plain bland.

This sort of prophecy tends to be messages of comfort or encouragement (just as well—can you imagine a whole congregation being let loose with utterances of condemnation or woe?) and I know many people who have found these encouragements immensely valuable. I know that many of these metaphorical 'pictures' have become powerfully lodged in their hearers' minds, enabling them to trust God in a new way.

These messages of comfort can be good and helpful and it is true that the biblical prophets sometimes spoke in these ways. But mostly they were doing something quite different—something much more odd and abrasive and risky and 'out there' in the public arena.

Take poor old Jeremiah. His very name has become a byword for gloom. Given his task, it is hardly surprising. He was called to speak for God at a time when the nation of Judah was sliding inexorably towards disaster. He had very few nice, comforting words of encouragement to bring, for the simple reason that there were practically none to be given. For forty years he listened for God's voice and watched the international scene and warned of what he could see was about to happen—and for most of those forty years, people took not a blind bit of notice. Prophets can be very unpopular people.

There were plenty of other 'prophets' around at the time to offer false hopes and Jeremiah was quick to express his fury at them.

*They have treated the wound of my people carelessly,*
  *saying, 'Peace, peace,'*
  *when there is no peace (Jeremiah 8:11).*

But when the inevitable did happen and in 587BC the Babylonian army destroyed Jerusalem and took the people captive into exile, Jeremiah did not busy himself saying, 'Told you so'. Rather he advised them to settle down, to accept their circumstances and not to expect any quick changes. The exile would last seventy years, he predicted, but after that he offered hope: 'For surely I know the plans I have for you, says the Lord, plans for your welfare and not for harm, to give you a future with hope' (Jeremiah 29:11).

It is a wonderful passage and one that has probably inspired millions of people since, but it is a terrible distortion of everything Jeremiah and the other prophets stood for to imagine that this was a typical message.

## A teller of the future

In practice, Jeremiah got his dates wrong. The Babylonian empire fell to Cyrus of Persia in 539BC and the first party of Jews returned to Jerusalem with Zerubbabel a year or so later. But in essence he was astonishingly right. What had seemed so hopeless and final was reversed within a generation and, remarkably, without bloodshed or struggle.

The prophets of the Bible did tell the future. On the whole, however, this was a byproduct. They were more concerned with getting people to change their ways *now*. Their words were occasionally mystical or ambiguous, but more often were a plain telling of what was likely to happen, based on experience and observation of what was already happening. It is more akin to scientists warning of a hole in the ozone layer, than some Mystic Meg with her crystal ball telling of meetings with a tall, dark stranger.

Again, most of the foretelling 'prophecies' I have heard in the contemporary charismatic church have been promises rather than warnings. They have foretold of great revival, great movements of God and often got the congregation very excited. These things have sometimes come amazingly true. They have also sometimes been wildly wrong.

There are three ways of reacting to predictions which fail to come true. The first is to become a sceptic (and maybe that's why you're reading this book). The second is to think yourself into a kind of religious fantasy world, where you leap from one great promise to the next, ignoring the fact that the previous dozen failed to materialize. The third is to say, 'Ah well, it just didn't happen in the way we expected. That's what happened to the prophets in the Bible, you know.'

There is some justification for this view. The latter half of Isaiah has an amazing passage on 'the suffering servant' (Isaiah 52:13—53:12). When the disciples re-read it after the death and resurrection of Christ, they were astonished to see how closely it tied in with the events they had just witnessed.

No one knows what or who Isaiah had in mind when he wrote that passage. (Scholars have tried very hard to discover whether he was writing about someone in his own generation, but have failed to come up with any evidence.) What we do know is that, in general, the biblical prophets were concerned with the *now*. They wanted to impact the behaviour of their generation. But they were also taking the long view. They were predicting what might happen generations and sometimes centuries ahead.

This is what makes the job of a prophet such a lonely one. The movers and shakers they are trying to influence, be they leaders of churches, local communities or governments, are by definition concerned with satisfying the people they lead now—before the next election, before they retire or move on, at the most within their own lifetime. The task of the prophet is always to ask the question of what might happen beyond that—to remind all of us that the way we behave now will have repercussions for centuries to come.

## A social activist

But returning to current views of prophecy and the layers of meaning we may need to strip off, what of those churches that do not have charismatic leanings? What is their take on prophecy? Most often, in these circles, prophecy is seen as synonymous with social action. It is to do with protesting about those evils that threaten to destroy or harm our world.

That may seem almost exactly the role I have just been claiming for the Old Testament prophets. But for them there was always more, and to reduce prophecy to protest is to miss a great deal of its significance.

First, what Old Testament prophets understood, and what today's charismatics also believe, is that God might have something *he* wants to say, and that if you can learn to discern these words and speak them out, they will have far more power than any amount of shouting of your own opinion.

Second, the Old Testament prophets were not just denouncing what was wrong. They were also offering an alternative. They spoke into a world where the Jewish people were continually compromising their beliefs and absorbing the ideas and practices of the worldviews around them. The prophets did not just tell them to live in a way that was moral and fair, they proclaimed living in a way that was radically different from the surrounding norms. Always they returned to the idea that a right way of living lay in obedience to God and in living by his precepts. It was not just the practices that needed changing but the deepest motivations behind them. Again and again the prophets preached a message of repentance, of actually admitting that you have been wrong and turning to God for help—never a popular concept, and certainly not a political one.

## Getting the message across

So how did these Old Testament radicals get their messages across? In what ways did they communicate their radical social comment?

### Unlikely origins

First they made it clear that the words they were speaking came from a higher authority than themselves. Sometimes they described the process that led them to speak in this way, and when they did so, it was clear they were not pursuing a cushy career option.

'Truly I do not know how to speak,' protested Jeremiah, 'for I am only a boy' (Jeremiah 1:6). 'Woe is me!' cried Isaiah, when faced with a vision of God, '...for I am a man of unclean lips and I live among a people of unclean lips.' Nevertheless, so powerful was the vision that he found himself volunteering for the task of messenger (Isaiah 6:1–8).

Sometimes the call came in the form of a dream, as it did to Zechariah, when a set of vivid images left him in dialogue with an angel to explore the meaning (Zechariah 1).

For Habakkuk, the call came when he complained to God about the injustice he saw around him. Perhaps to his surprise, God answered him, advising him to watch the international scene and to write down what he saw and was told (Habakkuk 1:1–5 and 2:1–2).

For Hosea, it was the unlikely circumstances of a bad marriage that provoked him to speak out. God had told him to marry 'an adulterous wife'—whether a woman who had already been unfaithful to another man, or one whom he suspected of the potential of unfaithfulness, is unclear. What is clear is that out of this painful experience of loving someone who did not love him, Hosea came to understand how he and his own people were hurting God with their disloyal behaviour (Hosea 1:2).

### Vivid poetry

Many of the writings of the prophets are in poetic form. Almost all of Isaiah is, as are Hosea, Joel, Obadiah, Micah, Nahum and Zephaniah. You can see in them the same two-part pattern displayed in Psalms and Proverbs, and the same metaphorical language—vivid imagery that has many layers of meaning and lends itself to being interpreted by the reader in many different ways.

Thus Lamentations (which is not, strictly speaking, a prophecy, but is written at the same time and in the same way) describes the city of Jerusalem—once a symbol of pride and integrity—as a promiscuous woman who has become a public embarrassment:

*All who honoured her despise her,*
    *for they have seen her nakedness.*
*She herself groans,*
    *and turns her face away.*
*Her uncleanness was in her skirts;*
    *she took no thought of her future (Lamentations 1:8–9).*

Somehow this conjures up for me an image of Monica Lewinsky, trying to maintain her dignity while dragging around with her for ever the image of that suggestively stained dress.

Lamentations describes how human life has become devalued:

*My people has become cruel,*
  *like the ostriches in the wilderness (Lamentations 4:3).*

Even I, who have absolutely no idea how ostriches behave in the desert, can somehow picture them pecking and kicking at each other under the blazing heat, squawking and squabbling over tiny scraps of food.

Isaiah takes more familiar images to paint a picture of God's faithfulness through even the hardest circumstances:

*When you pass through the waters, I will be with you;*
  *and through the rivers, they shall not overwhelm you;*
*when you walk through fire you shall not be burned,*
  *and the flame shall not consume you (Isaiah 43:2).*

Elements vital to life and universal to human experience are used to describe an emotion which is also universal—that of feeling engulfed, overwhelmed or consumed. I doubt if any human has ever lived for whom those words do not have resonance, if only to echo their longing for rescue.

## Straight-talking prose

In contrast, some prophets preferred to speak God's words in uncompromising prose.

*For if you truly amend your ways and your doings [says Jeremiah], if you truly act justly one with another, if you do not oppress the alien, the orphan, and the widow, or shed innocent blood in this place, and if you do not go after other gods to your own hurt, then I will dwell with you in this place (Jeremiah 7:5–7).*

Haggai had words just as blunt to say about the priorities of the returning exiles: 'Is it a time for you yourselves to live in your panelled houses, while this house [the Temple] lies in ruins?' (Haggai 1:3).

Malachi reserved his outspokenness for those who did not give the prescribed tithe (a tenth of their income) as a charitable offering to God.

*You are cursed with a curse, for you are robbing me—the whole nation of you! Bring the full tithe into the storehouse, so that there may be food in my house, and thus put me to the test, says the Lord of hosts; see if I will not open the windows of heaven for you and pour down for you an overflowing blessing (Malachi 3:9–10).*

Sometimes the messages were not moral but purely pragmatic ones. Jeremiah again: 'Those who stay in this city shall die by the sword, by famine, and by pestilence; but those who go out and surrender to the Chaldeans who are besieging you shall live and shall have their lives as a prize of war' (Jeremiah 21:9).

## Puzzles, pictures and parables

Sometimes God spoke to the prophets in pictures and showed them how to communicate in the same way. As part of his calling, God asked Jeremiah the question, 'What do you see?' (Jeremiah 1:11–14). Whether it was what happened to be in front of him at the time or was a visionary or imaginative experience, we do not know, but what he saw was a branch of almond blossom. From that God showed him the meaning, 'I am watching over my word to perform it.'

(This is one of the problems of reading a book in translation. In Hebrew we could see that the word for 'almond' is almost identical to the word for 'watching'. And if we lived in those climes we might also know that the almond is the first tree to blossom in spring.)

When God asked the question again, Jeremiah's eyes alighted on a boiling cauldron tipping dangerously on the fire. In God's hands it became an image of the political instability of the region, of the threat about to engulf them from the north.

Amos learnt to interpret locusts, a plumbline and a basket of ripe fruit (Amos 7:1–8 and 8:2); Ezekiel described a burnt and encrusted stock-pot (Ezekiel 24:3–12) and told a parable about a giant eagle landing on the top of a cedar tree (Ezekiel 17:1–7).

In the prophets' writings we are told the interpretations right away, but it is easy to imagine how the prophets themselves puzzled about these images and in turn invited their listeners to do so.

## Performance art

The Old Testament prophets would feel quite at home on today's arts scene. They were often asked to perform obscure and bizarre actions through which to make God's point. Jeremiah was told to bury an expensive linen loincloth (or 'belt', NIV) and dig it up dirty and mildewed some months later (Jeremiah 13:1–9). He also made a public ceremony of smashing a pottery jar (Jeremiah 19:1–10). Both acts depicted the destruction and ruin shortly to fall on the nation.

Ezekiel enacted the fate of Jerusalem in an even more wacky and dramatic way (Ezekiel 4). He was told to draw a picture of the city on a clay tablet and erect siege works in front of it, using an iron pan as an image of the enemy's military hardware. He then had to lay down in front of it for more than a year, eating meagre amounts of dry bread and drinking rationed water. Day by day the people saw him wasting away as the city would do under siege.

In a gesture worthy of Turner Prize artists, he was told by God to use human excrement as fuel to bake the bread. Even the foolhardy Ezekiel drew the line at that, so God relented and allowed him to use cow dung. The imagery still worked, predicting how the people would have to eat defiled food when they went into exile.

## Written compositions

Are we now getting to the point where we are reading documents actually written down by the person whose name they bear at the time of the events of which they speak? Well, yes and no. Some books—Nahum, Habakkuk, Zechariah, Malachi and Joel—appear to have been written compositions from the outset. Ezekiel, disjointed and written in the first person, reads very much like a journal. Others seem to have been the speeches of the prophets collected and assembled by their followers, often with added narrative sections to explain events. Jeremiah, for example, worked with a scribe, Baruch (Jeremiah 32:12–16; 36:4–32; 43:3–6; 45:1–2) but because these narratives refer to him in the third person, it seems that yet another hand assembled the final book

# An unenviable calling

It is hardly surprising the prophets brought their messages in such different ways—they were very different people. Isaiah was of royal blood. Jeremiah was part of the religious establishment, the son of a priestly family. Daniel was a statesman, quickly recognized as a high-flyer in the courts of Babylon. In contrast, Amos was a lowly shepherd and dresser of fig trees (Amos 7:14).

But whether they spoke with courtly wisdom or rough-hewn fury, in actions, metaphors or blunt no-nonsense statements, their fate was often the same. Jeremiah was outlawed and thrown into a sewer, Amos was banished and Daniel famously found himself in a den of lions. Some seem to have brought their message with impunity, others discovered its high cost to their personal lives. Hosea suffered the humiliation of an unfaithful wife. Jeremiah remained celibate, refusing to bring children into the world to face what was to come (Jeremiah 16:1–4). Being a prophet is not a calling to be chosen, they seem to indicate; rather, it chooses you. 'The Lord God has spoken; who can but prophesy?' asks Amos (Amos 3:8). These are the writings and actions of driven men.

It is worth noting that those prophets whose words were gathered into written books are not the only prophets in the Bible. In a sense, Moses was the greatest and earliest of them all, but the historical books tell of many others. Samuel, brought up to enter the priesthood, was a powerful and widely respected prophet at the time when Israel was first becoming a kingdom (1 Samuel 3:20). Nathan was a prophet with an unenviable task, to expose and reprimand King David's immorality (2 Samuel 12:1–15). Elijah and his successor Elisha both prophesied in the northern kingdom of Israel in the ninth century BC and many of their activities are recorded in the books of 1 and 2 Kings.

The prophets whose books became part of Scripture wrote over a period between 800 and 400BC. After that, perhaps because life was more secure, prophecy seemed to die away. In fact, a belief grew up that the times of God's speaking had ceased. That was why the appearance of John the Baptist four hundred years later caused such a stir. Did it mean a new era was dawning? the Jews asked each other—the common people with excitement, the secular and spiritual rulers with some discomfort. Naturally they respected Elijah and Elisha and the greats of yesteryear, but when it comes to it, what establishment wants a prophet in their own back yard?

# Signs of the times

'To open a prophetic book at random and start reading it,' says Chris Wright in *The User's Guide to the Bible*, 'is like turning on the radio to a heated and serious discussion programme where you haven't a clue what they are talking about' (Lion, pp. 2–3). Unless you have some idea of the social and political affairs at issue at the time, that prophetic book will probably make very little sense. And to get any idea at this remove from events is no easy task.

Sometimes the prophecy itself gives clues: sometimes it can be linked to events spoken of in other biblical books, sometimes to other historical evidence. Sometimes we are simply dependent on the best guessing of experts.

The historical events themselves are complicated enough. The Jewish people, by the beginning of this period, had divided into two nation states: Israel to the north and Judah, with its capital Jerusalem, to the south. As tiny nations at the crossroads of the Near East, they were always vulnerable to surrounding superpowers. Egypt to the south remained a constant but muted threat. To the north it was Assyria (today's Syria) with its capital Nineveh. Later, Nineveh was taken over by the Babylonian empire (today's Iraq), which in turn fell to the Persian empire (today's Iran).

(To give you a bit of help, I have included a timeline diagram, on the next page. I hope it helps!)

Even if the original circumstances are lost to you, reading at two and a half millennia's remove, never forget that there *were* real circumstances—complex, multi-layered, confusing as all real circumstances are. The prophets believed that God might have something to say into any arena—political, economic, social, spiritual, national, international, local—and were not afraid to step into those arenas and say it. Might it be that God still wants prophets like that today?

Timeline chart of Old Testament prophets and books

| | 800BC | 700BC | 600BC | 500BC | 400BC |
|---|---|---|---|---|---|
| International events | | *Israel falls to Assyria* | *Assyria falls to Babylon* · *Jerusalem falls to Babylon* · *Judeans taken into exile* | *Babylon falls to Persia* · *Zerubbabel leads return to Jerusalem* | *Ezra's group returns* · *Nehemiah returns* |
| Prophecies during exile | | | DANIEL · EZEKIEL · 2ND ISAIAH? · Lamentations | | |
| Prophecies to other nations | | JONAH? *to Nineveh* | NAHUM *to Nineveh* · OBADIAH *to Edom* | | |
| Prophecies to Israel (*Northern Kingdom*) | AMOS | HOSEA | | | |
| Prophecies to Judah (*Southern Kingdom*) | | ISAIAH · MICAH | ZEPHANIAH · JEREMIAH · HABAKKUK | HAGGAI · ZECHARIAH · JOEL? | MALACHI |
| Other Bible books | 2 Kings · 2 Chronicles | | | Ezra · Esther | Nehemiah |

# Books covered in this chapter

## Amos

Described as a herdsman and dresser of fig trees, Amos was compelled to leave his agricultural life on the edge of the Judean desert and journey north to the kingdom of Israel. Prophesying at the same time as Hosea, somewhere between 793 and 753BC, his straight-talking message was resented by the priest of Bethel, Israel's top shrine, who had him deported.

Amos warned of the impending collapse of Israelite society, a message that was left hanging in the air after his deportation and no doubt remembered in 722 when the Assyrians finally swept in, destroying the capital Samaria and dispersing the Israelites around the Middle East. The Kingdom of Israel was never to exist again.

## Isaiah

Scholars have had a field day discussing whether the book of Isaiah was the work of one author, two, three or even several. It is frequently divided into two parts: Isaiah, chapters 1—39, and Second Isaiah, chapters 40—66. The first part covers events between 767 and 698BC, and we can reliably date Isaiah's call to the year 740BC, 'the year that King Uzziah died' (6:1). Isaiah moved in aristocratic circles and tradition holds that he was the nephew of King Amaziah. Nevertheless, like all prophets, he seems to have been frequently ignored, but he did score one notable success. When the Assyrian army laid siege to Jerusalem and their triumph looked inevitable. Isaiah counselled the king to hold firm. As he predicted, the Assyrians withdrew and the city was saved (Isaiah 36—37). (The fact that this section refers to Isaiah in the third person indicates a later editorship.)

Many scholars believe that the second part of Isaiah was written during and after the exile, some hundred and fifty years later. Certainly Cyrus is named as the deliverer from Babylon (44:28; 45:13), a remarkable feat of foretelling if the book is all the work of one man.

But then again, this is a remarkable book, moving with abandon from near events to faraway ones. One minute it is talking about the threat from the Assyrians, the next of a deliverer who will gather the nations together and a day when 'the wolf shall live with the lamb' (chs. 10—11).

One minute it is talking about the return to the ruined Jerusalem, the next of the 'suffering servant' (chs. 52—53), a description which fits no one as closely as Christ.

## Jeremiah

Born of a priestly family in the southern kingdom of Judah, Jeremiah was in for the long haul. He began prophesying in Josiah's reign, around 627BC, and continued for more than forty years. In 587BC, he saw the Babylonians capture Jerusalem, as he had warned they must, and the people of Judah carried off into exile. He himself elected to stay behind, even though as a person of influence, life would probably have been far more comfortable for him in Babylon.

Jeremiah had an unenviable task and sometimes he wearied of it (12:1–4). He was beaten and put in the stocks for predicting the destruction of Jerusalem (20:2), imprisoned because he warned that the Egyptians would not save them (37:15–16), and branded a traitor and thrown in a cistern because he advocated surrender to the Babylonians (38:6). But his message was not all gloom. He predicted that the exile would not last for ever, and even bought a field at the height of the siege, to indicate his willingness to invest in better times to come (32:9). He saw things from God's everlasting perspective and was prepared to say so: 'For thus says the Lord: Just as I have brought all this great disaster upon this people, so I will bring upon them all the good fortune that I now promise them' (32:42).

## Zechariah

Probably among the first wave of people to return to Jerusalem after the Babylonian exile (around 538BC), Zechariah had a more encouraging message to bring than many of his fellow prophets. Like Haggai, his contemporary, he was instrumental in the rebuilding of the Temple (Ezra 5:1). But while Haggai puts his message in the bluntest of prose, Zechariah is a visionary like Ezekiel and Daniel. He speaks of a man on a red horse among myrtle trees, a plumbline, a golden lampstand, a flying scroll, a woman in a basket. He speaks not so much of bricks and mortar but of building a society where justice will prevail (Zechariah 7:9). He speaks of a city where the vulnerable will be safe and where scattered individuals will become one people once more (8:4–8).

There is a change in tone from chapter 9 onwards and some scholars believe this to be a much later addition. It speaks of judgment on enemy nations, before moving back to the theme of a holy city, a place where even the bells on the horses and the cooking bowls will be dedicated to God (14:20).

# Ways of reading

Most of the shorter prophetic books can be read at one sitting, and are probably best done so, at least at first, to get a sense of the overall purpose and message. In the longer prophetic books, the more historical and narrative portions are best read in large chunks to get a sense of the flow of events. Other more personal and symbolic poetic material may be better read in small segments.

- Try to find out the circumstances in which the words were written. Where possible, tie them in with parallel events in historical books.
- Try to define who the messages were for. Were they spoken to individuals or groups, to leaders or to the common people, to the kingdoms of Israel or Judah or to other nations?
- Was the message intended to change behaviour or simply to warn what would happen anyway? If there are promises, are they conditional?
- Which messages are universal and which are specific to that set of circumstances?
- What metaphors or images are used and what might they have conjured up for the original hearers? What do they conjure up for you?
- Trace the effects of right and wrong behaviour on the rise and fall of governments and nations.
- Read the books as a commentary on the repetitive nature of human weakness.
- See God as the parent of a wayward child: threatening, cajoling, promising, punishing, restoring, sometimes letting off the hook.
- Follow the thread of God's involvement at even the most godless times.
- Look for those sections which foretell the coming of Jesus.

# Exercises

## Drama and destruction (Jeremiah 17:19—21:14)

STEP 1:  Ask God to help you glimpse the prophet's world.

STEP 2:  Read the passage, perhaps a chapter at a time.
  - What imagery is used?
  - What methods of communication are used?

STEP 3:  In what circumstances was it spoken or written?
  - What can you deduce or guess from the passage itself? (See also Jeremiah 1.)
  - Are there any names or events you can trace to other biblical books?
  - Consult the timeline and book notes.

STEP 4:  What is the nature of the messages?
  - Are they spoken to a named individual, a government/nation, or ordinary people?
  - Are the prophesies intended to change people's behaviour or simply warn of what is to happen?
  - Are any promises conditional on action?

STEP 5:  Which statements are universal and which are particular to that situation?
  - Are there any evils or injustices denounced which are common to every society?
  - Are any promises made which express the unchanging nature of God?
  - Look at Jeremiah's complaint (20:7–18). What does this say about the demands of being a prophet? What does it say about Jeremiah's personality? (See also Jeremiah 1.)

STEP 6:  How does this relate to your experience?
  - Is there any behaviour in your life that you know you should change?
  - Can you see bad results coming from your behaviour? If so, could they still be averted?
  - Can you see any ways in which the society around you is heading for trouble?
  - If so, do you have the courage to stand up and make your voice heard?
  - Has God called you to speak out on any particular issue?

## Extraordinary imagery (Zechariah 1—7)

STEP 1: Ask God to help you see beyond the strange symbols.

STEP 2: Read the passage, perhaps a chapter at a time.
- What imagery is used?
- What methods of communication are used?

STEP 3: In what circumstances was it spoken or written?
- What can you deduce or guess from the passage itself?
- Are there any names or events you can trace to other biblical books? (See Ezra 5:1–2.)
- Consult the timeline and book notes.

STEP 4: What is the nature of the messages?
- Are they spoken to a named individual, a government/nation, or ordinary people? (See Ezra 3:8; 4:3. Joshua = Jeshua.)
- Are the prophesies intended to change people's behaviour or simply warn what is to happen?
- Are any promises conditional on action?

STEP 5: Which statements are universal and which are particular to that situation?
- Are there any evils or injustices denounced which are common to every society?
- Are any promises made which express the unchanging nature of God?

STEP 6: How does this relate to your experience?
- Do you look at your dream life to see if God could be saying anything through it?
- Do you think God could speak to you through everyday images?
- If you are a practical person, do you listen to hear if other, more imaginative, types of people have anything to say to you?

## Poetic promise (Isaiah 43—44)

STEP 1: Ask God to help you hold on to the promises he has for you.

STEP 2: Read the passage.

STEP 3: In what circumstances was it composed?
- Look at the timeline and book notes.

- Look at Isaiah 1:1; 2 Kings 19:20–21, 32–36; 20:16–17 (repeated in Isaiah 39:6).

STEP 4: What is the nature of the messages?
- Does this sound like prophecy for the immediate future or a longer view?
- Do you think they are predicting that bad things will not happen or depicting the restoration after the bad has passed?

STEP 5: Which statements and promises could be common to all human experience and which are particular to that situation?
- Are there any that have been fulfilled by the Jewish people in living memory?
- Would the promises have so much power if they were not locked into a real historical situation and a real geographical place?

STEP 6: How does this relate to your experience?
- Which manufactured 'gods' are offered to you by the media image-makers as you go through your day?
- In which area of your life do you most need a new beginning?
- Which promise here could you take and relate to your own need right now?

## Eleventh-hour entreaty (Amos 5)

STEP 1: Ask God to keep you from denial about the reality of the times in which you live.

STEP 2: Read the passage.

STEP 3: In what circumstances was it composed?
- Look at the timeline and notes.
- Look at 2 Kings 14:23–29 for a sketch of Israel's reigning king.
- Look at 2 Kings 17:5–8, 24–29 to see what happened to Israel some thirty to fifty years later.

STEP 4: What is the nature of the message?
- Which aspects of Israelite society does Amos condemn?
- Is he predicting the inevitable or suggesting that there is still a chance of averting the crisis?

- What action does he advocate for the Israelites at this time?
  (Note: Bethel, Gilgal and Beersheba were all well-known shrines. It was Amaziah the priest at Bethel, Israel's main shrine, who could stand Amos no longer and demanded he leave the country—see 7:10–12.)

STEP 5: Which acts of wrongdoing are common to all human experience and which are particular to that situation?

- Does compromised and formalized religion always go hand in hand with injustice? And vice versa? If so, why?
- To survive in a situation as bad as this, you have to 'seek', says Amos. What and who does he advocate seeking? Why doesn't he say how to seek?

STEP 6: How does this relate to your experience?

- Amos spoke into a situation where the rich were getting richer and the poor poorer. (See verse 11—stone mansions were the ultimate in wealth.) Can those of us who are comfortably off rather than filthy rich abdicate all responsibility for such a situation?
- Amos seems to be saying that, at this time in Israel's history, going to religious centres and taking part in religious ritual is not the way to seek God. Does taking part in Christian gatherings help in your seeking for God at this time, or should you be looking elsewhere?
- If someone told you that all your comfort and security were likely to be stripped away within your lifetime, how would you react? How would your faith hold up?

# Prophetic hope in politics, prison, and beyond

*In the first chapter of this book [*Pride and Perjury, *of which these are the closing words], I described an episode at the start of the Parliamentary Retreat of 1995 when Father Gerard Hughes SJ read out a text from Isaiah which mysteriously stirred me. Part of it is worth repeating here:*

*Do not be afraid, for I have redeemed you;*
*I have called you by your name, you are mine.*
*Should you pass through the sea I will be with you;*
*or through rivers, they will not swallow you up.*
*Should you walk through fire, you will not be scorched*
*and the flames will not burn you...*
*Do not be afraid, for I am with you (Isaiah 43:1–2, 5 [JB]).*

*With tremblings of wonder and tears of humility, I now accept that these prophetic words have come true for me. Redemption has been granted even though earthly punishment remains. I may have lost the whole world of my previous life, but I have found my own soul in a new life. Where that new life will take me is the next step of the mystery. Yet even if the road that has to be travelled lies through prisons, floods and more fires, I am not afraid. Having made the commitment to God, I now look forward to following him wherever he leads with trust, hope and joyful acceptance.*

JONATHAN AITKEN (EX-CABINET MINISTER, IMPRISONED FOR PERJURY), FROM *PRIDE AND PERJURY*, PP. 366–367

# Eleven

# Miscellany: books for all seasons

Simplifying to the extreme, the previous chapters have covered all the major types of literature in the Bible. There are, however, a few books which completely defy any of these categories. This chapter takes a brief look at four of the most obvious misfits.

## Song of Songs—a sensual extravaganza

What is a book like this doing in the Bible—a sensual and erotic love poem, with no moralizing and no mention of God at all?

Living, as we do, in an era where sexuality is permanently 'in yer face', it does not seem particularly shocking. For readers in other more prudish ages, it must have been something of an embarrassment. I have a Bible commentary written at the turn of the nineteenth century which comments primly, 'The imagery is too suggestive and the description of physical charms too minute for our taste… No doubt we should have welcomed a clear recognition of the intellectual, ideal and spiritual side of marriage…' The writer excuses the poem on the grounds that 'it was produced by an Oriental for Orientals' (J.R. Drummelow, *The One-Volume Bible Commentary*, Macmillan). Shades of corsetry, concealed table legs and the British Raj!

The early Church Fathers found the book just as difficult. After all, it hardly fitted with a monastic lifestyle. 'If these things are not to be understood spiritually,' asked Origen in the third century AD, 'are they not simply fabulous tales? If they have no hidden mystery, are they not unworthy of God?' So they allegorized it. It was, they explained, a picture of the love between Christ and his Church. Bernard of Clairvaux wrote no less than eighty-six sermons on the first two chapters of the book, simply to put this point across.

It is not too absurd a stretch of credulity to read the Song of Songs this way. It is, like the psalms, a book of poetry, rich in metaphorical imagery, and like the psalms, its metaphors are intended to be elastic. It portrays love—love deep and intense and passionate and yearning—and the early Church had learnt that nowhere was this love more fully embodied than in Jesus Christ. After all, both Paul and the book of Revelation set up the metaphor of Christ as the bridegroom and the Church as the bride—the Song of Songs merely fleshed it out (Ephesians 5:22–32; Revelation 19:7–8; 21:1–2).

The Latin word for the soul is *anima*, a word that has also been used by psychiatrist Carl Jung for the feminine side of personality. According to Jung, it is the *anima* that carries spiritual values, and must be awakened and integrated into the personality (of both men and women) for the wholeness of the psyche. So it is possible to give the Song a Jungian reading, of the female soul searching for her Lord and Master, and the man seeking to awaken the feminine side of his personality.

All very interesting, but obviously a long way from what the author originally intended. The poem is on the surface a dialogue between a man and a woman (the Lover and the Beloved), with occasional interspersions from onlooking friends. The background story, which may have been well known to the Song's original hearers, is far from clear, but may run something like this.

King Solomon (the Lover) owned a vineyard which he rented out to a mother and her two daughters: the Shulammite maiden (the Beloved) and her little sister. One day Solomon came to the vineyard disguised as a shepherd, and fell in love with the country maiden, returning later to take her as his bride.

There is also another suggested version whereby the Song contains three voices: Solomon—the villain consumed by lust—the maiden, and her true lover, a lowly shepherd.

Neither version is self-evident in the text, although since Solomon is recorded as having seven hundred wives and three hundred concubines, the latter has something going for it (1 Kings 11:3). Then again, perhaps it is the tale of a young Solomon, romantic and pure-hearted, before wealth and power turned his head and he started acquiring women as status symbols.

Forget the story—the beauty of this poem lies not in the narrative but in its lush, surreal imagery. It borders, of course, on the absurd—'Your hair is like a flock of goats' (4:1); 'Your neck is like the tower of David' (4:4). But in its many piled-up images it celebrates not only the intensity of physical passion but the surrounding beauty of landscape. It celebrates scents: cinnamon, myrrh, the fragrance of apples; tastes: milk, honey, spiced wine, the nectar of pomegranates; sound: the cooing of doves; and physical sensation: 'my head is wet with dew' (5:2); 'my heart began to pound' (5:4, NIV). It draws its images with reckless abandon from animals, plants, jewels and architecture.

And in all this abundance it teaches us something very important about the biblical mindset—something which, over the ages, the Church has often lost sight of.

One of the reasons that both the Old Testament and the teachings of Jesus are so gritty and honest is that within the Hebrew worldview there was no false divide between what was 'spiritual' and what was 'earthly'.

The 'dualist' split-vision worldview, which labels the material world as evil as compared to a purer heavenly realm, has often invaded the Christian Church. Its roots, however, are not Jewish but Greek. (There are, certainly, much stronger echoes of Greek thought in the writings of the apostles Paul and John, but even there the Greek ideas were transfused and transformed by a Jewish mindset.) It was Plato, writing around 400BC, who described the soul, immortal and infused with the divine, as being held in the 'prison-house' of the body, and it was Augustine of Hippo who brought these ideas into prominence in the Church some 800 years later.

This dualist worldview, at its worst, has driven believers deep into heresy, and at its subtlest has convinced them that some issues and ideas are not 'spiritual' enough to be brought into our relationship with God. It is dualism that has convinced good Christians that everything from bonnet ribbons to dancing to theatre to church organs are sinful. And, above all, sex.

Of course, humans are always tempted to excesses of vanity, lust, greed and sensual addictions, be it TV or tobacco. But a worldview which says that everything sensual and material and earthly should be shunned has nothing to do with the worldview of the Bible.

This is why I am so glad the Song of Songs was included in Holy Scripture. It celebrates human love as a God-given part of creation, and basks in exuberant delight at both the natural and manmade world around it.

## Lamentations—a time of waiting

Despite its position in the Bible, Lamentations is not a prophecy. Rather, it is exactly what its title suggests—a series of poetic laments over the fate of the Jewish people, now in exile, and over the ruined city of Jerusalem they have left behind. It takes its place in the Bible after Jeremiah, because it is historically attributed to him, although there is no outside evidence that he was the author

Lamentations may not seem to have much to interest or entice you. It offers no gripping stories, no wonderful promises, no wise advice, no challenge to action. But strangely enough, for me it is that very absence which is its charm. For it describes those times in human experience when all there seems to be *is* absence.

The worst has happened. The pain has subsided. But in its place comes a kind of numbness. All you can do is sit and wait, in the hope that better days will come. It is the experience of Easter Saturday, so often forgotten by Christians in their keenness to celebrate Good Friday and Easter Sunday. And that is a shame, because much of human life is lived in the 'between time' of Easter Saturday.

I am so glad that, just as it devotes a book to the experience of cynicism and the experience of sexual passion, so the Bible devotes a book to this experience of emptiness, depression, bereavement, loss. Because all of us are in that place at one time or another. Lamentations lets us know that no matter how we are feeling, first of all it is OK to feel that way and, secondly, no matter how it feels, God is faithful. The dawn *will* rise on a new day.

## Revelation—a weirdo's charter?

In his introduction to the book of Revelation for the Pocket Canons, writer Will Self comments on how often the mentally ill are to be heard muttering quotations from its text. Search for 'Book of Revelation' on the Internet, he points out, and over two million possible websites are offered. Even allowing for those which simply contain the word 'revelation', a startling number are 'the real McCoy: the apocalyptic visions visited on the wired generation in the here and now of Christian-defined 1998'.

'To think,' concludes Self in some horror, 'this ancient text has survived to be the stuff of modern, psychotic nightmare' (*Revelation*, Canongate, pp. xiii–xiv).

There's no getting round it—Revelation is weird. It has been the justification down the ages for any number of crackpot theories. Any number of small groups have gone and sat on mountain tops, convinced that the end of the world would come on a date deduced with absolute certainty from Revelation's strange numerical formulae. All sorts of identities have been claimed for its mysterious 'beast'—Popes, Protest-ants, Turks, Hitler, Stalin, rock music, the European Union—all these and many more have been claimed as the anti-Christ. Numerous events, from the Spanish Armada to the Israeli six-day war, have been claimed to have been prophesied in its pages. It features locusts with human faces wearing gold crowns, a dragon with seven heads and ten horns, rivers of blood and streets of gold, and a Lamb standing on a throne holding a scroll.

In the face of all this, it is hardly surprising that many Christians have treated Revelation with extreme mistrust, and sometimes avoided it altogether. Until recently, that would have summed up my attitude. This is the advantage of writing a book—you actually get to learn something! And what I've learned is more respect for this strange and uncomfortable book, and just a little more understanding of what it is all about.

## Who from? Who to?

So what *is* Revelation all about? Is it a drug-induced fantasy, or a timetable of the end-times in clever disguise? Does it have any value beyond a fundamentalist chocolate-box or a cabbalist's delight?

Perhaps the first question to ask is what it meant to its author and its first audience. Some have suggested that its meaning was just as obscure to them too, but there is plenty of evidence to suggest that this was not so.

The first thing to note is that Revelation falls within a genre of writ-ing that was familiar to its audience, that of 'apocalypse'. The word 'apocalypse' simply meant a revelation and many of these writings, equally strange and visionary, appeared in the two centuries before Christ and the one that followed. They portrayed world events from an other-worldly standpoint and were written for godly people who found themselves oppressed by a hostile regime. Where prophecies warned people of their own sin and of judgment to follow if they did not repent, apocalypses offer a vision of future deliverance that is to be waited for with patience.

The Old Testament book of Daniel contains an apocalypse, probably written in the second century BC, although the character and events it refers to happened some four centuries earlier. This is a familiar characteristic of apocalyptic writings, apart from Revelation itself, which were often written in the name of some famous figure from the past.

The second thing to note is that Revelation is steeped in references to the Old Testament. It is full of quotes and imagery which would have been familiar to its mainly Jewish audience, and allusions that would have been grasped without explanation.

Both the author and audience of the book are declared in its opening greeting: 'John, to the seven churches in the province of Asia...' It then goes on (in a straightforward section, much more akin to other New Testament letters) to send specific messages to each of these churches, all situated in present-day Turkey.

The John in question is clearly intended to mean John the apostle, author of the Gospel and letters, and very early Christian writings all support this view. The author clearly knows the Asian churches and describes himself as having received the vision while on the island of Patmos. There is a strong tradition that the apostle lived for some years in Ephesus (bringing with him Mary the mother of Jesus) and was exiled for a time on Patmos. Many people have questioned this identity, however, because the style and language of Revelation is so different from John's other writings. The book is reckoned to have been written sometime around AD90 (which would, of course, have made John a very old man at the time).

## What for?

So what can we make of the author's intentions? Was it an intentional commentary on events at the time, a symbolic representation of events applicable to all times, or a vision of the future faithfully transcribed without any understanding of what it might mean?

If it is simply the latter, it is hard to picture what his early readers made of it. 'It's about the Pope then? The atom bomb? Global warming? Oh, er, thanks, John.'

The images of Revelation are so strange and disjointed that it is hard to believe they are not the product of a dream or vision. On the other hand, if it is purely the writing down of an involuntary vision, then the many references to the Old Testament have emerged from his sub-conscious with remarkable accuracy and strategic placing.

As a writer of both fiction and non-fiction, I find no problem in the idea that this writing was both visionary and intentional. All writing is a mix of both inspiration and perspiration and, as in the prophets, it seems to me that here is the same interweaving of 'message received' (whether by dream or exercise of imagination) and intelligent, conscious thought.

It seems to me that what John was doing was something that con-temporary authors often engage in—'subverting a genre'. This is when an author takes a style of writing that is familiar and, working within its conventions, uses it to do something quite different from what has been done before. It can be seen in crime writers like P.D. James, who take the detective story established by writers such as Agatha Christie and use it to explore psychology, sin and guilt. It can be seen on the big screen with directors such as Quentin Tarantino, who in *Pulp Fiction* takes the gangster movie and both pays homage to it and twists it into something entirely different.

I think that John has taken the familiar genre of apocalypse and used it to do something quite different and radical—to announce that the events of history can now be understood in the light of Jesus Christ.

He declares his intentions early on:

*Look! he is coming with the clouds;*
  *every eye will see him,*
*even those who pierced him;*
  *and on his account all the tribes of the earth will wail (1:7).*

This is a combination of two quotes from the Hebrew scriptures—Daniel 7:13: 'I saw one like a human being coming with the clouds of heaven', and Zechariah 12:10: 'When they look on the one whom they have pierced, they shall mourn for him, as one mourns for an only child, and weep bitterly over him.'

Look, says John, *this* is who it was all about, *this* is the hinge of history—the Lamb whose sacrifice has changed everything.

(Of course, if this was his intention then it could account for the different style of writing. Most writers are able to take on a different writing 'voice' if necessary, and there is no reason why John should be an exception. No one questions that Tom Stoppard wrote the screenplay for *Shakespeare in Love*, despite its Elizabethan style, or that Yakomoto Ishiguri was capable of writing the voice of an English butler of the 1930s in *The Remains of the Day*.)

## Apocalypse now or then?

So is Revelation about the past, the present or the future?

Given the layers of meaning allowed for in such vivid imagery, it is probably all three. Many of its symbols would have had an obvious and immediate meaning to its readers and I have suggested some of them below. But there is something universal about such symbolism, which can be applied to almost every era. It is, at its most basic level, about the ongoing struggle between good and evil, about the suffering wrought by every regime that demands absolute allegiance, and the long-term triumph of God and his kingdom over any earthly power.

Clearly Revelation does speak of an end-time, but rather than offering a chronological brain-teaser, its main purpose is probably simply to announce that there *will be* one. Trying to decode Revelation as a secret purveyor of dates and times is a fruitless activity, not least because the signs spoken of are almost certainly not in any sort of linear sequence, and its many numerical references are intended not as mathematical clues but as poetic symbols.

These are symbols that John's readers would have understood from Jewish tradition—seven is the number of completeness, twelve (and its multiples) stands for the people of God. Apart from the obvious seven churches, John uses three main series of seven—seven seals, seven trumpets, seven bowls—to describe judgments falling on the earth. At first glance these could seem to be successive events, but it is more likely that John is writing in cycles, rather than in a linear way, so that these are all different perspectives on the same historical vision (shades of *Pulp Fiction* again).

Jesus was just as unequivocal in his announcement of a judgment to come (Matthew 24 and 25; Mark 13; Luke 21; although, curiously, no reference to speak of in John). He also made it abundantly clear that the time was to remain unknown:

'But about that day and hour no one knows, neither the angels of heaven, nor the Son, but only the Father' (Matthew 24:36).

'Beware, keep alert: for you do not know when the time will come' (Mark 13:33).

'It is not for you to know the times or periods that the Father has set by his own authority' (Acts 1:7).

Trying to use Revelation as a hidden timetable for the return of Christ is not only fruitless, it is a dangerous diversion from the main business of meeting Christ in our neighbour day by day (Matthew 25:31–46).


## So why read it?

For all its obscurity, Revelation does have some valuable things to teach. Here are just a few to look out for:

- Its observations on the strengths and weaknesses of church life.
- Its picture of heaven—perhaps the Bible's fullest picture of the after-life and its rewards (and judgments).
- Its repeated insistence that God will gather in people from 'every tribe and language and people and nation' (Revelation 5:9; 7:9; 14:6).
- Its viewpoint of even the most powerful earthly regimes as transient and doomed to destruction.
- Its reminder that good can ultimately triumph—without recourse to human violence (never once suggested).

---

## WAYS OF READING REVELATION

- Trying to see how it relates to the Old Testament.
- Referring it back to Jesus' words on the end-times.
- Seeing your own times in it without claiming it literally.
- Using imagination, rather than searching for reasoned argument.
- **Not** trying to find significance in things you don't understand.
- **Not** wasting time and energy on speculation irrelevant to your own life.

---

# Significant symbols

Many of the images contained in Revelation would have had relevance to its first readers. Here are just a few of them (from Marcus Maxwell, *The People's Bible Commentary: Revelation*, BRF).

**Babylon**, the empire which previously took control of the Jewish nation, taken here as a clear symbol for the Romans.

**Armageddon**, or Megiddo, the site of several ancient battles in Jewish history (Revelation 16:16).

**The Lamb that was slain**, an image of sacrifice as the means of rescue, familiar to the Jewish people through the Passover feast celebrating the escape from Egypt and from the Angel of Death when a lamb's blood was smeared on every Israelite doorpost.

**The four horsemen**, which refer back to Zechariah 1:8–10 and 6:1–8.

**The new Jerusalem**: by the time John wrote this, the actual city of Jerusalem had been besieged and laid waste by the Romans. John does not promise its earthly rebuilding but the possibility of a spiritual home.

**The Beast**, a composite description based on the four beasts in Daniel 7. Babylon is described as riding on it and its seven heads are aligned with seven hills, an unmistakable allusion to Rome and its machinery of domination (Revelation 13 and 17). Often also referred to as the anti-Christ, this term is not found in Revelation, however, but in John's letters (1 John 2:18–22; 4:3; 2 John 1:7).

**The second Beast (or false prophet)**, which appears to be the first Beast's propaganda machine—perhaps identified by the early Church as the emperor cult, which seemed harmless, but could inflict the death penalty on any who refused to worship Caesar (Revelation 13:11–15).

**666**: in the ancient world there were no universally recognized symbols for numbers and instead letters of the alphabet were used (a = 1 and so on). Adding up the numbers of a name, rather like astrological birth signs, was a popular way of describing character or telling fortunes. The name of Caesar Nero written in Hebrew adds up to 666, as does the word for Beast (Revelation 13:18).

**144,000**: the number 12 and any multiple of it always refers to the people of God—tribes, apostles and so on. In the Old Testament, the numbering of the different tribes was done at a time of war, to provide a census of the fighting force (Numbers 1). It may be that the description in Revelation 14 brought this to mind and implied that the 144,000 was God's fighting force of believers.

## Ecclesiastes—a post-modern worldview

I am so glad this book is in the Bible. It has to be said that it fits oddly: there is no voice of authority here, no deliverance, no commands, no comfort, no promises—just a lot of questions and very few answers. But even here God is to be found, and that, for sceptics like me, is a great encouragement.

The author of this book is the sceptic *par excellence*. He has tried everything—pleasure, wisdom, wealth, work—and watched them all evaporate into meaninglessness, or, in that wonderfully resonant word of the older versions, *vanity*. There is something curiously post-modern about Ecclesiastes. It seems to have been written by characters straight from a Douglas Coupland novel. It is Generation X grown old and bored.

It is, like Generation X, a voice from an age of unprecedented affluence. There are hints that the author, the mysterious 'Teacher', is Solomon 'son of David, king in Jerusalem' (1:1), and although the book probably dates from far later, we can see that Solomon, with his vast wealth and power, could easily have spoken these words. These are not the sentiments of someone struggling to survive. They are the words of someone who has it all and has discovered that having it all is not enough. This is the voice of someone questioning his own experience, searching for answers within himself, learning to live with lack of meaning, or perhaps to accept small meanings—the enjoyment of food and drink and honest toil (3:13; 8:15). God is not absent from these pages, but he is distant, unattainable. (Could it be this very affluence that makes it so?)

Like most of us, believers or not, the Teacher has no clear idea of what happens after death: 'All are from the dust, and all turn to dust again. Who knows whether the human spirit goes upwards...?' (3:20–21).

But at the end of all this existentialist *angst*, the Teacher concludes that true wisdom lies in taking a leap of faith. Ultimately, concludes Ecclesiastes, it is in God that meaning is to be found. There are ultimate values, however hazily we perceive them, and ultimately each of our lives does have meaning: 'The end of the matter; all has been heard. Fear God and keep his commandments; for that is the whole duty of everyone. For

God will bring every deed into judgment, including every secret thing, whether good or evil' (12:13–14).

I am glad Ecclesiastes is in the Bible. If there is room for Ecclesiastes within the Bible, then there is room for sceptics like myself within the Christian Church.

Ecclesiastes tells me that it is valid to test faith in the light of experience, that it is OK to ask questions and OK to be honest when answers are painfully lacking. Ecclesiastes tells me that even believers must sometimes live with a lack of meaning, and that even within that experience, the world is still a beautiful place to be in.

## Who, when, what?

Ecclesiastes, like Psalms, Proverbs and the Song of Songs, comes into the category of Wisdom literature. Like them, even though much of it is prose, it uses parallelism, the poetic repetition of phrases, to get its message across: 'The lover of money will not be satisfied with money; nor the lover of wealth, with gain' (5:10).

Like them, it is attributed to a great king of a former age, in this case Solomon, although this is merely a formal convention rather than the attempt to fake an antique. There are no clues as to the exact date of Ecclesiastes, but some hints that it has been influenced by Greek thought could put it as late as the third century BC.

The title is misleading, associated as it is to us with matters ecclesiastical or churchy. So too is the traditional translation of the speaker's title: 'the Preacher'. The original title is an untranslatable word, *Qoheleth*, which relates to the gathering of people together.

But forget churchmen in pulpits. Some contemporary versions give it as 'the Teacher'—closer, but forget also classrooms and pupils. Picture rather the orator in the town square, the adult disciples clustering round, debating and discussing. We can guess that it was these followers who put the book together. *Qoheleth*, like other great teachers—Jesus, Socrates and Confucius to name but a few—did not write his own words down. In fact, he was even sceptical when it came to books: 'Of making many books there is no end, and much study is a weariness of the flesh' (12:12).

One can only speculate what he would have made of the British Library, or even Waterstones!

## WAYS OF READING ECCLESIASTES

- Asking your own questions along with the Teacher.
- Examining your own experience and what has meaning for you.
- Extracting the juice from its pithy proverbs.
- Soaking up its wisdom and poetic beauty.
- Emulating its willingness to live with lack of meaning.
- Using it as a means of exploring life's paradoxes.

# Exercises

## The blossoming vineyard (Song of Songs 7 and 8)

STEP 1: Ask God to help you relate your most earthly and human experiences to him.

STEP 2: Read the passage.

STEP 3: Read it again, slowly and aloud.

STEP 4: Look at the imagery on which the poem builds.
- Are there any metaphors that seem absurd to your ears? (Navel like a rounded goblet, for example?)
- Are there any that seem beautiful?
- Are there any you don't understand?
- What picture do the metaphors conjure up of the writer's world?

STEP 5: How does this poem relate to wider themes?
- What does this poem have to say about love?
- What love relationship in your experience comes closest to it?
- Are there any things in this passage that you can relate to God or Jesus?

STEP 6: How does this relate to your experience?
- Do you ever take time to observe and delight in another human being (be it in a sexual or non-sexual relationship)?
- Do you take time to observe and delight in the world around you?
- Are you able to express that delight to yourself, to the person in question or to others? If not, what stops you?
- Is there anything in your experience of Christianity that has taught you to be ashamed, embarrassed or wary of

sensuality or sexuality? Is there any good reason behind this or is it something to be shaken off?

## I will survive (Lamentations 3:1–33)

STEP 1: Offer God your willingness to trust, even though you cannot see or feel.

STEP 2: Read the passage.

STEP 3: Pick out those words that best describe the feelings and situation of the author.
- These are the words of someone see-sawing between despair and hope—does the passage give any sense that such conflicting emotions are wrong?

STEP 4: Pick out those words that describe God's character.
- In situations such as these, can such words as 'love' and 'hope' carry any meaning? If so, how?

STEP 5: Pick out the word that best describes your feelings as you read this.
- Are they feelings you can share with others?
- How does knowing you are not alone change your reaction to these feelings?

STEP 6: Look at the words that offer hope. Pick out the phrase that most strikes you.
- What is there about this phrase that echoes with your experience?
- Can hope be hurried? Is it possible to shorten bad times or must they simply be lived through?
- Are you willing to let others take the time they need in this experience of waiting? Are you willing to share it in silence with them?

## Visions of earth and heaven
## (Revelation 13 and 21:1—22:5)

STEP 1: Ask God to give you understanding (and guard you from your own cleverness).

STEP 2: Read the passages.

STEP 3: Look at the imagery of the passages.

- In chapter 13, most of the imagery is about creatures. Picture these creatures in your mind. How would you feel about meeting them?
- In chapters 21 and 22, most of the imagery is about place. Build up a picture of this place in your mind. How do you feel about living there?

STEP 4: Look at the use of numbers in each passage.
- Why do you imagine the author was so fascinated with numbers?
- Do you think he intended them to be taken literally?
- What could be the value or danger of these numbers to contemporary readers?

STEP 5: Look at the contrast between earthly and heavenly realms.
- In each passage, look for the words which describe the relationship between the ruler and his subjects.
- Look for contrasts between the world of time and the world outside time.

STEP 6: Relate the passage to your own experience.
- Are there any ways in which the power structures described in chapter 13 can be recognized in the society you live in?
- Are there any ways in which you, in that society, have to stand against the power structures?
- Look at chapters 21 and 22. Which aspect of this picture of heaven is the one you most look forward to?
- Jesus talked of the Kingdom of heaven as already in operation on earth. Is there any way you can help build aspects of heaven into the society around you?


## The meaning of life (Ecclesiastes 2 and 3)

STEP 1: Ask God to show you what he wants you to take from this.
STEP 2: Read the passage.
STEP 3: Make a note of the questions asked here.
- Which of them relate most closely to your own questions?
- Which, if any, have answers?
- Which are the questions you would most like answered?

STEP 4: Look at the statements, sayings and summaries.
- Look at how the author explores time.

- Look at the basics that the author comes back to as the only meaning he can find.
- What do they say about our attitudes to time?
- What does the author see as the vital ingredient of enjoyment?

STEP 5: Look at the paradox contained in these passages.
- Achievement is meaningless but finding satisfaction in your work is paramount. Do these statements contradict or balance?
- A book of wisdom which claims that wisdom is meaningless—how does it add up?

STEP 6: How does this relate to your experience?
- How do you deal with thoughts of your own mortality? Should it make you give up trying or drive you on?
- Is there any way in which you can extract enjoyment from life's most routine moments? Try to find ways of doing so as you go through the rest of the day.
- Which sentence can you take from this passage as an idea to carry round and explore?

## How it works for me

*I don't always find Bible reading easy, but then most of the really important things aren't easy. However, I've been at this long enough now to realize the daftness of taking the lazy option. I used to think that if I missed a day I was letting God down, though I rather think now that it's more for my benefit than his. But I know that if I consistently choose to skip time with the Bible it's symptomatic of a bigger problem. I don't use notes or the Bible in a year plan because they make me feel guilty when I (inevitably) fall behind. I've found it helpful to read the Bible for themes rather than as a continuous text. For example, when I was really suffering in my job I found Ecclesiastes a great leveller. I find this route makes for better concentration because I am actively seeking solutions or inspiration rather than reading for general interest.*
RICHARD EYRE (CHIEF EXECUTIVE, PEARSON TELEVISION, PREVIOUSLY CHIEF
EXECUTIVE OF ITV)

*Probably about eight years ago, I used to get up at half past five every morning and spend half an hour reading my Bible with a set of daily reading notes. But*

I found I just couldn't keep it up. I became physically exhausted and ill and had to stop.

Now my Bible studying has changed. I now find it infinitely more rewarding and interesting to meet with a small group once a week. We choose between us what the book or section is going to be and we will work through it a passage each week, probably over a period of months. In that week we really study that passage, so I would probably read the same twelve verses seven times and also look up the various reference points that it says within the Bible. By the time I come to the group, I actually feel that I've learnt something in depth and I've understood it better.

ROSEMARY CONLEY (EXERCISE AND DIET GURU AND BESTSELLING AUTHOR OF *THE HIP AND THIGH DIET*)

I used to be a bit of a 'dipper'. The interesting thing is that before I became a Christian, every time I opened the Bible it was always terribly relevant. Since I became a Christian, every time I tried just opening it anywhere and reading, it was always something terrible! 'Have a continuity' is what I'm saying, don't just drop into the Bible in the hope of finding something relevant. There may well be, but that's not the way to do it. Have a scheme. Start with a book and read through that, chapter by chapter. I used to have Bible studies with a group of friends and that was tremendous. They meant a lot to me—I miss them. So when it comes to Bible reading my advice would be—it helps to have structure and it helps to have a group of people. You can't just do it by yourself.

ROBERT DUNCAN (ACTOR, BEST KNOWN FOR *DROP THE DEAD DONKEY* AND *CASUALTY*)

I don't read the Bible every day, my life doesn't permit it. But I do dip in fairly frequently. There really isn't an obligation to get through the whole lot. Little and often, I think, is a much better approach than long chunks. Although equally, there are some bits, particularly the Old Testament, which are actually quite exciting and you want to know what happens next. I think its horses for courses—some parts are quite easily read, but in others, like the denser bits of St Paul, you'd be a miracle worker if you could take on a whole lot in one go.

On the whole, however, my belief is that the word of God speaks to people as it is, and that if there's a particular passage that you're struggling with, he's not speaking to you through that passage. So just move on to the next one where you may find extraordinary revelation.

ANN WIDDECOMBE (CONSERVATIVE MP)

# Part Three
# WAYS OF READING

*Twelve*

# Imagining: using the right side of the brain

Some people are highly suspicious of any imaginative exercise. They claim that life is too short to waste time on 'make believe'. They want hard facts and logical explanation, reasoned conclusions rather than inconclusive fantasy. Perhaps they remember those ghastly Music and Movement sessions in primary school, when one was exhorted to 'pretend to be a leaf floating down from a tree'. Isn't it all rather soppy and self-indulgent?

### Not just for dreamers
As someone who resolutely refused to be a leaf and registers high on the 'thinker' scale of personality tests, I too was wary of flights of fancy. Until, that is, later in life when the craft of words grabbed me and I started devouring classes in creative writing, screenwriting or whatever.

You don't have to spend long studying fiction to realize that 'make believe'—be it film or fairy tale, sitcom or saga—far from being self-indulgent, fulfils a highly functional role in society. In fact there are several roles, but there are two in particular I want to focus on here.

The first concerns the understanding of others. 'You can never truly understand another human being,' goes the old saying, 'until you have walked a mile in his shoes.' This is the particular value of storytelling—to step for a short while inside someone else's world and view the human condition from a perspective that may be quite different from your own narrow viewpoint. Stepping in imagination into the shoes of someone in the biblical world is a great way to get a new perspective and understanding of what is really going on.

The second role of 'make believe' is to lead to a greater understanding of yourself. One of the greatest philosophers of all time, known down the centuries for his high respect for reason, coined a word for it— *catharsis*—'the purging of the effects of a pent-up emotion and repressed thoughts, by bringing them to the surface of consciousness' (Chambers). This was what was going on, said Aristotle, when the ancient Greeks watched one of their tragedies. This was the power and purpose of entering into a world of imagination.

Reading the Bible imaginatively may not leave you reaching for the tissue box like a good 'weepie' drama, but it can bring to the surface of your mind those thoughts and feelings about God that lie buried deep down.

Why not leave them buried? some might ask. Didn't we push them under for a reason? Yes, for many reasons: fear that this is not how good Christians 'ought' to think; fear that we might pursue a mental trail that leads to dangerous uncharted territory; fear that we will end up more confused than when we began.

Fear can be a useful safety mechanism and is not to be lightly despised. But ultimately, faith and fear live in opposition to each other. Those who want to move on in their spiritual journey, and not get stuck, sooner or later will have to face their fears.

As a compulsive people-watcher, I am fascinated by the fact that some religious lives seem to me to be far more attractive than others. They are often very flawed and frequently unprepossessing. There are others far more devoted and sacrificial, far more able to articulate their faith, far more determined and successful in their actions. These others are very admirable—the problem is that I don't necessarily *like* them.

I have come to the conclusion that this attractive quality is best labelled 'integrity', and that the people it shows up in are not always the ones you expect. It has to do, I think, with the fact that what these unlikely 'beautiful people' are giving you on the surface is completely in harmony with what is underneath. There is no conflict between what they claim to believe and what they actually believe deep down. (What really intrigues me is how on earth we so readily sense this. I haven't figured that one out. I only know that somehow we all can.)

Those who want to be people who attract rather than repel, grow rather than shrivel, and have a creed that survives whatever life can throw at them, must, it seems to me, allow their true feelings to surface. It is only once those feelings are out in the light of day that it is possible to see where they are out of kilter with professed beliefs and begin to make adjustments.

## Not self-help psychology

Did you notice that I said, 'allow' our feelings to surface? That is the beauty of this technique of imagining. I am not advocating a sort of amateur archaeology of the psyche—digging around our subconscious just to see what treasures we might find; nor self-help surgery—attempting to cut out our own tumours or siphon off our own poisons.

It is true that psychology has much to teach us of the value of images in exploring the self. But what I am suggesting here is somewhat deeper and broader than a christianized Rorschach test (those ink blots that are supposed to hold the key to personality), and something that goes back far further than the relatively recent wisdom of Freud, Jung and company.

## Not just for wimps

Ignatius Loyola was a medieval soldier-adventurer who experienced a dramatic conversion while laid up with a leg wound. He resolved to become Christ's soldier and went on to found the Society of Jesus—the crack assault force of militant Catholicism. The Jesuits were highly organized and fiercely disciplined, but the secret of their success lay in something more. Each recruit was required to go through Ignatius' training schedule—the Spiritual Exercises. Given Ignatius' activist personality, you might expect it to be a regime of study and practical work, but it is not. In order to be Christ's soldier, you must first spend time in passive reflection; exercising not intellect or muscle, but imagination.

In total, the exercises form a four-week retreat programme of meditation and instruction. Much of it, with its emphasis on sin and hell and penance, might seem outdated and authoritarian to 21st-century eyes, but there are some valuable techniques that we might borrow.

In essence, each exercise requires the retreatant to explore his or her faith by picturing a scene—some based strictly on a Bible passage, others a little looser in interpretation. Each meditation has three essential ingredients. The first is a preparatory prayer, asking God for 'the grace to direct my thoughts, activities and deeds to the service and praise of His Divine Majesty'.

Next comes the 'First preliminary—an imaginative representation of the place'. In this, you build up a vivid picture of the scene in question, often putting yourself in imagination right in there and using every faculty to build up the experience: 'What can I see/hear/touch/smell/taste?'

And always with it comes the 'Second Preliminary—asking the Lord God for what I want'. In Ignatius' eyes, this has little to do with self-seeking. It is prayer related to the subject-matter: asking for a share of Christ's joy or his agony, an understanding of the gravity of sin or the need for obedience.

If we are going to let our imagination loose on the Bible, then it seems to me that Ignatius offers some wise safeguards.

It is an activity to be tackled under the direction of God. Its purpose is not that we might gain some glowing moment of self-awareness or inspiration, but that we might grow into the human beings God intended us to be. It is not just for what we want out of it, but that what we want might be submitted to the greater wisdom of what God wants.

If this is how we approach it, then we need not fear that we are digging up thoughts and feelings best left buried. It is God who will allow to rise to the surface those issues which we are now ready to tackle.

## Not for solo navigation

Ignatius laid down that his exercises should only be done under the individual guidance of a spiritual director. Few of us will have that luxury, and there is no reason why we cannot undertake these limited versions on our own. However, we need to be aware that this method has its limitations and that there are circumstances when what we learn by this technique is best submitted to the wisdom and advice of others.

*An imaginative exploration of the Bible is not to be used as the grounds for theology or life choices.* Imagination can help us to understand ourselves and our relationship to God better, but it cannot give us either a true belief system or a wise way of making decisions.

True and workable revelation does not come ready-made from flights of imagination. It may be sparked off by it, but it is formed and refined by careful and thorough study, rational thought, and a long, humble process of sifting and submission. That is what the Church, with all its faults, is there for, and we go solo at our peril.

## Not just for experts

Some people claim they have no imagination. Not true. Of course, some people are more prone to imaginative activity than others, but imagination —the capacity to envisage something that does not exist in reality—is a God-given gift which all of us possess. It works very simply. Each of us has within our brain a huge memory bank of sensory input—visual images, scents, sounds, ideas, emotions—that we have been storing up from the day we were born (and perhaps before).

This imaginative envisaging is no more and no less than a sifting and reordering of the data in our memory bank to produce something new, something never experienced before. Whether it is used to create installation art or integrated circuits, to decorate cakes or design bridges, this imaginative right-brain activity is something every human being possesses. And it *is* God-given. The apostle Paul had worked that out. 'For by him [Christ] all things were created,' he wrote, 'things visible and invisible' (Colossians 1:16).

Imagination is not only one of the Creator's invisible gifts, it is also arguably the one most necessary for us to fulfil our human potential. Without this capacity to envisage something that does not already exist, we would still be in the Stone Age, waiting in vain for the wheel, the alphabet, the water closet, aspirin and sliced bread.

Allowing our imaginations the freedom to be playful is not a waste of time. It is a necessary prerequisite to progress.

# Ways of reading

## With understanding—background knowledge in place

This exercise may be best done after the passage has already been read in a more conventional way, so that you come at it already knowing:

* what was the author's intention;
* what is the historical setting of the passage;
* what are the events before and after;
* the significance of any words or customs peculiar to that culture;
* any other biblical passages which would throw light on this one.

## In freedom—no right or wrong answers

This is important. Having found out the basic information, give yourself freedom to embroider it. It may be that using imagination—to take the scene off in a new direction, or to feel things about the scene you suspect you are not 'supposed' to feel—will allow you to understand what is really there in a way you never have before.

## With time—to allow your imagination to roam

Exactly how long is up to you to determine. I would suggest that an hour is ideal. However, if that seems daunting, half an hour is perfectly adequate. I would suggest that twenty minutes is the absolute minimum. Decide on a length of time beforehand and stick to it. If you find it difficult, do not give up before the time is up, but determine to take even longer. See chapter 14 on meditation (p. 223)—this imaginative approach can also benefit from the techniques described there.

## Step into someone else's shoes

Obviously this technique works best for narratives. In a way, it is indulging in role-play, allowing yourself to 'become' someone in the story and experience it from their viewpoint. Incidentally, it is not sacrilegious to imagine yourself in Jesus' place. He came to set an example to others (John 13:15), and this is one way of exploring it.

First try to picture the scene. Ask yourself some of the following questions: What can I see around me? What can I hear? What can I smell, touch or taste? Am I warm or cold, comfortable or uncomfortable, pleased or reluctant to be there?

Then ask yourself where you are in the scene—right at the centre or watching from afar? Are you one of the main characters, a bit player or an unseen observer?

Allow the story or incident to unfold, asking yourself some of the following: Do I feel excited or depressed by what is going on? Am I threatened or encouraged by what I see?

Ask yourself what is left unsaid in the account of this story and allow yourself to fill in the gaps.

If you were one of the main characters, would you have done anything differently?

Which details of this scene particularly grab your attention? Whatever they are, give yourself time to explore them further.

Now take time to relate the happenings of that scene to something similiar in your own experience. Ask God to bring things to mind. Is this scene helping you to understand anything in your past? Is it throwing light on any of your present attitudes? Is it telling you anything about how you picture yourself? Is it telling you anything about how you picture God? Are there any issues raised by this exercise that you need to explore further?

# Exercises

## Jesus, an 'unclean' woman and society's taboos
### (Mark 5:21–34)

STEP 1: Ask God to help you enter into this woman's experience and to grasp the significance of the story.

STEP 2: Look at the context of the passage.
- What comes immediately before and after? See the other events in chapter 5 and the commission to the disciples in Mark 6:7.
  **Note:** contemporary translations lose what was a recurring theme in the original: 'uncleanness'. The man in the tombs was said to have an 'unclean' spirit; the disciples were sent to cast out 'unclean' spirits. Touching a dead body and a menstruating woman were both considered ritually unclean.
- It may be helpful to compare how this incident is described in two other Gospels (Matthew 9:18–22; Luke 8:43–48).
- Are there any other Bible passages that could shed light on this one? See Leviticus 15:16–30. What was the intention of these rules? Were they intended to stigmatize anyone?

Step 3: Set the scene: first build up a background picture of what life was like for this woman who had had menstrual bleeding constantly for twelve years.
- How many things can you list that are available in this day and age which could help with the problem?
- How do you think she managed without them?
- Imagine how life must have been for her. Did she ever have any romances, a husband? How did the other women treat

her when she came to the well for water? Did she get invited to parties?

- Next, in your imagination step into the story and picture the scene around you. What can you see as you look around?
- Why is Jesus wearing a cloak? What is the weather like?
- What is the atmosphere in the crowded street? Is it noisy or hushed? Are you pressed up against strangers, or people who are familiar to you?

**Note:** the other Gospels make clear that this was Jesus returning to his 'own town' or Galilean base of Capernaum.

Step 4: Allow the story or incident to unfold, running through your reactions to it—first from the viewpoint of a bystander.

- How do you react when Jesus is held up on his way to this life-and-death emergency by something relatively trivial?
- What do you make of the fact that Jesus needed to ask who touched him? Did he really have no idea what was going on and, if so, was he not as powerful as you might think? If he did know, why do you think he asked?
- What are your reactions to this woman, probably known to you, as she falls dramatically at Jesus' feet?
- Now imagine yourself into the role of the woman. What are your emotions as you put out your hand toward the cloak?
- How do you feel as all the attention suddenly focuses on you?
- What does it mean to you that Jesus calls you 'daughter'? (How old do you imagine you are?)
- The account does not say whether Jesus touched the woman. Do you imagine that he did?

Step 5: Relate this story to your experience. (Depending on your gender, this may be more or less easy!)

- If you are female, what does it mean to you that Jesus is concerned about 'women's problems'? What difference would it make to you to know he was concerned about yours?
- If you are male, does this behaviour of Jesus call for a change of attitude on your part?
- List the sorts of things that make people in our age feel unclean.

Step 6: What feelings and reactions has this imaginative exercise brought up for you?
- Are there any current things in your life, or any memories that make you feel unclean?
- How would you feel if public attention was drawn to them?
- How would it feel to know Jesus cared about them and wanted to deal with them?

## Jesus and his friends (John 13:1–17)

Step 1: Ask God to spark your imagination in new ways.

Step 2: Read the passage slowly and carefully.
- Look at some of the tumultuous events that have led up to this quiet and private moment.
- Look at what comes next.

Step 3: Imagine the scene around you.
- What sort of room are you in? How is it lit? Is it sumptuous or poor?
- How are you feeling—tired, exhilarated, anxious, confused?
- The room is full of unspoken tensions—what are they?
- Your head is full of memories of the last few days—what are the predominant ones?
- Who are you in this scene? Are you an unspecified disciple or one of the named characters?

Step 4: Allow the incident to unfold around you.
- How do you react when you see Jesus pouring water into a basin and kneeling down to begin his task?
- How do you feel when you see him serving Judas? (You do not yet know what Judas will do, but you must surely have some suspicions that all is not as it should be.)
- How do you feel when Jesus comes to you?
- If you are imagining yourself as Jesus, what are your feelings and thoughts as you wash the feet of each of these, your followers and friends?
- After Jesus has finished his task and finished speaking, there is a silence. What are you thinking?

Step 5: Relate this story to your present-day life.

- Has anyone ever washed your feet for you, or given you a pedicure or foot massage? How did it make you feel?
- Can you remember a time when you have seen someone of high status doing a lowly task?
- Has anyone ever humbled themselves to serve you in a way that was unexpected?

Step 6:  What thoughts and ideas does this story stir up in you?
- Does anything in this story make you need to revise your image of God?
- Does this story tell you anything about your own reactions—pride, embarrassment, passivity, your need to serve, your unwillingness to serve or be served?

## Elijah and a mountain retreat (1 Kings 19:1–18)

Step 1:  Ask God to let you engage with this ancient tale and relate it to your life.

Step 2:  Read the passage slowly, perhaps twice over.
- Read the previous chapter, at least from verse 16, to see the momentous event in which Elijah had just taken part.
- Read the last verses of chapter 19 to see what happened immediately afterwards.

Step 3:  Picture yourself huddled in the mountain cave.
- Imagine yourself just waking up. How do you feel—cold or warm, stiff or relaxed, safe or scared, exhausted or energized?
- Picture the surroundings of the cave—what can you see, smell, feel beneath your hands?
- Picture the view from the cave entrance. What do you see? Is it barren or wooded, rocky, sandy or covered with vegetation? Is the sky dark or bright?

Step 4:  Allow the events to unfold before you.
- When the Lord asks you, 'What are you doing here?' how do you feel—angry, awestruck, too tired to care, self-pitying, guilty?
- Watch as the earth is riven by wind, earthquake and fire. How do you feel, alone on the mountainside watching all this power?

- Imagine yourself hearing the gentle whisper. Is it in words, or just an impression? What is it saying? Can you catch it? Does it bring peace or challenge?
- Again God says to you, 'What are you doing here?' You say the same things, but have your feelings changed as you say them?
- God tells you to return. Do you feel encouraged, apprehensive, ready, uncertain, resentful, excited?

Step 5: Relate this to your own experience.
- Have you ever had a time of exhaustion and depression following some big achievement or major event in your life?
- Have you ever felt that you were the only one who cared about something, or that you were alone battling on in a difficult situation?
- Have you ever taken time out to be alone in the natural world and watch the wonders of creation? How did it change your perspective on your situation?

Step 6: What thoughts or ideas does this story provoke in you?
- Imagine God saying to you, 'What are you doing here?' Hear him speak your name to preface the question. What is your answer?
- Imagine a whispering voice coming to you. What does it say?
- Imagine God saying to you, 'Go back...' What does he tell you to do as you go back to the particular challenges of your life? Is he telling you to do anything differently or see anything in a different way?

## Jesus and a paralysed man (Luke 5:17–26)

Step 1: Pray that God brings this story alive to you.
Step 2: Read the passage. To put it in context, read the beginning of the chapter and the following section about the calling of Levi. Look particularly at verses 31–32.
Step 3: Think yourself into the story. First, picture yourself as one of Jesus' audience in the crowded house.
- Imagine yourself as one of the crowd. Who else is around you, listening to Jesus' teaching?

- What does it feel like in the room? What can you smell? What can you see? What are you touching?
- Can you guess at some of the reasons that have drawn people to come? What is your reason?
- Now imagine yourself as the paralysed man. The day starts as normal. You are lying or sitting as you always do. Where is it? What can you see? Who is around for you to watch, or speak to? What is the thing you most long to do?

Step 4: Now allow the story to unfold, first from the perspective of the paralysed man.
- Suddenly your friends come rushing up. They are excited but you find it hard to grasp their garbled message. What are they saying to you as they bundle you on to the mat?
- You are being carried, jolting along, unable to see much except the sky and your friends above you. How do you feel about being carried in this way?
- You are carried up to the roof. The next thing you know, you are being lowered down into a room full of gawking strangers. How does this make you feel?
- Then you see Jesus leaning toward you. How do you react to meeting him?
- 'Friend, your sins are forgiven you.' Is it what you wanted to hear?
- Now picture yourself in the crowd. How do you react when Jesus says these words about forgiveness? Are you shocked, surprised, watching for the reaction of others, wondering if he could wipe out your sin too?
- How do you feel as you see the man get up and walk? Are you joyful, sceptical, excited, troubled?
- Picture yourself as the man once more. What do you do after this and where do you go?

Step 5: Relate this to your experience.
- Are there any aspects of your life in which you feel paralysed—unable to function normally or fully?
- Have you ever been in a situation where you have been unable to function and needed help from friends? Have you been willing to accept help? Have you been able to ask for it?

- Are there any areas of guilt that you carry? Are there any ways in which these prevent you from functioning fully and normally?

Step 6: What thoughts or ideas does this story evoke in you?

- If you could ask Jesus to heal any part of yourself, what would it be?
- Would you pay the price of embarrassment in front of a crowd of people in order to be made whole and fully functioning?
- In both this story and verses 31–32 Jesus implies a link between health, forgiveness and repentance (turning away from wrongdoing, turning toward God). Can you see any such links in your life?

## Expecting the unexpected

*There's an extraordinary feature of the great stories from all round the world—that you can never know them in an ultimate way—there's always more to discover. The golden rule from a writer's point of view, and I think also from the point of view of a spiritual pilgrimage, is to engage in a kind of radical unknowing, a letting go of what you think you know: your experience, your remembered sermons and illustrations, even the images from art history. When you encounter these great stories of the Bible you almost have to block your ears and close your eyes to these memories, wonderful though they may be. Something different may be about to happen if you free yourself to enter into the story.*

*The incident of Elijah and the earthquake, wind and fire is a good example. Elijah thought he knew God better than anyone. Hadn't he himself just been the instrument of God's power? So he thought God would speak in power, but when he got there it was something quite different. When I had to write this story as a script for an animated film, I discovered that some translated the 'still small voice' as the 'thin sound of silence'. It set me thinking very deeply, made me realize, 'I don't know this story at all.' It connected in my mind with a description of the isle of Iona as a 'very thin place', in other words where the veil between heaven and earth is transparent, and made me explore the the idea of seeking out such a place. For me that was a bench mark in encountering the nature of God, by imagining Elijah's role. It was the shock really, of all your ideas being turned upside down.*

MURRAY WATTS (PLAYWRIGHT AND SCREENWRITER FOR THE *TESTAMENT* SERIES AND *THE MIRACLE MAKER*

# Thirteen

# Trawling: searching systematically

## What does it really say?

The Bible says homosexuality is wrong. *Does it?*

The Bible says all those who don't believe go to a place of eternal torment. *Does it?*

The Bible says you should never get angry. *Does it?*

The Bible says you should always forgive everyone unconditionally. *Does it?*

There are plenty of people keen to tell you what the Bible says. Sometimes they are correct and helpful. Sometimes they are not. I have often discovered people who are quite convinced they know the Bible's viewpoint on a particular issue. When pressed, they rarely know any actual sources for their opinion, or perhaps can quote, or misquote, only one verse.

The only way truly to find out what the Bible as a whole has to say on a subject is to read it for yourself. But you can't read through the whole Bible every time you want to know what it says on a particular subject.

You might be able to find a book by a contemporary author giving a biblical perspective on the issue. But does the fact that someone has bothered to write a book on the issue mean they have an axe to grind? How can you be sure you are getting the Bible's full range of voices on the subject?

## Why bother to search?

I have chosen my four examples for study at the end of this chapter not because they are necessarily the most important or contentious, but because they are all issues I have had to grapple with at some time or another, for a variety of reasons. I thought it was worth explaining those reasons, and why I believe a search is worthwhile in these cases.

## Finding a moral code for today's world

I don't believe the Bible is the *only* place we should look to when working out our ethics, but I do believe it is a solid starting point. It was Karl Barth, I am told, who suggested that we should do our ethics with a Bible in one hand and a newspaper in the other. It seems like sound advice.

Every generation has particular issues which rise up like mountains as the tectonic plates of society and technology radically reshape the landscape. For a far earlier generation, it was the authority of the Bible itself, brought into sharp focus by the invention of the printing press. A couple of centuries ago it was slavery, made possible by exploration and improved trade routes, made visible by improved communications, and made an issue by democratic government. This last century, it has been about the role of women, brought about by contraception, education, washing machines and vacuum cleaners.

And for this century, partly because of the above, sexuality and sexual relationships have become the big issue. And as part of that—homosexuality.

Many Christians whom I respect feel that all homosexual practice is taboo. I know other Christians, also ones I respect, who have, not without pain and a great deal of internal struggle, decided that it is possible for them to live in a homosexual relationship and still retain their faith. I have heard people on either side of the argument claim the Bible on their side.

And so I felt I needed to see what it really said. I discovered that the issue needed to be seen as part of a much wider picture, not least because the Bible has very little to say on homosexuality *per se*. Gay practice as we know it today (promoted as an alternative and equal life-choice and a possible stable relationship akin to marriage) was simply unknown in biblical times (or if known, then never spoken about).

That being the case, has the Bible anything authoritative to say on this issue anyway? Well, I believe so, because it seems to me that it gives some underlying principles—on relationships and on sexual morality in general—that matter a great deal. Maybe it is not quite as clear cut, in either direction, as some people would like to think. And maybe that is not such a bad thing, if it forces us to grapple really honestly, to listen and struggle and try to understand, rather than trotting out glib answers.

## Holding a creed

I don't think being selective with the Bible really works. Yes, there are some passages which I don't find easy, some beliefs which are hard to swallow. But ignoring them and concentrating on the ones that are helpful seems to me, in the long run, a false policy. Sooner or later those hard issues are going to confront you, so you may as well face them at a time when you can do so, calmly and with your emotions unengaged.

To me, the afterlife is one of those issues. For many years, it seemed to me far more important to get on and live in a right way than to worry about things that couldn't possibly be known anyway. But when a friend died—someone who led a decent life but subscribed to no faith—the questions could no longer be ignored.

What did the Bible really say about the afterlife? If it consigned my friend to eternal torment, simply because she was not signed up to the same set of beliefs as me, then could I subscribe to these beliefs at all? Any God who would condemn someone to an eternity of horrible suffering as punishment for threescore years and ten of trivial sinning and honest doubt could not possibly be fair, let alone loving. Since I couldn't believe in a God like that, it was very important to me to find out whether the Bible really did support this idea of hellfire and damnation.

Well, I found some hard passages that couldn't be ignored, and certainly no sense that God forgives everyone no matter what. But as you can see, I went on being a Christian, and in my own mind came to an understanding of what those difficult passages were really saying. So that is why I have shared my exploration of the idea of hell—a concept many people may be surprised to learn comes almost entirely from the New Testament and not from the Old.

## Living in balance

My background is English, non-conformist and very 'Let's-be-civilized' stiff-upper-lip in style. I therefore grew up thinking that good Christians never got angry. However, I soon began to notice good Christians stabbing each other in the back, while smiling politely to each other's faces. It didn't seem so much better than a good shouting match.

Psychology told me another story—that bottling up your anger was repression, and repression didn't do you any good at all. So can good Christians get angry? Should they, and if so, when?

And what about forgiveness? There are not that many people I find it hard to forgive, but I admit I have had great difficulty with one or two. Does God really expect us to forgive in every circumstance? If so, then how, for goodness' sake? It certainly doesn't come naturally, however holy you try to be.

And should you really lend your neighbour the lawnmower again when it comes back broken for the third time?

These high principles are all very well, but do they work? Is God *really* demanding things that seem to run contrary to psychology and common sense? Does the Bible actually say what I think it does and if so, why?

I don't know what answers you need in order to live your life and see the world aright. The subjects that burn for me may not be the ones you feel are important, but whatever the questions you need to explore, I hope this means of discovery may yield some answers.


## Tools for the task

This is where the one extra tool that I advocated in the opening chapter comes in—a concordance. The beauty of a concordance is that it is a totally neutral device—it simply lists each time a certain word is mentioned with an extracted phrase to show you the immediate context. From there it is admittedly a rather tedious and time-consuming task (although nothing like as endless as it first appears) to look up each reference. (For this study I have used *The NIV Complete Concordance*, which is the one I happen to have.)

If you are online you can get the information you need over the Internet. Bible Gateway (part of something called the Gospel Communication Network) offers exactly the same search facility as a concordance, with a choice of different Bible versions. A click on the reference brings the whole verse up on screen. You can find this site on www.Bible.gospelcom.net and there are probably others out there that I haven't come across yet.

If you have a computer but not yet a modem, it is also possible to buy programmes such as *The On-line Bible*, that provide the same facilities. This particular one makes it even easier by bringing the verse up on the screen immediately. (However, that brings its own drawbacks: sometimes it is more useful to see the whole passage in front of you and to be able to glance at what comes before and after.)

Whichever way you trawl through, those passages that are irrelevant can be quickly discarded. From those that are relevant, a picture can be assembled of what the Bible has to say.

Of course, there are often times when the Bible has something to say on the subject without mentioning the actual word. In fact, in some cases it barely mentions the word at all (homosexuality being a case in point). In that case, you will need to think of any possible related words that might help—sexuality, sodomy, prostitution, promiscuity, men, males and so on. Some of these may not appear at all, or offer little of use, but with a little ingenuity and persistence, this method will usually yield the information you need.

I have called it 'trawling' because it reminds me of dragging a net through a great ocean full of words, trying to catch just the ones you want. Of course, others which are no use to you will come tangled up in the netting as well, and there are times when you will catch nothing at all. In order to draw wise conclusions from what you find, it is a technique that must be handled with care. Still, it is a useful starting point and a technique worth trying.

(I have in one instance here used an extra tool, which is perhaps worth explaining, if only to make it clear that I am not an expert in New Testament Greek! The tool in question is a book called *An Expository Dictionary of Bible Words* (W.E. Vine, Marshall, Morgan & Scott), which can be used to find out what the particular shades of meaning of a word were in the original text. I don't advocate you buying this unless you really want to study the Bible in detail, in which case it is an excellent resource.)

## How it works here

I am assuming that right now you do not have a concordance at hand, and so I have listed the references on a particular word or subject for you. In the interests of time and space, I have edited out some of the complete irrelevancies, and in order to give you an idea of the technique without getting bogged down, I have done some of the donkey work and suggested those passages that are most important to look at. I have also suggested other words and passages that are relevant, and explained how and why I arrived at them.

However, don't take my word for it, any more than anyone else's. If you possibly can, check all references and trawl as broadly as you can.

# Ways of reading

## Context

First, you will need to bear in mind the context of the references you drag up. Make sure you keep a eye on the following things.

- The overall message of the incident or passage: Is this subject the main import of the passage, or an aside? What was the author's intent in including it?
- The type of literature: Is the word used in a poetic, metaphorical way, or is it part of a clear, unambiguous instruction?
- The framework of ancient Middle Eastern society: Did the word carry the same meaning and connotations in that society as it does in ours?

## Counter-balance

Secondly, it is useful to keep in mind the Bible as a whole and the broad principles it lays down. Even if you're not sure what these are, it may be useful to try to look at some contrasting concepts and ideas and use them as a counter-balance. For example:

- How does the idea of hell relate to the concept of a God of compassion and forgiveness?
- If the Bible has little to say about homosexuality *per se*, what are the principles of heterosexual relations that it considers important and are they relevant?
- Does the Bible's emphasis on forgiveness mean that criminal justice isn't necessary?

This may be too much ocean to fish on one voyage, but it is at least worth keeping in mind for later expeditions.

## Christ

Thirdly, even if you cannot trawl these vast expanses of ideas, I would suggest that every time you look at a subject, you make a point of looking not only at what Jesus said on the subject, but at what he did and what he said on more general subjects that might be related. Perhaps every time you trawl for a subject, you could also skim through at least one Gospel, searching for clues.

For example:

- Did Jesus get angry? What at?
- How did Jesus react to those on the outside of sexual respectability?
- What did he say to the thief on the cross about the afterlife?
- Did Jesus practise forgiveness? If so, when?

## The importance of absence

One last suggestion:once you have searched out all the references you can, ask yourself what *isn't* there.

- What does the Bible not say, that you might expect it to?
- Does it leave this thing unsaid because it takes it for granted? Is it an issue that simply didn't exist in biblical times? Or could it be that the Bible actually considers it far less important than we do?

# Exercises

## Homosexuality

Step 1:  Ask God to help you approach this study with openness of mind and free of preconceptions.

Step 2:  Look up all references first to the word itself and then if necessary to other related words.

- Homosexuality: none.
- Homosexual: 1 Corinthians 6:9.

- Sex: Genesis 19:5; Judges 19:22.
  **Note:** Incidentally, both these stories raise some big questions of the sexual morality of the period, with their horrific depiction of women treated as sex objects.
- Sexual: Exodus 19:15; 22:19; Leviticus 18:6–23; 20:10–19; Numbers 25:1; Deuteronomy 27:21; Matthew 15:19; Mark 7:21; Acts 15:20, 29; 21:25; Romans 1:24–27; 13:13; 1 Corinthians 5:1; 6:13, 18; 10:8; 2 Corinthians 12:21; Galatians 5:19; Ephesians 5:3; Colossians 3:5; 1 Thessalonians 4:3; Jude 1:7; Revelation 2:14, 20; 9:21.
  **Note:** In the Leviticus passage, the word 'sexual' only appears from verse 15 onwards, but looking up the passage revealed a reference to male homosexuality in verse 10. This raises up the question of whether the word 'lies', as in 'a man lies with a man', will yield any more information, but since in fact it doesn't, I have spared you that extra search!
- Sexually: 1 Corinthians 5:9–11; 6:9–18; Hebrews 12:16; 13:4; Revelation 21:8; 22:15.
- Lust: Proverbs 6:25; Isaiah 57:5; Ezekiel 20:30; 23:8–19; Nahum 3:4; Romans 1:27; Ephesians 4:19; Colossians 3:5; 1 Thessalonians 4:5; 1 Peter 4:3; 1 John 2:16.
- Promiscuity/Promiscuous: Deuteronomy 22:21; Ezekiel 16:25–29.
- Prostitutes (male): Deuteronomy 23:18; 1 Kings 14:24; 15:12; 22:46; 2 Kings 23:7; Job 36:14.
  **Note:** Since the word for male prostitutes was rendered as 'sodomites' in the King James translation, we can safely assume that this was gay prostitution rather than toy-boys for rich women. Incidentally, these passages, and the many others referring to female shrine prostitutes, shed some light on why the worship of pagan idols was so strongly taboo in the Bible. It usually entailed far more than harmless superstition.

Step 3: Try to find anything that might give background information or shed light on general principles.
- Sodom: Genesis 13:13; 18:20; Ezekiel 16:49–50.

**Note:** We have already found the story in Genesis 19 which resulted in the town giving its name to a sexual act. There are many other references to Sodom throughout the Bible as a symbol of God's judgment on a wicked city. However, it is worth asking whether homosexuality was the wickedness for which the city was destroyed. The above selected quotes shed a little light.

- Creation: Genesis 2:18—3:24.
  **Note:** Despite its simplicity, the Bible's account of origins has some deep things to say about what it means to be human. It is often worth referring back to as a starting point, on this issue as on others.

- David and Jonathan: 1 Samuel 20:17, 41.
  **Note:** Some people have claimed that David and Jonathan had a homosexual relationship. The expression rendered 'but David wept the more' is translated as 'but David exceeded' in the King James version, leading some to argue that David had an orgasm. The original is unclear, but the orgasm theory seems pretty unlikely, first because of that society's taboo against homosexuality, and second because David showed himself to be a hot-blooded heterosexual in later life (2 Samuel 11:2–4). This passage does indicate, however, that the Old Testament world saw nothing taboo about a strong, loving (in a non-physical sense), same-sex friendship.

Step 4: What did Jesus say or do that relates to this issue?
- Marriage, divorce and adultery: Matthew 5:27–30; 19:1–18.
- Sinners and outcasts: Luke 7:36–50; John 8:1–11; Mark 2:13–17.

Step 5: What conclusions can you draw from these references? How does their context affect their relevance for today? Is there anything the Bible does not say on this issue?
- Did the attempted gang rape described in Genesis 19 have any connection to other homosexual practice, and could it have been this practice that caused the downfall of the city of Sodom?
- Are the Levitical laws on this issue ones that govern the basics of all human society, like not murdering or stealing, or

pragmatic ones for that particular circumstance, like not eating pork or wearing garments made from different yarns?
- Paul makes it abundantly clear that 'sexual immorality' is wrong, and unarguably clear that same-sex relations come within that. However, you may need to try to discover whether homosexual practice as Paul knew it was always linked to promiscuity and general debauchery and decide whether that makes a difference.

STEP 6: What can you take from this study that relates to your life personally? You may like to look again at the following.
- On sexual practice in general: Matthew 5:27–30; 1 Corinthians 6:18–20; 1 Thessalonians 4:4.
- On relating to those who are seen, for whatever reason, to be outside society's norms: John 8:1–11.

# Hell

STEP 1: Ask God to open your mind and help you deal with this difficult subject.

STEP 2: Look up all references to the word itself and if necessary to any associated words.
- Hell: Matthew 5:22, 29–30; 10:28; 18:8–9; 23:15, 33; Mark 9:43–49; Luke 12:5; 16:19–31; James 3:6; 2 Peter 2:4.
- Torment, Tormented: Revelation 14:9–11; 18:9–10, 15–16; 20:10.
- Fire: Matthew 3:7–12; 7:19; 13:40–43; 25:41–46; Luke 3:7–17; 12:28, 49; 17:29–30; John 15:6; Acts 2:3; 1 Corinthians 3:13–15; 2 Thessalonians 1:7–9; Hebrews 10:26–31; 12:29; James 5:1–3; 2 Peter 3:7–12; Jude 7, 23; Revelation 1:14; 20:11–15.
  Note: There are many other Old Testament references to fire, but although many of these relate to fire as punishment or destruction, or fire as an image of God's holiness, these are on the whole to do with earthly punishment. The Old Testament has no concept of hell or eternal fire.
- Hades: Matthew 16:18–19; Revelation 1:18; 6:8.

STEP 3: Try to find anything that might give background information or shed light on the general principles. If the Old Testament does not show any indication of a belief in hell, what does it believe?
- Shadows: Job 10:21–22; 34:21–27; 38:17–18.
  **Note:** It is worth bearing in mind that God points out in this final reference, and elsewhere (38:2; 42:7) that Job and his 'advisors' do not have any knowledge of what they are pontificating about!
- Grave: 1 Samuel 2:6; Job 7:9; 14:13; 17:13–16; 24:19; Psalm 6:5; 9:17; 16:10; 49:14–15; Isaiah 14:9–15; 38:18; Ezekiel 32:21; Hosea 13:14.
  **Note:** Many of the words translated 'grave' in the NIV are rendered as 'Sheol' in other older translations (a Hebrew word rendered as Hades in Greek). It does not literally mean a burial plot, but carries the idea of a place of the dead—a shadowy, unhappy place to which the wicked go, and from which God's redemption might be possible.

STEP 4: What did Jesus say or do that relates to this issue?
- Look at Matthew 7:13; Luke 13:23–30; 23:43; John 8:51.
- What do you make of the sharp contrast between Jesus' uncompromising statements and those that seem to express mercy?

STEP 5: What conclusions can you draw from these references? How does their context affect their relevance for today? What does the Bible *not* say on this issue?
- Are the words being used literally, or metaphorically to paint a picture?
- Think particularly carefully about the metaphor of fire. What is the nature of fire and what happens to things thrown in a fire? Does the Bible speak on the whole of eternal fire or eternal torment and is there a difference?
- If *anyone* is promised eternal torment, who is it?
- In Matthew 25:46, Jesus speaks pretty unequivocally of opposing possibilities of eternal punishment or eternal life. He's telling a story—is he speaking in hyperbole just to make his point?
  **Note:** The original Greek word for 'punishment' in this case

is *kolasis*, a word which primarily means 'pruning, curtailing, docking' and, as a secondary meaning, 'restraining, checking, punishing'. The only other place it is used is in 1 John 4:18: 'Perfect love drives out fear, because fear has to do with punishment', in a passage that starts with the assertion, 'God is love'. Could it be that this is a punishment only for those who are unable to accept God's love? I admit that this is a question, not an answer—but for me at least, this one reference to eternal punishment sticks out as inconsistent with what the rest of the Bible says about God's character, and I can only leave it as a question mark.

STEP 6:  What can you take from this study that relates to your life personally? Doing this as an isolated Bible study could give you a very lop-sided impression. Whatever you conclude about hell, you may need to balance it with a look at the many references to God's mercy and Christ as God's escape plan. Here are just a few.

- Merciful/Mercy: Deuteronomy 4:31; Daniel 9:9; Luke 6:35–36; Ephesians 2:4–9; 1 Peter 1:3–5.
- Compassion: Psalm 103:8–13; 145:8–9; James 5:11.
- Saved/Salvation: John 10:9; 1 Thessalonians 5:9–10; 1 Timothy 2:3–6.
- Eternal life: John 3:16–21; 6:35–40.

## Anger

STEP 1:  Ask God to help you be honest about your own anger, and to teach you how to deal with it.

STEP 2:  Look up all references to the word itself and, if necessary, any associated words.

Note: The concordance yields nearly four hundred references to anger/angered/angry and so on, and a large proportion of them relate to God's anger. This raises a lot of questions and could be a study in itself, but for this purpose I am suggesting that we look at what the Bible has to say on human anger. Quite a few of the other references to anger come within a historical story and do not have a great deal to teach, so I have therefore been quite selective in my choice of references.

(Sorting through that number of references is not as laborious as it might seem, as the extracts quoted by each reference in the concordance make them relatively easy to sift, and do not involve looking up every one.)

- Anger: Psalm 4:4; 37:8; Proverbs 15:1; 21:14; 27:4; 29:8, 11; 30:33; Ecclesiastes 7:9; 10:4; 2 Corinthians 12:20; Ephesians 4:26, 31; Colossians 3:8; 1 Timothy 2:8; James 1:19–20.
- Angered: Proverbs 22:24; 1 Corinthians 13:5.
- Angers: Proverbs 20:2–3.
- Rage: Galatians 5:20.

STEP 3:   Try to find anything that might give background information or shed light on the general principles.

**Note:** Although I have not included references to God's anger above, and there are far too many to investigate in full here, it is worth looking at a few, to see if we can learn anything about the manner of God's anger and what provoked it. Here are just a very few references on the subject:

- God's restraint: Exodus 34:6 (also Numbers 14:18; Nehemiah 9:17; Psalm 86:15; 145:8; Joel 2:13; Jonah 4:2; Nahum 1:3); Psalm 30:5; 78:38.
- Things that provoked God's anger: Exodus 22:22–24; Leviticus 26:27–28; Numbers 25:1–3; Deuteronomy 4:25; Judges 2:18–20; Ezra 8:22; Isaiah 5:24–25; Zechariah 10:2–3.
- If anger can be a sin, then provoking it certainly is. When looking at anger, it is worth also looking at what provokes it. See Proverbs 27:3; Galatians 5:26; Ephesians 6:4.
- Some of us are so passive that anger might be a good thing, if it provokes us into action. For examples of motivating anger, see 1 Samuel 11:1–8; Nehemiah 5:1–13.

STEP 4:   What did Jesus say or do that relates to this issue?

- Teaching on anger: Matthew 5:22; Luke 6:27–36.
- Times when he was angry: Matthew 23:13–39; Mark 3:1–5; 11:15–17.
- Look closely at who and what provoked Jesus to fury and, equally importantly, who and what did not. Does it seem to you that his anger was controlled or not?

- Times when Jesus was not angry: John 8:3–11; Matthew 26:49–53; Luke 23:34.

STEP 5: What conclusions can you draw from these references? How does their context affect their relevance for today? What does the Bible *not* say on this subject?

- Look particularly at the social context of anger—are there some circumstances where anger is more appropriate than others?
- What can you learn about the control of anger?

STEP 6: What can you take from this study that relates to your life personally?

## Forgiveness

STEP 1: Ask God to show you any areas where you harbour unforgiveness and to help you deal with it.

STEP 2: Look up all references to the word itself and, if necessary, to any associated words.

**Note:** Out of 131 references to forgive/forgiveness and so on, 68 are about God's willingness to forgive us; 12 are warnings of circumstances where God may not forgive; 28 are requests for God's forgiveness; 4 are requests for forgiveness from another person; 13 are about the need for us to forgive others; 5 are miscellaneous.

- Forgive, forgiving (related to others): Matthew 6:14–15; 18:21–35; Mark 11:25; Luke 6:37; 11:4; 17:3–4; 2 Corinthians 2:7; Ephesians 4:32; Colossians 3:13.

STEP 3: Try to find anything that might give background information or shed light on the general principles.

- Steps toward forgiveness: Romans 12:14–21; Ephesians 4:26; James 5:16.
- Results of unforgiveness (bitterness): Hebrews 12:15; James 3:14–16.

Obviously, Jesus linked forgiving others very closely with receiving forgiveness from God—and the converse!

Therefore it is worth looking at God's forgiveness and the times when he withholds it. Following are some references on the subject.

- God's forgiveness: 2 Chronicles 7:14; Nehemiah 9:17; Psalm 86:5; 99:8; Jeremiah 33:8; Daniel 9:9; Matthew 9:2–5; Hebrews 8:12; 1 John 1:9.

STEP 4: What did Jesus say or do that relates to this issue?
- Jesus' example: Luke 23:34.
- The power of forgiveness: John 20:23.
- Steps toward forgiveness: Matthew 5:38–44; Luke 7:47–48.

STEP 5: What conclusions can you draw from these references? How does their context affect their relevance for today? Is there anything the Bible does *not* say on this issue?
- Some of Jesus' commands to forgive relate specifically to when someone comes asking to be forgiven. Does that mean that the others only relate to that circumstance, or should you be prepared to forgive unconditionally?
- Can forgiveness be given if there is a refusal to receive it?
- Do the references to God's forgiveness teach you anything related to this?

STEP 6: What can you take from this study that relates to your life personally? It might be good to explore further and meditate on the circular patterns of relationships that the Bible sets up.
- Receiving love–being willing to repent–feeling forgiven– being able to forgive–receiving forgiveness–being able to love.
- Anger–broken relationships–unwillingness to forgive– inability to receive forgiveness–spoilt relationship with God–guilt.

## Forgiveness at the sharp end

*When I look at the Lord's Prayer, the phrase that sticks out at me has to be the one about forgiveness. It's emphasized at the end: 'Forgive us our sins as we forgive those who sin against us'.*

*It's tempting to maintain hate or dislike when someone's really done us down, yet somehow we all have to learn, in the light of this verse, that unless we're prepared to forgive others, God is not prepared to forgive us the things that we do wrong.*

*I don't want to sound trite, because forgiveness is still such a difficult thing to do. The opposition to my single release of the Lord's Prayer—the 'Millennium Prayer'—and the criticism I received were very hard for me to understand. I have to say that I tried hard to forgive and I honestly think I have forgiven them. I had to say, 'It's OK. That's what you think and that's fine.' It did hurt, though. I guess I'm going to remember this period as one of the most painful hits I've ever had. I don't think I can forget it. Perhaps that's the difference between me and God.*

*But the more I've talked about it, the more I've come to realize that it's not really that difficult a thing to do. I mean, why should I hold a grudge?*

SIR CLIFF RICHARD (SINGER AND ENTERTAINER)


## Motivation for forgiveness

*My favourite Bible verse is Romans 5:8, 'But God proves his love for us in that while we were still sinners Christ died for us.' This truth of God's immense capacity to love just overwhelms me.*

DESMOND TUTU (ARCHBISHOP OF CAPE TOWN, CHAIRPERSON OF THE TRUTH AND RECONCILIATION COMMISSION)

# Fourteen

# Meditating: giving it time to breathe

If you have worked your way through the exercises in the previous chapter, congratulations! After writing it, I found myself in need of something a little less heavy. After reading it, I guess you might too. This chapter offers something a little simpler. Simpler—but perhaps not easier.

The thought of meditating frightens some people. It conjures up images of perching precariously with ankles on thighs, chanting for endless hours until you drift into some exalted state of cosmic consciousness. It implies something deep and esoteric, only to be obtained by long practice of mysterious techniques.

Not so. 'Meditation is really very simple,' said Thomas Merton, a Catholic monk who knew more about it than most, 'and there is not much need of elaborate techniques to teach us how to go about it' (*Spiritual Direction and Meditation*, A. Clarke Books).

'Meditation has no point and no reality unless it is firmly rooted in life,' concluded Merton (*Contemplative Prayer*, Darton, Longman & Todd, p. 45), highlighting the difference in the Christian approach from Eastern forms of meditation, with their emphasis on detachment from the world and loss of personal identity. Nevertheless, Eastern spirituality has some valuable things to teach Christians and unbelievers alike and, while opening our minds up to any and every influence should be treated with caution, meditation itself is nothing to be afraid of.

Often, however, it is not fear of the cultural unknown which frightens people away at all. It is fear of something far simpler—solitude, stillness and silence.

# Stillness and silence

'Hurry is not *of* the Devil,' Carl Jung is reputed to have said. 'Hurry *is* the Devil.' But most of us have chosen, or been forced into, lives that are constantly under pressure. Most of us are bombarded with more mental stimulation in a week than our ancestors had in a decade. We are accompanied by words and images wherever we go—radio, TV, video, Walkman, hoardings, packaging, newpapers, magazines, books—on and on from waking to sleeping. We are surrounded by so many words that words are cheap. We are surrounded by so much noise that we no longer hear birdsong or the tick of a clock.

So meditating—sitting for even fifteen minutes in stillness and silence—can be an extremely uncomfortable experience. It can be frightening, if salutary, to discover how little concentration you really do have, how much your mind wanders, how hard you find it to relax without sleep or something to distract you, how little point all of that busyness really has when you step back and reflect on it.

But if you discover words in the Bible which are profound, and if you want them to change your life profoundly, then the only way to do it is to give them the time and space to sink in. The Church Fathers had a delightful phrase: 'holy leisure'. If we want to become 'holy' (or, in a word that sits more easily with our generation, 'whole'), then, in the words of Richard Foster, 'We must pursue "holy leisure" with a determination that is ruthless to our datebooks' (*Celebrations of Discipline*, Hodder, p. 21). In other words, we must plan space for meditation and book it in the diary, even at the expense of other activities.

I confess, I don't find this easy. I'm a cerebral person. I like being busy. I'm inquisitive. I like knowledge and acquiring more and more. Words are my trade, after all, and moving images are my passion. Given half a chance, I will surround myself with them at all times. But more and more I am aware how much I need times of stillness. The more you surround yourself with words, the cheaper words become. I need time to open myself up to God to allow him to speak just those few words I really need to hear.

When I do it, I enjoy it. Nevertheless, I find it extraordinarily difficult to get round to doing it. Particularly, I suppose, because I work at home, it is often a real struggle to relax and switch off. Therefore, for me, this ruthless pursuit of holy leisure has meant putting into the diary the occasional day, perhaps two or three per year, specifically for prayer and meditation. I go to a retreat centre, not that far from where I live, but just far enough to have no distractions and no excuses for my ridiculous, endless busyness.

It is worth it. The words that enter me at these times stay with me. They have often given me reassurance, challenge and a fresh sense of direction. Their impact is far in excess of their number.

## God and you

For the whole of this book so far, I have been going on about the importance of understanding the origins and context of a biblical passage. I now want to be awkward and say, forget all that!

Yes, intellectual understanding is important, and a knowledge of the background will help a great deal, but just for now, leave those things completely aside. In meditation the goal is to receive these words as though God has written them just for you, just for this moment in time.

Dietrich Bonhoeffer explained it thus: 'Just as you do not analyse the words of someone you love, but accept them as they are said to you, accept the word of Scripture and ponder it in your heart, as Mary did. That is all. That is meditation' (*The Way to Freedom*, Harper & Row, p. 59).

This sort of acceptance is far more than an intellectual one. 'I treasure your word in my *heart*,' says Psalm 119, 'so that I may not sin against you.' For the psalmist, the word 'heart' had many meanings—the entirety of mental and moral activity, emotions, reason and will, the inner life, the hidden centre of personality, the spring of all desires.

It is one thing to know something in your head, quite another to *know* it deep in your being. 'It is unlikely, but possible,' says priest and author, Gerard Hughes, 'that someone should know the Bible by heart, the Christian creeds, the works of all the theologians and commentators who have ever lived, yet keep that knowledge sealed in the top layers of their mind, so that it did not affect them at any emotional or gut level' (*Oh God, Why?* BRF, p. 11). The journey from the top of our heads to the deepest level of our being is a long one, and one that needs time—time to ponder, time to prove, and time to pray it in.

This sort of Bible reading is indissolubly linked with prayer. In a way, it *is* prayer, the best sort of prayer—listening rather than talking.

It may be that God has some big message he wants to impart to you: stop worrying, learn to play, hang on in there. It may be something practical, almost mundane: get up five minutes earlier, learn to touch-type. It may be just one small step: phone a neighbour, write to your MP, take two minutes to look at the changing colours of the seasons.

'If you feel that we live in a purely physical universe,' says Richard Foster, 'you will view meditation as a good way to obtain a consistent alpha brainwave pattern... But if you believe that we live in a universe created by an infinite-personal God who delights in our communication with him, you will see meditation as communication between the Lover and the one beloved' (*Celebration of Discipline*, pp. 17–18).

Even if you have difficulty in believing in a God who loves you and wants to communicate with you, can I challenge you to try the exercise of meditation? Maybe you need to stop running, for God to have a chance to break through.


## Meditation and me

I have explored meditation in various different ways—sometimes positive and enjoyable, at others more like a frustrating waste of time. For me, writing my thoughts or chewing over the words while going for a walk has often worked best. But I have gradually discovered that, even if they seemed to yield little insight at the time, words and ideas worked over in this way have often suddenly popped up again later in a new light that has made me say, 'Ah, *now* I see!'

One example is some strange words of Jesus in Matthew: 'The eye is the lamp of the body. So, if your eye is healthy, your whole body will be full of light; but if your eye is unhealthy, your whole body will be full of darkness' (6:22–23). For a long time those words made no sense to me at all. But because they puzzled me, I kept chewing over them. And then it suddenly became obvious: *It's the way we see things!*

I realized that as I faced all life's varied experiences, I made choices about how I interpreted them—or indeed, whether I bothered to interpret them at all. I realized that sometimes we just don't look. And if we don't look, then we just don't see. And then our understanding can be at best cloudy, at worse, dark.

Perhaps that seemed glaringly obvious to you all along. But because it was something that had taken time to emerge from the grinding cogs of my own mind, rather than an idea handed to me as a cosy soundbite, it had an impact. I realized that looking closely at the world and trying to understand what I saw wasn't just curiosity, academic interest or aesthetic exercise. There was actually something spiritual about it. And I gradually realized also that 'seeing' with my own understanding was not enough. God often had a very different perspective from my own. Those times I gave to silence, prayer and contemplation were often those when my perceptions were most radically transformed. What I *saw* through my meditation made a difference.

# Ways of reading

## Rest and receive

Meditating involves stopping and relaxing. But then what? What do you actually do? Well, in essence the important thing is to find some words that seem to have something to say to you, and them give them the time, space and conditions in which to say it.

## Choosing the words

Obviously there is not a great deal of juice to be sucked from a dry passage of regulations or a long saga of bloodthirsty history. The best way, in whatever part of the Bible you are reading, is to look out for those things that strike you in some way. It may be because they hit home or reverberate with a longing deep within. It may be just that they puzzle or intrigue you. The sayings of Jesus—deceptively simple and paradoxical as they are—are especially rewarding if read in this way.

It was Mark Twain who sagely remarked, 'It ain't those parts of the Bible I can't understand that bother me, it's the parts that I do.' In this book I have, for obvious reasons, spent a disproportionate amount of time on the parts that are hard to understand. Important as it is to grapple with these difficult bits, it is also vital to take time to fully absorb those parts you do understand—or think you do.

## Finding a space

Choose a place where you will not be interrupted—the laundry cupboard or the garden shed if necessary. Perhaps fill a thermos flask and drive to some out-of-the-way place. Find somewhere where chores can be forgotten and with a pleasant and peaceful atmosphere. If possible, create a regular space for worship and prayer, even if it is only in the act of turning a chair round to face the window. *Definitely* choose somewhere out of reach of the phone. If not, unplug it!

## Giving it time

How much time is entirely up to you, but if you are new to meditation, I would suggest between half an hour and an hour. Don't push yourself to sit in solemn silence if you really find it impossible to concentrate. Instead, do something that helps you focus on the words—write, draw or speak (see below). Or do something that allows your mind freedom— go for a walk, or do a simple repetitive task like ironing or weeding. Don't, though, completely switch off and give up.

## Prepare yourself

I have claimed that meditation is not all about techniques. Yet here I am, about to offer you some. These techniques are not ends in themselves. They are simply means, first, to help you relax your body and quieten your mind, and second, to focus on the words in order to take them in. They are tried, tested and recommended from a variety of wise and experienced sources. Try what you fancy; use or adapt those which work for you.

### Relaxation

Shake yourself out. Stretch up to the ceiling and out to the sides. Lie on the floor or sit on an upright chair with both hands at your side and both feet on the floor. Work through the body, tensing and then relaxing each part of it: feet, legs, pelvis, abdomen, hands, arms, shoulders, neck, face. Drop your shoulders and let your arms flop out.

### Focus

Give yourself a visual focus—light a candle, put a single flower in a vase. Look out at the sky or a tossing tree. Focus your touch by holding a smooth pebble, a shell or a fir cone, or perhaps stroking the cat! Put on some music that you find beautiful or soothing. Whatever the focus, give it just a few minutes of your undivided attention.

## Breathing

Breathe slowly and steadily—in through the nose and out through the mouth with a sigh, each to a count of four. Picture yourself breathing out all the strain and pollution of the day and breathing in the Holy Spirit of God. Imagine him being taken down into the lungs and transferring from them into the bloodstream and so round the whole body.

# Absorbing the words

The aim of the exercise is to allow the words to travel from your mind to your heart. If you can do this by simply sitting, kneeling or standing in silence (see 'posture', below) and holding them in your mind, great! At least give it a try. However, you may find that the first thing that happens is that your mind either goes completely blank, takes off at a wild tangent or is filled with urgent tasks you have forgotten to do. (If so, write down all the tasks and put them firmly to one side. Examine the other thoughts to see if they do have any connection with the words you are trying to meditate on—there may just be a connection. If not, put them on one side too.) But never fear, it really does become easier with practice. And if stillness and silence just don't work, here are some aids to concentration.

## Speak the words

Speaking something *out* has a surprisingly powerful effect on absorbing it *in*. Reread the whole passage aloud, slowly several times over. You may want to use this as a means to memorize it. Speak it a word at a time, taking time after each word to digest its meanings and connotations.

(I am not talking about auto-suggestion here—the sort of technique that led psychologist Emile Coue to suggest that his patients repeat fifteen times a day: 'Every day in every way I am getting better and better'. Rather, I mean something much more open, gentle and questioning.)

## Put it on paper

Write the phrase or sentence, being creative with the way you do it. You may like to draw the images and ideas it evokes, or create a spider diagram with the passage in the centre and associated thoughts and ideas coming off from it. Or you may like just to write a stream of consciousness of thoughts evoked by the words.

## Posture—praying the words

Once you have read the words and helped your mind to focus on them, you may find it helpful to move your body into a posture specifically recommended for meditation and prayer. Sitting is the obvious one, but rather than slumping into an easy chair, try sitting upright, with feet on the floor and hands on your lap, palms upward in a gesture of receiving. Or lie on the floor—face down for the traditional prostrate posture of worship and awe, face up and arms outstretched as a gesture of wanting to receive. (Don't make yourself too comfortable, though, or if you are like me, you are liable to fall asleep!) Kneel, either upright leaning on a table, or bent over with your lower arms and the top of your head touching the floor. Or stand, feet slightly apart, hands raised.

There is no magic in any of these positions—they are simply a way of saying with your body, 'These moments are different. This is a time I give to God and God alone. I want to open all of myself to all God has to give.'

## Return, re-activate and realign

It is important that this first time of meditating is unhurried. But to really absorb the passage it is good to return to it again and again over a period of days, weeks or months. You may choose to do this in what Richard Foster calls 'little solitudes' (*Celebration of Discipline*, p. 93), those times in the day when you find yourself in a sudden pool of aloneness and quiet. Early in the morning before the rest of the household is awake, stuck in rush-hour traffic, sitting on the train, queuing for the bus, walking the dog—whatever those moments are for you, these are times when the words can be brought back to your mind and pondered. Return to them, like a cow chewing the cud, over and over again, until they have been turned into rich, nourishing milk.

# Exercises

## Using your gifts (Matthew 25:14–30)

Step 1: Relax. Take time to relax mind and body using some or all of the techniques above.

Step 2: Read. Read the passage once to yourself. Then read it a second time—this time aloud if possible. Notice any sentence or phrase that jumps out at you or sticks in your mind. Now read just that phrase again—slowly, several times over.

Step 3: Respond, rest and receive. Ask God what he has to show you from these words. Pray that they be taken from the top of your head to the deepest part of your being.

Take a moment to rest, not in the words themselves but in God, the ultimate author. Picture him speaking them with your name attached.

Step 4: Recite and remind. Repeat the phrase aloud, several times over.

Write it down, in a notebook/journal with a date beside it, and/or on a piece of paper to pin up or place somewhere where you will see it regularly.

Step 5: Reflect. Spend some time in silence in a posture of prayer. Simply mull the words over in your mind. Take it word by word, trying to suck the meaning out of each one before moving on to the next.

Make a note of any associated, or even seemingly disconnected, thoughts or images or feelings that come to you.

**Later**

Step 6: Return, re-activate, realign. Re-read the phrase, both on its own and in the context of the passage, over a period of several days, weeks or months. If you have different Bible versions, it may be helpful to read it in these.

Repeat the phrase and reflect on it in moments of stillness and solitude—as you look in the mirror, make a cup of tea, walk to work and so on.

Use the steps above for the following exercises:

- Whatever, whenever, wherever (Philippians 4:4–19).
- Being rooted (John 15:1–16).
- Being a child again (Luke 18:15–17).

# Taking time to remember the simple things

*A passage especially relevant to me is the one in Matthew where Jesus tells us not to worry. He reminds us to look at the simple things, the flowers and the birds, and just to trust our heavenly Father (Matthew 6:25–34).*

*We actors are terribly insecure: we're ruled by ego, we constantly need to be told 'Well done'—if we say we're not, we're not being truthful. That's why faith is so important to me. It's so easy to be materialistic and to get in a tizzy worrying where the next job is coming from. Then we forget the simple things, we forget to take time out to think—or read the Bible. We just don't stop and see what it's doing to us—and of course, in that situation you cut out God. It's not that he's gone—he's there all the time—but we've forgotten to trust him.*

*I had a recent situation which bore this out. I'd had quite a lean year, I'd done lots of theatre, but compared to the more commercial work, my income was less than halved—and I'd just bought a house! I'd decided not to do panto, but when it came to Christmas I found myself wishing desperately that I hadn't. On 21 December I had a phone call, telling me that a lead actor had been taken ill and asking me to take over. I found myself on stage within hours, terrified, and opening the show as Abenezar in Aladdin. I don't for one moment believe that God brought illness on the other actor (and he's now fully recovered), but I do believe it was tangible evidence of the way God was looking after me. He can affect your life—sometimes when you least expect it.*

ROBERT DUNCAN (ACTOR ON STAGE AND TV, INCLUDING DROP THE DEAD DONKEY AND CASUALTY)

# Fifteen

# Character building: walking in someone's shoes

### Warts and all

There was a time when the character sketches I met in the Bible disappointed me. Why were they not tidier, more triumphant? Why were they not like the biographies I found at the religious bookshop? You may know the sort—the ones where people become Christians and all their troubles disappear, the ones where missionaries are all super-holy superheroes. I devoured these biographies when I first became a Christian, but they soon lost their charm. It was not only because I discovered that, despite my best efforts, I was not reaching these glowing heights. I also noticed that the people around me in the church fell well below the standard too.

Still I thought that somewhere these amazing heroes of the faith existed. My wishful thinking was often compounded by the way Bible stories were told to me in church, not only as a child but even as an adult. I was, I now realize, often given a censored, sanitized version, as if the harsh reality would damage my fragile faith, as if my middle-class sensibilities would be bruised by the raw, uncut version.

I concluded that these lofty heroes and heroines of the faith must be the ones who spoke to me from big conference platforms. But then I got to know some of *them* better and noticed that their feet were distinctly clagged with clay.

But as I went back to the Bible and reread its stories, I realized that God had far less of a problem with these clay feet than I did. God not only communicated with flawed characters with mixed motives and see-sawing emotions, but these were the people he actually chose to accomplish his will in the world.

What I have come to love about the Bible is the reality of the characters you find there. They are such terribly unsuitable heroes: scheming Jacob, naïvely arrogant Joseph, foot-in-mouth Peter, self-righteous Paul—would any of us have picked them as religious role models?

And they live such messy lives: Moses, killing a man and running away; David, committing adultery and sending the cuckolded husband conveniently to the forefront of the battle.

The Old Testament is full of stories that start magnificently and end in a most unsatisfactory way. Noah is so wise and obedient that he survives the destruction of humankind, managing a floating zoo in the process. What does he do then? Gets out-of-his-skull drunk (Genesis 9:21). Solomon, renowned for wisdom, mighty king, builder of the great Temple. How did he end his days? A playboy with seven hundred wives, whose influence led him to compromise the faith that had once seemed so dear to him (1 Kings 11:4–6).

The New Testament provides us not so much with inconvenient endings as no endings at all. What did happen to the rich young ruler or Lazarus or the woman at the well? Did Peter really fulfil his promise as the Church's rock, or did he just fade out in favour of Paul? Where did Paul get to in the end anyway?

The Bible is like this because life is like this—full of loose ends and anti-climaxes, spectacular failures and unpromising starts. Its world is not some amazing parallel universe where everything happens as we feel it ought. Its world is the real one.

## Human interest

The reason I devoured Christian biographies and the reason I enjoy reading about the characters I find in the Bible, is the same reason I watch fly-on-the-wall docusoaps and yes, I admit it, enjoy a good gossip—I am fascinated by how people behave and what makes them tick.

Like most of the rest of the population, I learn more by watching and listening to people, real and imaginary, than by any amount of theory. Valuable as psychology, theology, biology, sociology and any other 'ology' are, for most of us the ideas that these disciplines generate need to be related back to the real world of human relationships and tested there.

Where does our nation now work out its ethics? In the churches, in parliamentary debate, in academic papers? No, for most people the forum where contemporary issues are debated is the soap opera.

This is why the chronicles of human experience in the Bible are so important. It is in these experiences that the earliest tentative beliefs in the one true God were tested and refined. It is in these stories that those developing beliefs were absorbed and understood and handed down from generation to generation.

## Choices and consequences

Somewhere between the beginning of my Christian journey and now, I have spent quite a lot of time studying the craft of writing and, in particular, telling a story. I learned that before you create a protagonist for your story, you need to know not only how they might act in certain situations, but why they would behave that way. You need to know what motivations are driving them, what is the world they grew up in and what influences it had on them, what are their weaknesses and how could those weaknesses be turned into strengths.

As the story continues, you need to work out what circumstances they could encounter that would test their character to the limit, what choices they could make that would make them grow and gain fresh understanding (or alternatively prove their downfall).

You need to be able to describe your fictional character's journey in a way that your readers relate to because that is their journey too. The same is true of biography: those things that you put into fiction—motivations, strengths, weaknesses, tests, choices, consequences, growth and downfall—are also the things you seek to draw out in biography.

As a spin-off from this desire to write stories, I have also spent some time looking at myths and at Jungian psychology. From this I have learned the importance of archetypes—those classic characters, be they from history or folk-tale, that are important to us because they embody some vital truth about what it means to be human.

Having learned all this, I came back to the Bible's stories with a great deal more respect. Whether instinctively or because God inspired them, these are well-crafted stories. Economic with words as many of them are, they highlight motives, choices and consequences with a clarity that the most skilled screenwriter might envy and a compassionate honesty that the best biographer could take as a model.

The faith journeys these characters take still resonate with us down the ages because they so often mirror our journeys too. And they give hope. If God could work with these people, he could work with anyone. If God didn't give up on them, he will not give up on us.

# Ways of reading

The questions I learned to ask in creating fictional characters could be adapted, I discovered, to help in understanding characters elsewhere, both real and fictional. The questions I list below are no more than a set of tools. They will help you dig beneath the surface of events, to learn not only about the person and what drives them, but about God and how he sets about working with raw human material to achieve something memorable.

Sometimes the answers to these questions are not found in the passages themselves. Sometimes you may need to guess or imagine them. Don't be afraid to do this. As we explored in Chapter 12, imagination is a God-given tool like any other. Because it draws out our own background knowledge and experience of what it is to be human, it allows us to combine that with what we are reading and thereby enrich the whole exercise.

## Questions to build up a character

- How was this person formed by their childhood, their family history, their cultural surroundings?
- What motivates them? What are the forces, both positive and negative, which drive them?
- What are this person's strengths and weaknesses and how does God use each of them?
- How does God use the bad things that befall them and their own failures to help them grow and develop? How does God use these things for the benefit of others?
- What choices is this person confronted with, and how do their decisions affect outcomes?
- What has this person learned by the end of the story? How did their experience teach something about God's character or about following God's way that had not been known before?

# Exercises

Note: If the story is a long one, as with Joseph or Peter, it would be foolish to try to study it at one sitting. The exercises below may work better if Steps 2 to 4 are done separately. In that case, start and finish each day's study with Steps 1, 5 and 6.

## Joseph (Genesis 37, 39—50)

Step 1: Ask God to help you walk in this character's shoes.

Step 2: Find out all you can about this character's background, origins and early life.
- In order to understand the intense rivalries that influenced Joseph's early life, you need to start before his appearance on the scene, with his complex family history. Read Genesis 29:16—30:24 and 35:16–26.
- In order to discover what religious understanding he inherited, read Genesis 35:1–14. This passage (plus v. 21) also give some clues as to the family's mode of life.
- How did this background shape Joseph's character?
- What motivated him? What were the forces, both positive and negative, that drove him?

Step 3: How was this character tested?
- Read Genesis 37 and 39—41.
- What were Joseph's strengths and weaknesses and how did God use them?
- How did the bad things that befell Joseph help him grow and develop? How did God use these things for the benefit of others?
- What choices was Joseph confronted with, and how did his decisions affect him for good or ill?

Step 4: What did this character learn?
- Read Genesis 42—45, 47 and 50.
- What has Joseph learned by the end of the story?
- What did his experience teach him about God's character or about following God's way?

Step 5: What did this person's story teach later generations and why was it such an important one in their history?

- You may like to ponder what effect the situation in chapter 47 had on events probably as much as four hundred years later at the time of the Exodus. How was it that the Israelites were able to keep their identity and beliefs throughout this long period of assimilation in a foreign land?

STEP 6: What can you personally draw from this story?
- You may like to do a meditation exercise on Genesis 50:20.

## Gideon (Judges 6—8)

STEP 1: Ask God to help you walk in this character's shoes.

STEP 2: Find out all you can about this character's background, origins and early life.
- Read Judges 6:1–10.
- How did this background shape Gideon's early life?
- What might have motivated him? What were the forces, both positive and negative, that drove him?

STEP 3: How was this character tested?
- Read Judges 6.
- Might it be a more appropriate question in this case to ask how Gideon tested God?
- What were Gideon's strengths and weaknesses and how did God use them?
- How did the circumstances that Gideon encountered help him grow and develop? How did God use these things for the benefit of others?

STEP 4: What did this character learn?
- Read Judges 7—8.
- What choices is Gideon confronted with, and how do his decisions affect him and his people for good or ill?
- What has Gideon learned by the end of the story?
- What did his experience teach him about God's character or about following God's way?

STEP 5: What did this person's story teach later generations and why was it such an important one in their history?

STEP 6: What can you personally draw from this story?
- The idea of 'putting down a fleece'—asking God to perform some arbitrary action as a sign—is one that some

Christians quote as a method of finding God's will. Do you think this is wise or appropriate as a general practice? Are there circumstances when it might be right?

## Ruth (Ruth 1—4)

STEP 1: Ask God to help you walk in this character's shoes.

STEP 2: Find out what you can about this character's background, origins and early life. Note: Moab, to the east of the Dead Sea in present-day Jordan, was a neighbouring people group to the Israelites when they settled in Canaan. Like most neighbouring tribes, their relationships were somewhat tense.

- For some of the tribal background, see Numbers 22:1–12; 25:1–3; Judges 3:12–30.
- How might this background have shaped Ruth's early life and her relationship to the Israelites?
  Note: The whole story is set in a world with vastly different customs to our own, particularly regarding marriage and courtship. Marriages were arranged and women had little way of supporting themselves independently (other than, perhaps, the oldest profession).
- To see what the law said about responsibilities to widows, read Deuteronomy 25:5–10.
- Take some time to imagine yourself into the conventions of this pastoral world.
- Read Ruth 1:1–6.
- What circumstances motivated Ruth? What were the forces, both positive and negative, that drove her?

STEP 3: How was Ruth (and Naomi) tested?

- Read Ruth 1:6—3:18.
- What were Ruth's strengths and weaknesses and how did God use them?
- How did the things that befell Ruth help her grow and develop? How did God use these things for the benefit of others?
- What choices is Ruth confronted with, and how do her decisions affect her and others around her?

STEP 4: What did this character learn?

- Read Ruth 4.
- What do you imagine Ruth has learned by the end of the story?
- What did her experience teach her about following God's way?

STEP 5:  What did this person's story teach later generations and why was it such an important one in their history?

STEP 6:  What can you personally draw from this story?
- Seen through contemporary eyes, Ruth may seem an outmodedly passive and dependent character. Her roles are certainly the traditional ones of child-bearing and home-making. Nevertheless, is there anything about the values of this ancient society that still have something to say to you?

## Peter (Gospels, Acts, 1 and 2 Peter)

STEP 1:  Ask God to help you walk in this character's shoes.

STEP 2:  Find out all you can about this character's background, origins and early life. Note: Capernaum was a small lakeside town, with its own synagogue (see Mark 1:21)—possibly a radical one if it invited Jesus to speak there. It lived with the familiar presence of Roman occupying forces (Matthew 8:5) and with the puppet government of Herod Antipas (son of the hated Herod the Great, who massacred the babies in Matthew 2:16). Antipas was based in Galilee (Mark 6:21) and built a base at the spa town of Tiberias, named after the current Roman Emperor (John 6:23). There were even moves to rename the lake Tiberias (John 6:1). Capernaum's position at the north-west of the Sea of Galilee meant that it was well placed for communications within the region. (Matthew 4:25). The Decapolis, a region directly across the lake, was, as its name suggests, a Greek area of ten cities. Possibly Peter the fisherman traded there, and so had contact with Greek culture.
- How might this background have shaped Peter's early life?
- Read John 1:19–42; Matthew 4:18–22; Luke 4:31—5:11.
- What clues do these passages give you to Peter's character?
- What motivated him? What were the forces, both positive and negative, that drove him?

STEP 3: How was this character tested?
- Read Matthew 16:13–20 and 17:1–9—a confession of faith and a supernatural experience.
- Read Matthew 26:31–46, 69–75—boasting and failure.
- Read John 21—reinstatement and commission.
- What were Peter's strengths and weaknesses and how did God use them?
- Read Acts 1:15—5:32.
- What do these chapters tell you about Peter's qualities of leadership and capacity to respond to new situations?
- How did the things that Peter experienced help him grow and develop? How did God use these things, including his failure, for the benefit of others?
- Read Acts 10:1—11:18 and 15:1–21.
- What choices was Peter confronted with, and how did his decisions affect him for good or ill?

STEP 4: What did this character learn?
- Read 1 Peter. Note: 2 Peter is generally thought not to have been written by Peter—see the Appendix. Some have also claimed that 1 Peter was not really written by Peter, on the grounds that its language and thought are too sophisticated for an uneducated fisherman. However, as we have previously seen, Peter grew up in a cosmopolitan environment, and tradition has it that by the time he wrote this letter he was in Rome. Moreover, he would not be the last person to have gained an education and realized their hidden potential after being converted. This letter is written to believers in today's central and northern Turkey. Could it be that these were churches founded by those who first heard the Gospel at Pentecost (Acts 2:9–10), whom Peter had visited and kept in touch with over the years?
- What has Peter learned by the time we last meet him?
- What did his experiences teach him about God's character or about following God's way?

STEP 5: What did this person's story teach later generations and why was it such an important one in Christian history?
- What, if any, difference would it have made to the Christian Church if the person whom Jesus had chosen as

leader of the disciples had been an educated, establishment figure?

STEP 6:  What can you personally draw from this story?

- What aspect of Peter's character, or incident from his story, do you most identify with?

## Men (and women) behaving rightly

*Ruth is a particularly meaningful book of the Bible for me. I think it's an astonishingly good and riveting read, because it says so much about having faith and doing the right thing and being obedient. I would recommend that anyone would definitely have a good read of Ruth. It shows a lot of very good people being obedient to God and behaving in an entirely proper way and that's excellent.*

ROSEMARY CONLEY (EXERCISE AND DIET GURU AND BESTSELLING AUTHOR OF *THE HIP AND THIGH DIET*

# Sixteen

# Thread gathering: tracing the big ideas

This chapter bears some similarities to the one on 'Trawling', with one big difference: that chapter was about searching for references to issues that *we* find important; this is about tracing through those issues which *the Bible itself* considers important.

At this point, the fully paid-up sceptic may ask: but who decides what the Bible thinks is important? I confess—for the purposes of this chapter, it has to be me. But I have selected the themes for exploration because they are some of those that the main protagonists of the New Testament picked out and returned to again and again.

## A Jewish mindset

The New Testament writers referred to these themes because (with the possible exception of Luke) they were Jews writing for a Jewish audience. They understood—Jesus and John the Baptist beforehand, but the disciples only afterwards—how the events of the New Testament linked in with and continued from the Old. They wanted to explain this continuity to their audience. They were gathering the threads of what the Jewish nation had learnt over century after century and showing how, in Jesus, they became woven into a radically new but stunningly fitting design.

The only way for you to find these threads for yourself is simply to look out for recurring themes and ideas as you read. If you have a Bible with references in the margins, that will help a great deal, as it will often refer you back to the origins of an idea. If not, a concordance or biblical computer search can be used in the same way by tracing a particular word.

Look, though, for images as well as ideas—often it is a similarity in the situation or train of events that may alert you to some big theme of the Old Testament being fulfilled or re-enacted in the New.

## A universal journey

These are big themes because they are universal, perhaps not to all human beings, but certainly to all human beings who have set out on a journey to discover the divine and, having discovered, to live in relationship with God.

I guess that that too is why I have chosen these themes. Despite their uncompromising Jewishness and their sometimes unfashionable language (being 'cleansed by the blood of the Lamb' sounds a long way from modern psychology, although in practice it is surprisingly close), they get to the very heart of what it means to take a spiritual journey. As I've travelled haltingly over the years, I have come to realize that I know what they mean. I've been there.

You may need to work at it to get behind the archaic language and unfamiliar images, but perhaps you too will find that their journey is your journey, and that the promises that excited them will become reality for you.

# Ways of reading

## Picking up the thread

My starting point in these exercises has been to look at something that was said or done by one of the first proclaimers of the Christian religion and seemed to be of vital importance to them.

## Tracing it back to its origins

The next step is to follow the idea back to the Old Testament. Often it goes back to one big seminal event or story—the exodus from Egypt is the classic example.

## Finding the pattern

The next move is to see whether other biblical writers also picked up the same theme and what it meant to them. Sometimes it will recur in a variety of ways and be referred to over and over. You cannot hope in one study to gather all of these threads, and it would be tedious to try. But once noticed, you may discover them in other parts of your reading and, having done so, begin to piece the bigger design together. (Note: you may prefer to work through these other readings at several sittings.)

### Returning to the start

Having done all that, return to the passage you started with and see what light your study throws on it.

### Bringing it into the present

Like all the exercises, the final step is to see how the theme relates to your own life and your own spiritual journey.

## Exercises

### The sacrificial Lamb

STEP 1: Pray for God's help in grasping this ancient theme.
STEP 2: Picking up the thread.
- Read 1 Peter 1:18–19.
- Why did Peter consider this idea of Christ as Lamb to be such an important one?
STEP 3: Tracing it back to its origins.
- Read Exodus 12.
- God could have effected an escape from Egypt without this ritual. Why would he choose to include it?
STEP 4: Finding the pattern.
- Read Leviticus 4—5.
- Why were these rituals such a vital part of the Jewish religion? What roles did they play?
- Read John 1:29.
- John the Baptist must have known that introducing Jesus in this way was not only shocking to his hearers, but putting Jesus on the spot. Do you think it was a long-considered statement or a spur-of-the-moment recognition?

- Read Acts 8:26–35; 1 Corinthians 5:7; Hebrews 9:11–14, 28.
- Why do you think the idea of Jesus as a sacrificial Lamb was such a welcome one to these people and their listeners/readers?

Step 5: Returning to the start.
- Why was this belief so important to Peter? How had he come to understand the truth of it?

Step 6: Bringing it into the present.
- The idea of Christ as someone on whom to off-load all guilt is an attractive one. What things make it difficult for you to appropriate it?
- Is it possible to live with guilty feelings without any way of off-loading them?

# Death and rebirth

STEP 1: Ask God for the courage to die to old ways and be reborn to new.

STEP 2: Picking up the thread.
- Read John 3:1–8.
- Jesus' statement seems very adamant. Is it just for Nicodemus or is it a process that everyone must go through?

STEP 3: Tracing it back to its origins.
- Read Genesis 2:7.
- I'll admit that at first glance this appears something of a tenuous connection—but bear with me. What does this verse have to say about being alive and being human?

STEP 4: Finding the pattern.
- Read Exodus 3:1–12 and Jonah 1:1—3:3.
- Each of these stories shows a character who was 'reborn' from someone weak to someone strong. What is the pattern of change? What is the central turning point?
- Read 1 Peter 1:3–4; 1 Corinthians 15:8; 1 John 2:29; 3:9; 5:18.
- What light do each of these passages shed on the concept of new birth?

STEP 5:  Returning to the start.
- Is the rebirth that Jesus speaks of a once-for-all experience, or something that may need to happen over and over?

STEP 6:  Bringing it into the present.
- Have there been any rebirths in your experience?
- Have you ever seen anyone else who appeared to become a new, 'reborn' person? What was their experience?

## Water and wilderness

STEP 1:  Pray for the willingness to journey where God takes you, even into the desert.

STEP 2:  Picking up the thread.
- Read Matthew 3:1—4:11.
- This could be more properly described as two threads rather than one—a sequence of events rather than one concrete idea. Is there any connection between the baptismal 'water' experience and the following desert 'wilderness' experience?
- How would you describe in general terms what is going on in the baptism?
- How would you describe in general terms what is going on in the desert?

STEP 3:  Tracing it back to its origins.
- Read Exodus 14—16.
- What was accomplished by the 'water', the crossing of the Red Sea, in the history of the Jewish people?
- What was accomplished during the forty years of 'wilderness', of wandering in the desert?

STEP 4:  Finding the pattern.
- Read Joshua 3—4.
- Coming immediately after the forty years in the desert, this event does not repeat the two-step pattern. How does it repeat the pattern of the 'water' crossing and why was this experience such an important one in Jewish history?
- Read Acts 9:17–31; 11:25.
- Can you see a faint echo of the pattern of baptism and wilderness (withdrawal) here? Why was it not only safer

but also beneficial for Saul (later renamed Paul—see Acts 13:9) to withdraw to Tarsus, out of public view for a while?

STEP 5: Returning to the start.
- How do the Old Testament events, with their significance of travelling 'from' and 'to', throw light on events in the New?
- Each of these incidents comes at the start of some huge leap forward in spiritual events. Is it coincidence?

STEP 6: Bringing it into the present.
- Do these themes relate in any way to your experience in your faith journey?
- Have you ever taken a retreat before moving on to some big new venture? What would be the purpose and value of such a time?

## Get up and go

Step 1: Pray for courage to go where God calls you.

Step 2: Picking up the thread.
- Read Mark 1:14–20.
- What made these fishermen so ready to get up and go?

Step 3: Tracing it back to its origins.
- Read Genesis 12:1–9.
- The journey of Abram (an earlier name of Abraham) would have had little significance were it not for the birth of a nation and a religion that came from it. What is it about 'getting up and going' that opens the door to big initiatives?

Step 4: Finding the pattern.
- Look at Moses—Exodus 13:20–22; 14:31; 16:35; 23:20–22; Elijah—1 Kings 17; Ananias—Acts 9:10–19; and Paul—Acts 16:6–15.
- What came from the willingness of each of these characters to follow the prompting to go somewhere unexpected?

Step 5: Returning to the start.
- What useful characteristics does this point up for anyone who wants to be a follower of Jesus?

Step 6: Bringing it into the present.
- How would you feel if today God asked you to go and do something totally unexpected?

- Is there a difference between faith and foolhardiness? If so, what?

## A brand new experience

*For me, the idea of being 'born again' was very important. I was ashamed of my past and wanted God to bury it as deep as possible. In fact I love the bit in the Bible that says that God takes our sins and totally blots them out. God does not remember them any more. That was just what I needed. I wanted to be washed inside and out and to stand before my God as if I was brand new— born again!*

*It's important to understand that it's not like deciding that you're going to be good from now on, like a New Year's resolution. People can be God-fearing and church-going and yet not be born again...*

*Only God's Holy Spirit can enable us to be born again and it's still a revolutionary thing today. We're so used to handling things ourselves, in our way and our time. Sometimes we are too proud to let God into our lives. We must learn to 'let go and let God'—not just once, when we accept God into our lives, but every single day.*

BOBBY BALL (COMEDIAN AND ENTERTAINER), IN *THE BIBLE SPEAKS TO ME*, PP. 8–9

# Seventeen

# Exploring: making your own itinerary

Well, my job as tour guide is all but done. There is, I know, a vast amount still to discover: some places left unvisited, others whizzed through with barely a glance to left or right. But I hope it has given you a taster, shown you which sites would be worth a further visit, which alley-ways you want to take time wandering through, which will become home from home, places you will want to return to again and again.

And I hope it has given you some suggestions for *ways* in which to revisit—which journeys need to be taken at walking pace, with plenty of time to stop and stare; which can be zoomed through, taking in the scenery at a glance; which ones you need to return to in the company of an expert. I hope above all that you will want to return and explore the Bible for yourself in your own time and your own way.

I could say that you are on your own now, but that would be untrue. There are a huge number of other maps and guidebooks available, many people, professional and amateur, willing to guide you and many fellow travellers curious as you are to find out more.

Give a thought to this last one. I have been struck by how many of those who have contributed quotes to this book have said that getting together with a group of like-minded people to read and discuss the Bible together has been the thing that has helped them most. I would certainly endorse that myself, as an activity that has not only helped me to understand the Bible better, but also to stretch my brain, have a fun evening and deepen friendships into the bargain!

## The elusive companion

But there is one companion above all others to take with you as you travel through the Bible. In fact without this companion, the journey might be interesting, informative, even fun for a while, but will probably prove ultimately unsatisfying.

The companion I am suggesting is the Holy Spirit.

Now the minute I say this, I feel myself slipping into difficulties. I am using a term that conjures up wildly different ideas and associations— good, bad and off-the-wall. I am talking about a companion who is unseen, undefinable, elusive to reason.

I had been casting round, wondering how on earth I could express this idea, when quite by chance, someone lent me a book. It is called *A Matter of Life and Death* by John V. Taylor (SCM Press), and as I read its first few pages, I suddenly had my explanation:

*I was returning by train from Oxford to London on a late summer evening. My mind wandered from my paperback to the stubble fields where the stooks of corn cast long blue shadows towards the glowing trees. As so often before, I was moved and held by the beauty of it, and I began to think about what actually happens when a landscape or a great tree or the spectacle of the night sky presents itself and commands attention. That quite ordinary scene beyond the railway track had ceased to be merely an object I was looking at. It had become a subject imbued with a power that was affecting me, saying something to me in the way that music does. Something had generated a current of charged intensity between it and me. If I said that the significance and value that it had taken on was all a project of my imagination, I knew that that would be understating the truth. In all such experiences a kind of mutual communication or exchange was taking place which did not originate entirely in myself. I was also quite sure that this was a very ordinary, almost universal human experience. I was not an animist so I did not credit the corn stooks with consciousness. Then what was the source of this current of communication that makes a landscape or a person or an idea act upon me, or upon you, in this way? Who effects the introduction between me and that which is there, turning it into a presence towards which I surrender myself?*

*As soon as the question took that form the answer fell into place. So this is what is meant by the Holy Spirit!*

If that is true, then the Holy Spirit is not only to be found at Pentecostal meetings or at the fingertips of specially gifted individuals. The Holy Spirit is a natural presence, the breath of the Creator God, breathed into us to make us more alive and more aware, as the first breath of God transformed Adam from a heap of dust to a human being. If that is true—and everything in my experience and instinct echoes that it is—then God can breathe this life, this awareness, into any moment when we give ourselves fully to what he has to give.

For some people, an awareness of being bathed in the Holy Spirit has come as a dramatic moment of ecstasy. For those who experience it, that may be wonderful. But those who do not have such an experience need not fear that they are missing out. Jesus promised the Holy Spirit as an ongoing companion and an all-time presence:

*And I will ask the Father, and he will give you another Advocate, to be with you for ever. This is the Spirit of truth, whom the world cannot receive, because it neither sees him or knows him. You know him, because he abides with you, and he will be in you (John 14:16–17).*

## The unpredictable moment

I don't want to suggest that all you have to do is to invoke the Holy Spirit and suddenly every act of Bible reading will be spine-tinglingly relevant. If that is anybody's experience, it is certainly not mine.

Perhaps the problem with us sceptics is that we hover between worlds, using part logic and part sense, part doubt and part hope, so that if the Holy Spirit does show up, we only catch the merest glimpse. I take heart that this seems to be many people's experience. The following poem is on the subject of prayer, but I think it could equally apply to Bible-reading or any act of spiritual search.

### Disclosure

*Prayer is like watching for the*
*Kingfisher. All you can do is*
*Be where he is likely to appear, and*
*Wait.*

*Often, nothing much happens;*
*There is space, silence and*
*Expectancy.*
*No visible sign, only the*
*Knowledge that he's been there*
*And may come again.*
*Seeing or not seeing cease to matter.*
*You have been prepared.*
*But sometimes, when you've almost*
*Stopped expecting it,*
*A flash of brightness*
*Gives encouragement.*

**ANN LEWIN**

So am I suggesting that you should sit for hours, restless and uncomfortable, with this ancient, confusing book, in the hopes that just now and then there will be a 'flash of brightness'?

Yes. Because even in those times when there is no magical glimpse of shimmering turquoise wings, sitting there will still be a good experience. There is still the river—that stream of words, sometimes turbulent, sometimes restful. You will be learning to read its subtleties and nuances, starting to see what is under the surface, storing up memories that you will carry with you back into the busy, complicated world.

## The unlikely journey

Near the beginning of this book, I picked up a phrase written by the apostle Paul in one of his letters: 'All Scripture is God-breathed...' I suggested that in Bible reading this God-breathedness might come at both ends of the exchange—into the author and into the reader—and that it is this that makes Bible reading special. A fanciful hypothesis, maybe, and I have no way of proving it. It is one that can only be accepted by faith.

In fact, the whole hypothesis of the Bible is just as incredible. Its theme from beginning to end is that there *is* a God—all-present, all-powerful—and that this God can and does relate in a personal way to human beings as they go on their meandering, faltering journeys through life. The Bible claims that this is not only possible, but that it has happened since the earliest time to the unlikeliest people. It claims that this relationship begins with a leap of faith.

For years I have had a little saying pinned to my notice board: 'Trusting God is not a feeling, it's a decision'. I can't remember now where it came from, but it seems more true as the years go by. Alongside it are a series of slightly blurred action photos. They are of our son Simon aged about 13. It was the year we went to France and for the first time he managed to do a back flip off the diving-board into the river. I can picture him now, standing there, hovering, shivering, almost going for it then stepping back. Day after day he would almost make it, wanting to but not quite daring. But eventually there came that glorious moment when he launched himself backwards, somersaulted over and landed triumphantly in the water. Of course, as soon as he had done it, he was back up on the board doing it again over and over. I keep the photos and the faded saying alongside them, because between them they remind me daily what faith is about.

The Bible is *about* faith and can only be understood if it is read *with* faith. How can anyone understand what swimming is like, if they have never taken the plunge and let the water carry them?

I hope that you will go on turning the Bible's pages, and that as you do so you will take a risk, a scary, blind leap, and find yourself immersed in God's love and care.


## The ongoing exploration

Following are the last four exercises in this book and they come without any guide or suggested routes. Just to recap, the questions I suggest you ask yourself before you set out are these:

- What sort of literature is it—an eye-witness report, myth, instruction, history, poetry, social comment or something that doesn't quite fit any of those categories?
- Is it best explored by taking in the whole thing at a sweep or looking at it minutely bit by bit?
- Is it poetry to be taken metaphorically or prose to be taken literally?
- What was the author's intention and who were his audience?
- Can I use my imagination to get into this more vividly?

- Are there subjects or ideas that I need to trace through to see what other biblical authors thought and said?
- Could I learn more about this passage if I followed its central character throughout his or her story?
- Are there any big themes here that recur throughout the Bible?
- Which are the words that especially leap out at me, and can I usefully spend time meditating on them and returning to them again and again?

## Exercises

- Building a place to be (Isaiah 58)
- Behaving with integrity (James 2—3)
- Acting crazily (Genesis 22)
- Living radically (Matthew 6—7)

Happy exploring!

# Satisfied customers

*The Bible is guidelines on life. It's God's word, God's love letter to me and to everyone. It gives the answers to my life, it solves my problems in life. That's what God encourages me to do and encourages everyone to do—to turn to his word and seek him.*

VA'AIGA TUIGAMALA (RUGBY PLAYER, NEWCASTLE FALCONS, NEW ZEALAND ALL BLACKS AND SAMOA)

*I think the Bible can be to many people a dusty old book, but there are many, many times in my experience when it comes to life, and you realize it's not a dusty old book at all. Not so much individual words but stories and scenes that suddenly become relevant and real and jump into your life and mean something.*

PAM RHODES (TV PRESENTER)

*Christians talk about God speaking to you, but how do you know God's voice? For me it is essentially the Bible. Not to rule out that God can speak in other ways but primarily a Christian's focus must be on knowing God's word and applying it. That really gives me total direction. If I am looking for an attitude or have a big decision to make, I'll pray, but I also need to know from God's written word. The Bible plays a very important role in telling me what my attitudes, my actions, the way I live my life, should be. The basic philosophy of what I try to do is to glorify God through every aspect of my life, and the Bible helps me know how. It's fundamental.*

JONATHAN EDWARDS (OLYMPIC SILVER MEDALLIST, WORLD RECORD HOLDER IN TRIPLE JUMP)

*I've read every word of the Bible, because it occurred to me one day that what I didn't want to hear when I died was God saying to me, 'Ah, I had a special message for you on page 571, but you never read it.' Since then I have found many messages that are special to me, often hidden in verses you might not expect.*

SISTER WENDY BECKETT (NUN, ART HISTORIAN AND TV PERSONALITY)

# Background on Bible books not covered elsewhere

## History

### Joshua

The author of Joshua is unknown, but the book is probably a compilation gathered in the same way and around the same time as the first five books (see Chapters 6 and 7).

The book of Joshua covers the period of conquest of the promised land, around 1200BC. It features valiant heroes who brought even their warfare under God's direction, and introduces an ongoing dilemma—the choice between serving the one God with his high values, or the surrounding pagan gods with their easy morality.

### Judges

Judges, like the Pentateuch, was probably compiled from a number of sources, but bears the marks of a single writer/editor. This could have been Samuel or one of his contemporaries, since the book itself clearly places its time of writing after the destruction of the sanctuary at Shiloh (Judges 18:31) and before David captured Jerusalem (Judges 1:21).

There seems little sense of a loving God or of a morally upright people in these chronicles of cruel tribal warfare. Yet there is an ongoing belief that God is involved in human affairs, an acceptance that he might work through the most unlikely heroes, and the recurring theme that following foreign gods could only lead to weakness, while strength came from faithfulness to the one true God.

# Ruth

This story has echoes of folk-tales from other cultures, but it is set firmly in a historical framework: 'In the days when the judges ruled...' (Ruth 1:1). The phrasing of this opening implies that it was now in the distant past, and the explanation of forgotten customs in 4:7 confirms it. It has been suggested that the book was written around the time of Ezra and Nehemiah, as an oblique protest against their strict laws forbidding intermarriage. If so, the author was content to let the story speak for itself.

This gentle pastoral tale stands in quiet contrast to the aggressiveness of Judges and deals with issues of loyalty and obedience. In the subtlest of ways it makes a strong statement: God can and does use people from any nation—and both genders—to fulfil his purposes.

## 1 and 2 Kings

These accounts were probably compiled by a prophet during the Babylonian exile. Tradition attributes them to Jeremiah, and although there is no evidence for this, his views on idolatry and unfaithfulness to God certainly find echoes here.

These books cover a long sweep from David's death in 971BC to the fall of the southern kingdom in 587BC. At a time when the Jewish nation had all but died away and the Temple lay in ruins, the author lays great stress on God's promise to David to maintain 'his house' for ever. The promise, however, as given to Solomon is seen to be conditional:

*If you will walk before me, as David your father walked... keeping my statutes and my ordinances, then I will establish your royal throne over Israel for ever... If you turn aside from following me, you or your children, and do not keep my commandments and my statutes that I have set before you... the house that I have consecrated for my name I will cast out of my sight (1 Kings 9:4–7).*

1 and 2 Kings tell a story of how those conditions were sometimes kept and sometimes abandoned and how God eventually and reluctantly fulfilled his warning to withdraw support.

# 1 and 2 Chronicles

These volumes were written rather later than Kings, although they cover a lot of the same ground. Tradition has it that they were written by Ezra, and it is a common view that these books, together with Ezra and Nehemiah, form one long history, perhaps begun by Ezra and finished by Nehemiah.

Written for a people who had at last returned to Jerusalem to rebuild their Temple and their faith, Chronicles lays great stress on the original building of the Temple. Although it covers the same period as Kings, after the division of the kingdoms it focuses entirely on Judah. Its message is the same recurring one: when the people and their leaders are faithful to God, they prosper; when they follow false gods, decline and defeat are never far behind.

# Ezra

Here, for the first time as we go through the Bible, we arrive at a book which bears the name of its author. Even if some later hand was responsible for editing (and it is commonly held that the same editor did the final compiling of Ezra and Nehemiah and probably also 1 and 2 Chronicles), it is clear that this is the personal memoir of Ezra, a priest and scribe who gave up the security of life in Babylon to restore a city in ruins. It was a task that he shared with his compatriots Nehemiah, Haggai and Zechariah.

Ezra tells the story of a people suddenly and miraculously free to return to their homeland. The first wave arrived around 538BC to find Jerusalem a heap of rubble and the neighbouring peoples in fierce opposition to their plans. Their first task, however, was not to build fortifications or homes for themselves, but to rebuild the Temple, the spiritual heart of the city and the focus of their nationhood. But while the physical building was a potent symbol, the social and ethical framework of the nation also needed to be rebuilt. That is why Ezra, arriving eighty years later, pronounced a ban on intermarriage. It is an edict that sounds harsh to our contemporary ears, but Ezra realized that any dilution or compromise of the Jewish faith and moral code at this point could have fatal repercussions for generations to come, and jeopardize its eventual survival. Ezra showed the Jews the importance of repentance and obedience to the one true God.

For Nehemiah, see Chapter 9.

## Esther

The author of this story is unknown, but a storyteller he or she most certainly was. Of the right length to be told at a sitting, this tale has an '*Arabian Nights*' feel to it. How closely it was based on history is unknown, but it appears to be told some time after the events by someone well acquainted with life in Persia and at pains to explain its details to an audience which was not.

Although God is not mentioned, the subtext of this story is his provision for his people via the right person in the right place—in this case, Esther the beautiful Jewish girl who won the heart of King Xerxes of Persia and managed through cunning and courage to avert a plot to destroy the Jewish people. The annual Jewish festival, Purim, celebrates this deliverance.

# Prophets to the northern kingdom

## Hosea

It was around 760BC and, on the surface, things in the northern kingdom of Israel were fine. But the rich were getting richer and the poor poorer, and injustice was rife. The one God was still worshipped, but so too were a host of other pagan gods, and religion had become adulterated—at best easy-going, at worst positively immoral. Hosea demonstrated God's love through his own marriage to an unfaithful wife. He put forward a radical new concept: not only was God angry at the people's wayward-ness, it also caused him pain.

However, the people showed no more willingness to be faithful than Hosea's erring wife, and their prostitution to false gods and false values soon proved their downfall. This is a love story without a happy ending.

See also Amos (Chapter 10).

# Prophets to the southern kingdom

## Micah

Micah was a contemporary of Isaiah in the south (see Chapter 10), and of Amos and Hosea in the north. Unlike Isaiah, though, he was a peasant, a countryman from a humble village. He saw the corruption of his nation at grassroots level—fraud, false measures, witchcraft and paganism, prophets who told the people what they wanted to hear and not the truth. He also saw the international picture—the gathering threat of Assyria—and the bigger spiritual one—a merciful God who pardons and forgives.

Micah saw it all, and reduced his message to one glorious soundbite: 'What does the Lord require of you but to do justice, and to love kindness, and to walk humbly with your God?' (6:8).

## Zephaniah

For fifty years after Isaiah and Micah, there followed a long prophetic silence. It coincided with some of the darkest days in Judah's history, when the evil King Manasseh and his son and successor Amon took the nation deep into spiritism and pagan practices (2 Kings 21). It was towards the end of these days that Zephaniah grew up, and the beginning of his prophetic activities probably coincided with the accession to the throne of the young King Josiah in 640BC.

It may even be that Zephaniah was an adviser to Josiah. Certainly Josiah turned out to be a good guy, discovering the book of the Law and calling the people together to renew their allegiance to its teaching (2 Kings 22—23). Equally clearly, this book of Zephaniah's was written before that turning point in 621BC. It prophesies the destruction of the pagan worshippers, the downfall of corrupt Jerusalem, and a vast generic doom encompassing also the neighbouring nations of Philistia, Moab, Ammon, Cush and even the mighty Assyria. Even in this bleak prediction, though, there is hope. The people will be restored, they will experience God's care: 'He will rejoice over you with gladness, he will renew you in his love; he will exult over you with loud singing as on a day of festival' (3:17–18).

## Habakkuk

Nothing is known about the personality of this questioning prophet, but he seems to be writing just after Micah and at the same time as Jeremiah (see Chapter 10). He sees the rise of the Babylonian empire (also known as the Chaldeans), and God tells him that his own eyes will watch this feared and dreaded people sweep right across the land (1:5–11). In fact, Assyria fell to them in 612BC and by 597 they had arrived at Jerusalem.

This gives Habakkuk a problem—surely God is not saying it is part of his plan that 'the wicked swallow those more righteous than they' (1:13)?

Rather like Job before him, Habakkuk dialogues with God, concluding, like Job, by standing 'in awe, O Lord, of your work' (3:2) as he contemplates the mysterious forces in the created world.

# Prophets to other nations

## Nahum

Perhaps prophets *against* other nations would be a better description. Nahum is writing about Assyria and the fall of their capital Nineveh. (This is the same Nineveh as that in the tale of Jonah—see Chapter 6. Now, however, not a glimmer of hope for Nineveh remains.)

Previously, in 663BC, the Assyrians had pushed right down to Thebes in Egypt (3:8–10). Now, however, the Assyrians themselves were about to be conquered. Nineveh was destroyed by the Babylonians in 612BC.

Nahum wrote between these two events, but little else is known of him, other than that he was a Judean. His book could be seen as little more than strutting patriotism. But Nahum had watched smaller nations like Israel swallowed up and destroyed by mighty Assyria. He had been angered by injustice and oppression and he dared to believe that God felt the same.

## Obadiah

Obadiah prophesied against Edom, a small nation hidden in mountain strongholds to the south-east of the Dead Sea. Their capital Sela (forerunner of Petra) was perched high on a plateau above a rocky cliff and approached by a narrow gorge and the Edomites thought they were invincible. 'Your proud heart has deceived you,' says Obadiah, 'you that live in the clefts of the rock, whose dwelling is in the heights' (1:3).

The occasion for Obadiah's anger was the fact that the Edomites had swept down to wreak havoc on Judah at the time of their weakness, while the Babylonians were laying siege to Jerusalem in 587BC. Obadiah was not the only prophet to speak out against Edom. A passage remarkably similar is to be found in Jeremiah 49, and Isaiah, Ezekiel and Amos also had things to say about this people, who were descended from Esau, brother of Jacob. If nothing else, this book reminds us how much pain and hurt can be unleashed by petty sibling rivalries and the bearing of grudges.

In the fifth century BC, the Arabs took Edom, and in the third it was overrun by the Nabateans, who built the rock city of Petra. By AD70 the Edomites had totally disappeared from history.

# Prophets of the exile

## Ezekiel

The book of Ezekiel is written almost entirely in the first person and reads like a journal. Its opening could not be more specific. On 31 July 593BC, seated by the Kebar river (strictly speaking, a canal) in Babylon, Ezekiel had his first vision (1:1). Ezekiel had by then been in exile for five years—he was one of the first to leave with King Jehoiachin (1:2).

The book falls roughly into three parts. The first talks of the punishment the Israelites must suffer; the second deals with God's judgment on the surrounding nations. When Ezekiel first started prophesying, the Temple was still standing. Six years later he heard of its destruction. But twenty years after he first started seeing visions, he was rewarded by a joyful one—that of a new Temple, with its glory restored. Amid the measure-ments and statistics, he describes a river flowing from the Temple refreshing everything around (ch. 47). It was a vision that John was to pick up six hundred years later, as a revelation of heaven. In Ezekiel's hands, though, it predicted accurately that the Israelites were not a spent force, that their glory would rise again, and their influence spread far more widely than even Ezekiel's fertile imagination could ever have pictured.

## Daniel

Daniel is, strictly speaking, not a prophecy at all. The book falls into two distinct halves. Chapters 1—6 form a narrative about the activities of Daniel and his compatriots in the Babylonian court. Chapters 7—12 record a series of visions: these, however, have far more in common with the type of apocalyptic writing found in Revelation than with the usual style of prophecy. There is a good reason for this. The book of Daniel, many scholars now agree, was probably written in the second century BC, nearer to the time of Revelation's writings than to the exile. The Jewish canon recognizes this and places Daniel within the 'Writings' rather than the prophets, after Esther and before Ezra.

Since the book was probably written at such great remove, 450 years after the events it describes, we have no way of knowing whether they are fact or fiction. Daniel *was* a historical figure, well-known at the time of the exile—Ezekiel mentions him, first as a byword for righteousness and resourcefulness (Ezekiel 14:14, 20), and later for wisdom (Ezekiel 28:3). Presumably such legendary status was based on something, and therefore the picture we have of Daniel as a statesman in the Babylonian court, and a man of courage, integrity and wisdom, could well be based on fact.

When it comes to the visions in the latter half of the book, if we take the scholars' suppositions as accurate, then we are likely to be disappointed. Were these visions, then, written after the events and if so, what was the point of that? It makes better sense if we understand that this technique of setting words in the mouths of historical characters was a familiar one to the Jewish people and not one that they regarded as cheating. It was not written with any intention of fraud.

So why was it written? Daniel was probably written about 167 to 164BC, a time of great persecution from yet another oppressor, Antiochus IV, who tried to impose Greek religion on the Jewish people by force, slaughtering eighty thousand of them. Judas Maccabeus led a successful revolt which led to the purification of the Temple and a revival of faith. Apocalypses were always written at a time of persecution. They encouraged the people to take the long view of history, to see that the oppressor would fall and that the righteous would eventually be rewarded if only they would hold on. Both the stories and the visions of Daniel carry this message and, viewing history from our longer perspective, we can see that they were right.

# Prophets of the return

## Haggai

The first group of exiles had returned to Jerusalem. For nearly twenty years they had toiled there, trying to scrape a living in a ruined land. They had survived; they had even built panelled houses. But times were hard. Haggai tells them the remedy. If they really want to live in abundance they must build God's house. What does their religion really mean to them if the Temple has fallen so low in their list of priorities? Haggai is not advocating an ecclesiastical building programme as the answer to all ills. He is saying in this specific instance what Jesus says more generally in the Sermon on the Mount: 'But strive first for the kingdom of God and his righteousness, and all these things will be given to you as well' (Matthew 6:33).

## Malachi

The word Malachi is not a name at all, but a title meaning 'my messenger'. Most experts date it when Nehemiah was governor of Jerusalem, perhaps eighty years after Haggai and Zechariah (see Chapter 10). The Temple had been built by then, and the worship rituals had become part of everyday life once more. The people were keeping the letter of the law, but they had lost its spirit. 'Bring the full tithe...' says Malachi (3:10). (A tithe is a tenth of income, the offering brought to the Temple as the people's gift to God.) It is once again the message of the Sermon on the Mount: 'Strive first for the kingdom...' The Old Testament ends typically, showing the same pattern—right living, degeneration into selfishness and false values, collapse of society, repentance, restoration, right living, degeneration, downfall and so on—that pervades its history.

The cycle is about to repeat itself yet again. But yet again God sends someone to point the way back, and as always there are a faithful few who fear the Lord, listen and remember (3:16).

## Joel

No one knows when this book was written. It refers to 'Zion... my holy mountain', implying a time when the Temple still stood on Jerusalem's mount. But whether it was before or after the exile, no one can be sure. Perhaps this very lack of information emphasizes the cycle of wrongdoing–punishment–repentance–redemption as a pattern for every generation.

Joel sees punishment on the way—a cloud of locusts, whether literal or metaphorical, sweeping in to destroy the land. But it is not yet too late. 'Return to the Lord,' says Joel. And even if the worst happens, there is a promise of better days to come. The Spirit will be poured out. Jerusalem will be holy and prosperous once more. Joel's promise for Jerusalem echoes on for all time and for all those working their way painfully through this endless cycle. God can restore 'the years that the swarming locust has eaten' (2:25–27). He can make people joyful again and take away their shame. As the cycle continues, Christ promises the same.

# New Testament letters
For Paul's letters and 1 Peter, see Chapter 7.

## Hebrews
Although Hebrews was originally attributed to Paul, since it reflects neither Paul's style of language nor his thought, this theory is almost universally dismissed. Perhaps the author intended to be anonymous: the letter has no written introduction and no specific target audience, other than that which forms its original title: 'To the Hebrews'. The author knew Timothy (Hebrews 13:23), wrote polished Greek and knew his Old Testament backwards. It was almost certainly written before AD70 as it refers to Temple practices, but does not mention the destruction of Jerusalem by the Romans. More than that is not known.

The author's intention was to explain to his audience—perhaps educated Jews hovering uncertainly between Judaism and Christianity—just exactly what this new religion of the Christ had to do with the old. He has clearly thought long and hard about its significance, which is why he majors so much on 'priest' and 'sacrifice', having grasped in a giant mental leap how Jesus had taken on the role of both.

## James
This is thought to be not James the fisherman and disciple, but James the younger brother of Jesus. It seems that during Jesus' lifetime he was an unbeliever (John 7:5), but was converted when he saw the risen Christ (1 Corinthians 15:7) and went on to become leader of the church in Jerusalem (Acts 12:17; 15:13). The historians Josephus and Hegesipus tell us that he was held in great esteem by his fellow country-men, Jew and Christian alike. This esteem was not enough, however, to prevent him being condemned by the high priest and stoned to death in AD62.

His death marked the turning point of relations between Christians and Jews. Up to that point there was no great divide. Followers of Christ considered themselves Jewish and continued to worship at the synagogues, and the great controversies over whether Jesus was the Messiah had yet to arise. This explains why James' letter is so practical and devoid of doctrine. It appealed chiefly to that which Christians and Jews had in common.

Of all the letters, this one bears the most allusions to the teachings of Jesus, on quite a few occasions quoting them almost direct. He may not have believed at the time, but he was certainly listening. Perhaps it is not fanciful to suggest that he, as a brother, out of all the New Testament writers was the one who knew Jesus best.

## 2 Peter

There have been doubts over many centuries as to whether Peter was the genuine author of this letter. Its language and subject matter are quite different from 1 Peter, and suspiciously close in places to that of Jude. Both 2 Peter and Jude seem to have been written in response to some sudden danger that had arisen from 'false teachers' (2 Peter 2:1) and 'ungodly intruders' (Jude 1:4), who threatened to subvert the flock. Whether these were the same dangers, it is impossible to tell. The Church has been dogged from the first century to the twenty-first with heresies, exploitation and immorality. Whoever wrote 2 Peter, and whenever, the warning it gives—to stick to simple faith and a virtuous life—is timeless.

## 1, 2 and 3 John

These letters bear clear marks of the same authorship as John's Gospel. If you assume that this was the same John who was one of Jesus' favoured disciples, and there is no evidence to the contrary, then he was by this time an old man, perhaps the last of the original apostles alive, living out his last years in Ephesus in modern Turkey. It was now some fifty years since John saw his master crucified, and he was keen to remind his readers that Jesus was not only a man who came 'in the flesh' but also the Christ, who rose from the dead for them. He was trying to counter an early form of Gnosticism, a misleading teaching which tried to divide the spiritual (which was seen as pure) from the material (which was seen as evil).

John's many years have made him focus on the importance of one simple thing: love. 'Love one another,' he repeats. Follow Christ's example. Love people, not things, for 'love casts out fear'.

John's third letter, little more than a personal note to a friend, shows, by its affection, that love in action. Love does not mean indiscriminate tolerance, however. A church member 'who likes to put himself first' is given short shrift (3 John 1:9–10) and John promises that if he ever gets to visit the otherwise unknown Gaius and his fellow believers, he will have something to say to the self-important Diotrephes.

## Jude

Jude describes himself as a servant of Jesus Christ and a brother of James, and is assumed to be a younger brother of them both. He wrote to an unknown destination to counter false teachers (see note on 2 Peter). His allusions to both Old Testament and apocryphal writings show him as someome steeped in the Jewish scriptures. Like all the New Testament writers, he wanted to show how the mercy and justice of 'our Lord Jesus Christ' were indissolubly linked to the mercy and justice of the God of the Old Testament.

# Notes for groups

The exercises in this book were designed primarily for individual study, but it may be that some would like to use them for group study and discussion. They have not been 'field tested' in this way, although I have often used similar material with groups and, with appropriate adaptations, they would lend themselves to this use. Following are a few suggestions on their group use:

## Reading the passages

- Ideally, get the members of the group to read the passages before they come. However, this will only work if the majority of members agree that this is something they want to do. A leader imposing 'homework' on people with otherwise busy lives is not a good idea.
- If not, delegate one person to be leader for that week and to do the research, selecting which verses or passages actually need to be read out during the session. For exercises such as the History and Character Building sections, this person could act as a sort of 'storyteller'.
- To save time during the discussion, write out the Bible references on small Post-it notes and give them out to the group members to find and mark before the actual discussion begins. (There's nothing worse than a whole group waiting while some poor embarrassed soul tries to find Zephaniah!)

## Ringing the changes

Don't try to do all the studies in the same way.

- Those exploring Imagining and Meditating are best done in the context of an evening of meditation. In this case, create an atmosphere with candles and music, open the session with relaxation exercises, and allow plenty of silence. It may be best not to discuss or share at all, but simply to allow people space with their own thoughts. Otherwise suggest a time of conversation at the end, perhaps in pairs, when people can share what the study brought to them.
- Those which explore or raise specific topics—anger, homosexuality, the expressing of doubts and pain in prayer, God's involvement with warfare—may be best dealt with as a full-scale debate. Like the Bible passages on which they are based, make sure that people are free to say exactly what they think, without censure.

## Remaining constant

All the exercises in this book have two things in common. Each starts with prayer and each ends by relating the study to the individual's personal life here and now. Effective groups need to do the same.

- The prayer can be done as a formal reading, an extempore conversation with God, a moment of silence or a song—and a variety of all of these is probably best of all. The important thing is that God be acknowledged as part of the process right from the start.
- Relating back to people's personal lives can be done in discussion, by each person writing down what they think God is saying to them, by a time of silence, even by revisiting the passage at the next meeting to find out what people carried away with them. However, make sure that no one feels pressured to produce some life-changing insight out of every session!

## Receiving from others

The book of James has some good advice which all group members should heed: be 'quick to hear, slow to speak' (James 1:19). There's nothing worse than a group where everyone is busy thinking about what they want to say next and no one is actually hearing what the others are saying. One of the greatest gifts we can give another is that of truly listening to what they have to say—considering it, respecting it, and esponding to it, as Gerard Hughes puts it, 'from your midriff rather han from your head' (*Oh God, Why?* p. 156). What he means is that nstead of trying to analyse and offer advice, you just listen, taking note of what gut feelings and reactions it evokes in you—something that can ell you a great deal about yourself. He also suggests (in the context of people sharing quite deep things about themselves) having a brief moment of silence after each person speaks, as a mark of respect for the speaker and to allow what they have said to sink in more deeply. I have ound that this principle translates well into any group situation.

I do not mean by this that those in the group who feel that their role n life is to be listened to (and there always seems to be one!) should be allowed free rein. They may well need to be gently silenced in order that others may be heard. Nor do I mean, however, that the most timid and tentative group member should be put on the spot and commanded to share their deepest secrets.

The model of a group leader is perhaps best found in Isaiah's description of the Lord's servant: 'A bruised reed he will not break and a dimly burning wick he will not quench' (Isaiah 42:2). Both those who talk too much and those who talk hardly at all have probably come to the group already bruised in some way and will need handling with care— and a sense of humour. Perhaps the best gift anyone can bring to a group s that of laughter, especially the ability to laugh at themselves.

There are many lessons to be learned from the Bible, but perhaps almost as many from those who are on a faith journey alongside us. It is not necessarily those who have the greatest knowledge or the greatest eloquence who have the most to teach. If you listen carefully, you may hear the voice of God speaking from the most unlikely mouthpieces.

# Recommended Further Reading

**On the Bible in general**
Eds. David Alexander and Pat Alexander, *The New Lion Handbook to the Bible* (Lion)
Eds. Robert Alter and Frank Kermode, *The Literary Guide to the Bible* (Fontana)
The *People's Bible Commentary* series (BRF)

**On the Gospels**
Richard Burridge, *Four Gospels, One Jesus* (SPCK)

**On the Old Testament**
Etienne Charpentier, *How to Read the Old Testament* (SCM Press)

**On the Psalms**
C.S. Lewis, *Reflections on the Psalms* (Fount)
Walter Brueggemann, *Praying the Psalms* (St Mary's Press, Christian Brothers Publications)

# Acknowledgments

Charles Handy, for extract from *Thoughts for the Day*, Arrow Books, 1999
Chris Gidney, for extracts from *The Bible Speaks to Me*, 1998, Marshall Pickering.
Ann Lewin, for the poem 'Disclosure'.